FREUD AND
AMERICAN SOCIOLOGY

FREUD AND AMERICAN SOCIOLOGY

PHILIP MANNING

polity

First published in 2005 by Polity Press

Polity Press
65 Bridge Street
Cambridge CB2 1UR, UK

Polity Press
350 Main Street
Malden, MA 02148, USA

ISBN: 0-7456-2504-5
ISBN: 0-7456-2505-3 (pb)

A catalogue record for this book is available from the British Library.

Typeset in 10.5 on 12 pt Sabon
by Servis Filmsetting Ltd, Manchester
Printed and bound in Great Britain by MPG Books, Bodmin, Cornwall

The publisher has used its best endeavours to ensure that the URLs for external websites referred to in this book are correct and active at the time of going to press. However, the publisher has no responsibility for the websites and can make no guarantee that a site will remain live or that the content is or will remain appropriate.

Every effort has been made to trace all copyright holders, but if any have been inadvertently overlooked the publishers will be pleased to include any necessary credits in any subsequent reprint or edition.

For further information on Polity, visit our website: www.polity.co.uk

Contents

Acknowledgments

I owe a great debt to my teachers, colleagues, and students. In particular, I would like to thank the wonderful group of sociologists at the University of Durham who set me on this path 20 years ago. Harriet Bradley, Dave Chaney, Bob Roshier, Irving Velody, and Robin Williams taught and inspired me at the same time. Charles Turner, now a professor at Warwick University, also taught me a lot and insisted on the seriousness of social theory. At Cambridge I was lucky to be taught by Anthony Giddens and Derek Gregory, and to have Chris Philo, Peter Rush, and Alison Young as intellectual companions.

When I began this project I knew relatively little about Freud and psychoanalysis. I was therefore in need of all the help I could get from the Cleveland Psychoanalytic Institute. Vera Camden, Scott Dowling, Javier Galvez, Murray Goldstone, and Sara Tucker all helped me read and understand Freud and psychoanalysis in an informed way. At Cleveland State University Bill Morgan was particularly important in helping me think through some of the ideas presented in this book. Jim Chriss also happily listened to my ideas and offered useful criticisms. Teresa LaGrange asked me every day for six months whether the book was finished and that needle was a remedy for my laziness.

Colleagues from nearby Chicago also helped. Fred Strodtbeck and Andy Abbott both spent several hours listening to my ideas and offering suggestions. Gary Fine has participated directly, as he and I co-authored several papers while I worked on this project. Gary alerted me to the importance of Philip Rieff's work and invited me to present a paper on Rieff at the American Sociological Meetings in Chicago in 2002. There I met Charles Camic, Lauren Langman,

Howard Kaye, Alan Woolfolk, and Jonathan Imber. I would like to thank them all for their help, particularly Jonathan Imber who answered many of my questions by phone and email long after the conference was over. I also benefited from my work as an editor of *Symbolic Interaction*. Over a two-year period I had countless exchanges with Kathy Charmaz and Dave Maines. Although this work was often tiring and frustrating, it was an excellent education, and Kathy and Dave gave me a powerful demonstration of intellectual commitment and fair-mindedness.

I presented parts of this book at seminars at Cleveland State University, the University of Durham, the University of Leicester, and the University of Salford. I would like to thank Robin Willams, Greg Smith, and Jack Barbalet for allowing me to speak at their respective universities and for ensuring a lively exchange of ideas. I would also like to thank Emma Longstaff of Polity Press and the anonymous reviewers of drafts of this manuscript.

Chapter 3 incorporates some material I have published elsewhere. See my papers "The Institutionalization and Deinstitutionalization of the Mentally Ill: Lessons from Goffman," in James Chriss (ed.), 1999, *Counseling and Therapeutic State* (New York: Aldine de Gruyter); "Ethnographic Coats and Tents," in *Goffman and Social Organization: Studies in a Sociological Legacy*, edited by Gregory Smith, 1999 (London: Routledge); and "Credibility, Agency and the Interaction Order," *Symbolic Interaction*, 2000, 23(3): 283–97. Chapter 5 draws heavily on my paper "Philip Rieff's Moral Vision of Sociology: From Positive to Negative Communities – and Back?," *Journal of Classical Sociology*, 2003, 3(3): 235–46.

Lastly, I would like to remember the friends and family who had little interest in this project but who kept me happy and motivated. These include my cycling friends Joanne Cohen, Chris and Rich Elliott, Lou Giesler, Jim and Susan Hughes, and Morris Wheeler. My extended family is now spread out across England and Greece. Thank you to my stepmother, Julia Manning, my brother John, and Olga, Harry, Irene, Venetia, and Orestes, with whom we spend our summers. To my wife, Maria Hatzoglou, and my sons, Simon and Triantaphilos: I love you all.

I dedicate this book to the memory of my wife's parents, Triantaphilos and Venetia, who traveled to the United States to help raise our children but who have both died without seeing the real fruit of their labor, and to the memory of my father, Brian Manning. At all the turning points in my life I remember him by my side. The structural engineer in him would no doubt have found most of the ideas in this book to be dodgy, but he would nevertheless have ordered a copy for every public library he could get to.

Preface

This book attempts to show that qualitative sociology can benefit from ideas derived from a stripped-down, non-clinical version of psychoanalysis. I argue that the fusion of theoretical, methodological, substantive, and moral concerns that emerged under the banner "symbolic interactionism" reached its highpoint with Goffman's powerful study, *Asylums* (1961). This study was the first "ethnography of a concept" (Manning, 1992) – in this case of the total institution – rather than an ethnography of a place at a certain time. In this book I argue that once the extent of this achievement is realized, it is worthwhile extending this already rich qualitative tradition by incorporating the psychoanalytic understanding of transference and counter-transference into it. This will result in a blurring of genres: specifically the line between traditional ethnography and the new-fangled "auto-ethnography" will be erased as new and old forms of data are intermingled. This book is therefore an exploration of the intellectual history of this proposed theoretical fusion.

Symbolic interactionists share some of the theoretical, empirical, and methodological concerns of psychoanalysts, especially those analysts with a "relational" approach. Although symbolic interactionists do not perform clinical work, their interest in symbols, meanings, and groups is reminiscent of psychoanalysis. George Herbert Mead's famous discussion of the self as a reflexive entity with an "I" and a "me" bears more than a surface resemblance to Freud's later structural model of the self as a composite of the id, ego, and super-ego. In fact, the similarity was noted by Mead himself and later pursued by Shibutani and others. There are also methodological similarities: both symbolic interactionists and psychoanalysts have employed a qualitative methodology that has been out of step with the statistical, quantitative, and experimental ambitions of their respective colleagues.

However, as I explore in chapter 1 of this book, what seems reasonable is not always perceived to be so by the parties involved. Although American sociologists were alerted to psychoanalysis by Freud himself during his visit to Clark University in 1909, his message fell on deaf – or at least unresponsive – ears. For the most part, pre-World War II American sociologists did not view psychoanalysis as a cognate discipline. Rather, they tended to see it as an inferior version of their own activities, spicier but less reliable.

As I show in chapters 2 and 3, the Meadian, post-social behaviorism, soon to be symbolic interactionism, that emerged at Chicago in the first half of the twentieth century, often defined itself, albeit elliptically, in opposition to Freud and psychoanalysis. Nowhere was this clearer than in the work of both Herbert Blumer and Erving Goffman. In a sense, these two men mark the passing of the guard, as Blumer is a key link back to Mead and Goffman is the messenger from the future. They both agreed that psychoanalysis had no role to play in any kind of sociology.

As I suggested in the opening paragraph, in my view, Goffman's *Asylums* (1961) marks a critical moment in the history of symbolic interactionism and American sociology in general. In part this is because it clearly signaled the transition to a post-Blumerian era, with Goffman as the new key figure. "The King is dead. Long live the King." But, even more significantly, *Asylums* marks the culmination of the non-psychoanalytic, symbolic interactionist research program. In a brilliant fusion of theoretical, methodological and moral insights, Goffman produced a new kind of ethnographic study, no longer of a place at a certain time but of a concept. Goffman did not write an ethnography of St Elizabeth's Hospital in the 1950s. Rather, he wrote an ethnography of the concept of the total institution. This was a tremendous advance over what had come before. Although it is certainly true that it was Everett Hughes who taught him to think in this way, it was Goffman's singular achievement to realize the project in so spectacular a fashion. The introduction of comparative data generated both empirical and theoretical developments. *Asylums* also made it plain that sociology is a moral practice. Goffman felt an obligation to side with the underdog and resist the abuses of 1950s psychiatry. The moral lesson Goffman taught sociology is the same one Philip Rieff offered to psychoanalysts who mistakenly thought that their rightful home was in a medical school or biology department.

Goffman's invention and demonstration of a new way of doing

symbolic interactionist ethnography could have marked a transition to a new gold standard for qualitative research. However, for unclear reasons, this did not occur. As has been pointed out from time to time (for example, Fine and Manning, 2000: 457) there is not a "Goffman school." This may be because Goffman is thought of as an energetic writer rather than as a methodologist. It is also true that Goffman did not try to build a school, in the way that Durkheim, Parsons, or Garfinkel did, perhaps because he believed that there was no work for what Peter Winch called "under-laborers." However, I believe that the most important factor is that Goffman did not represent himself as a methodological innovator. He wrote very little that was explicitly and exclusively methodological – just a bootlegged talk (1989) and the introduction to *Relations in Public* (1971). This represents a gigantic failure of marketing. Instead he became one of the preeminent theorists of face-to-face interaction. This is true but it does not do justice to the range of his achievements.

However, there was an additional problem with Goffman's comparative ethnography of concepts. This problem surfaced in many different and apparently unrelated criticisms of his work. Goffman was accused of analyzing social interaction but of ignoring the people who do the interacting. His books, Sennett elegantly said, had "scenes but no plots." Some people found his analysis of St Elizabeth's Hospital so abstract that they wondered whether he ever visited the place. Others made much the same point when they complained that Goffman did not present field notes in *Asylums* (in fact he did, but there are few).

Goffman thought of the ethnographer in contradictory ways. For the most part, he suggested that the ethnographer should be a fly on the wall who is easily missed and so can observe the social world without affecting it. However, Goffman also suggested that the ethnographer should feel able "to settle down [in the group being studied] and forget about being a sociologist" (1989: 129). His definition of participant observation emphasized this, as he described it as a technique requiring ethnographers to subject themselves and their bodies to the demands placed routinely on members of the groups being studied (1989: 125).

Even if Goffman followed his own advice, very little if any information about his own experiences appear in *Asylums* or elsewhere. Even the deeply personal essay that drew on his own experiences, "The Insanity of Place" (in Goffman, 1971), about the challenges of living with someone who is mentally ill, is written with misleading detachment. Goffman had certainly been subjected to the life he described.

This issue is the connecting door to psychoanalysis from sociology that I discuss in chapter 6. Stripped of nineteenth-century mechanistic metaphors and deterministic, developmental schemata, psychoanalysis is a relational theory in which transference and counter-transference are the central ideas, as Chodorow argued recently (1999). With no clinical responsibilities and no (traditional) clients to serve, sociologists have the opportunity to use their own counter-transferential reactions to the social and bodily experiences of group membership as valuable data for their disparate projects. I take this to be the line separating ethnography and auto-ethnography: the ethnographer is primarily an observer, whereas the auto-ethnographer shares in the experiences of the group as a group member. These experiences must therefore mean the same cluster of things to the auto-ethnographer as they do to group members. The auto-ethnographer should not write autobiography, which we read because of the uniqueness of the author's experiences. By contrast, the auto-ethnographer, like sociologists in general, must strive to identify the typical. Goffman understood this as a methodological precept but he did not integrate it into his writing. As a result, his classificatory approach that is so reminiscent of Simmel is in many ways the culmination of the project initiated by William Sumner toward the end of his life that resulted in the publication of *Folkways* (1906). One of Sumner's greatest admirers, Charles Cooley, was nevertheless able to recognize the importance of the sociologist's own experiential data. His now forgotten *Life and the Student* (1927) contains the auto-ethnographic voice that is suppressed by the otherwise extraordinary Sumner-Goffman tradition.

There is of course a second, more dominant sociological tradition that has sought to integrate psychoanalytic insights into mainstream sociology. This is the grand sociological theory of Talcott Parsons that monopolized sociological thinking in the late 1940s and 1950s and that I discuss in chapter 4. In many ways, Parsons' action theory is what every sociologist in principle wants: a single framework in which varied empirical projects can be integrated. Parsons' background in biology allowed him to understand the incredible promise of breakthroughs in molecular biology and to want them for sociology. In Parsons' view, psychoanalysis, particularly object relations, could play an important subsidiary role in action theory. Freud and Mead converged and made an important contribution. Freud in particular was promoted to the rank held by Durkheim and Weber. However, the key test for Parsons' action theory, as it is for molecular biology and Goffman's ethnography of concepts, is the empirical realization of the ideas. Molecular biologists have been able to generate a cascade of results. Goffman produced *Asylums*. Parsons, however, struggled and toward the end of his career made a final effort with Gerald Platt to show his ideas in action. Their study, *The American University* (1973), is an overlooked classic that was often insightful. However, as I discuss in chapter 4, as a demonstration of action theory it was a failure, albeit an instructive one.

Parsons' failure was conceptual, in that his complicated scheme of interlinked two-by-two classificatory boxes could not capture the complexity of social life. However, Parsons also clung to the natural scientific assumption that his work was morally neutral. He read Freud in this way, unable to grasp, as Rieff did brilliantly, that Freud was a moral teacher (perhaps *the* moral teacher), albeit one in need of radicalization. Rieff is primarily remembered for his extraordinary study *Freud: The Mind of the Moralist* (1959), but I emphasize in chapter 5 that his later work may be more significant because it is there that his own cultural critiques were expressed most powerfully. Rieff was a model for a certain kind of rigorous teaching, but he was also a powerful theorist in his own right, despite his self-deprecating claim to have discovered nothing new.

In the final chapter of the book I attempt to thread together these disparate themes, highlighting work from Arlie Hochschild, Nancy Chodorow, Jeffrey Prager, and Loic Wacquant. The first three exemplify the version of psychoanalysis that can connect to the best of symbolic interactionism (which I identify as the breakthrough ethnographic work of Goffman). Wacquant is the wild card. He does not appear interested in fusing psychoanalysis and ethnography and is not interested at all in auto-ethnography. However, I believe that his study of the social world of boxing shows the contribution that is missing from Goffman. I understand this contribution to be the counter-transference that Chodorow and Prager identify as one of the keys to contemporary psychoanalytic practice.

I do not know whether my overall argument will carry the day. If it fails, I hope that I have at least rekindled interest in some extraordinary sociological works. I remember in particular picking up Sumner's *Folkways*, Cooley's *Life and the Student*, Rieff's *The Triumph of the Therapeutic* (1966), and Parsons and Platt's *The American University*. In each case I began reading with a slight grimace, skeptical that the book could still speak to me. By contrast, Freud, Goffman, and to a lesser extent Parsons seem all too familiar. Part of the pleasure in working on this project was the revelation that all these voices are still relevant. At a minimum, I hope that I am able to persuade people to read or reread these and other treasures from sociology's rich intellectual history.

I

An Uncertain Place: Freud in American Sociology

For we do not consider it desirable at all for psychoanalysis to be swallowed up by medicine and to find its last resting place in a textbook of psychiatry under the heading 'methods of treatment'. . . . It deserves a better fate and, it may be hoped, will meet one. As a 'depth psychology', a theory of the mental unconscious, it can become indispensable to all the sciences which are concerned with the evolution of human civilization and its major institutions such as art, religion and the social order. . . . The use of analysis for the treatment of the neuroses is only one of its applications; the future will perhaps show that it is not the most important one.

Sigmund Freud, Standard Edition, 1966, vol. 20: 248

Had Freud lived long enough to enter more deeply into the technical analysis of the object-systems to which the individual becomes related, he would inevitably have had to become, in part, a sociologist, for the structure of these object-systems is – not merely influenced by – the structure of society itself. Essentially, Freud's theory of object-relations is a theory of the relation of the individual personality to the social system. It is the primary meeting ground of the two disciplines of psychology and sociology.

Talcott Parsons, Social Structure and Personality, 1964: 107

Introduction

This book is an investigation of some of the responses made by American sociologists, most of whom are associated with symbolic interactionism, to Freud and psychoanalysis. The premise of this project is that (1) elements of psychoanalysis can strengthen symbolic interactionism; (2) these elements were anticipated in some form by the founding figures of symbolic interactionism; and (3) there are non-clinical but empirical ways of pursuing symbolic interactionism "after Freud." This project therefore offers, in Foucault's suggestive phrase, a "history of the present" of one strand of the development of American sociology. Like other aspects of the emergence of American sociology, it is a complicated story relating how once famous but now largely forgotten figures argued about the value of psychoanalysis and its relevance to the social sciences.

From the first published responses to Freud by American sociologists there was disagreement, if not outright controversy, about the importance of psychoanalysis. For some, Freud was a potential ally, someone who had demonstrated that apparently medical conditions were in fact better understood as variations of normal behavior. However, for others, Freud was an imperialist who threatened to undermine sociology's autonomy. Both these views are, in a sense, predictable responses. What is more surprising is that another group of American sociologists found Freud's arguments to resonate with ones with which they were already familiar. Contrary to what we might expect, Freud was not understood by them as a revolutionary thinker, but rather as one among many contributors to an analysis of the "social self" that was already well under way. It is this last viewpoint that guides much of the discussion in this book. My intention is to show that the reception given to psychoanalysis by American sociologists reveals the strength they perceived in their own homegrown sociology. The task of this book is therefore to assess whether their perception was well founded.

The most prominent attempt to integrate psychoanalysis into American sociological thinking was undertaken by Talcott Parsons, who captained this group initiative in the mid-1940s and after, beginning at a time when his influence was at its zenith. However, even then the proposed integration brought out what he and other American sociologists perceived to be the inherently sociological character of psychoanalysis at its best. Even Parsons' own formal training in psychoanalysis did not convert him. Despite the fact that psychoanalysis was from 1909 until the 1960s an increasing part of the intellectual context of American sociology, Parsons, and American sociologists generally, largely retained their confidence in their distinctive approach to the study of human behavior and social interaction.

I think that it is helpful to anticipate the arguments that will be presented in this book. I will argue that the first distinctively American contribution to sociology was symbolic interactionism. This "somewhat barbaric neologism" was first coined in 1937 by Herbert Blumer and defined by him in two different, but interconnected, ways. The first definition stressed that the term is a "label" for the "great" similarities between a group of American scholars clustered in the Chicago area whose work shows affinities with the ideas of Blumer's mentor, George Herbert Mead (1969: 1). The second definition was more formulaic. Blumer stated that symbolic interactionism is based on three premises: (1) that we act according to the meanings objects have for us; (2) these meanings emerge in social interaction; and (3) meanings are modified over time (1969: 2). For critics, this language qualifies everyone and no one as a symbolic interactionist; however, in the context of his first definition, Blumer's approach has real teeth. This is because symbolic interactionism was not just a general set of assumptions about the social world; it was also a way of studying the social world, of doing sociology. It fused theoretical and qualitative methodological concerns, allowing both innovative theoretical extensions to Mead's framework and methodological extensions to the pioneering empirical work of W. I. Thomas and others.

I consider one endpoint of this line of inquiry to be the incredible study by Erving Goffman, *Asylums* (1961a). This book extended both the theory and method of symbolic interactionism by being both an ethnography of St Elizabeth's Hospital in Washington, DC, and a comparative ethnography of the concept of the total institution (Manning, 1992). Further, Goffman was not just an observer; he was also a moral critic. Later, Goffman ridiculed sociologists who thought of their discipline as a kind of chemistry, likening them to children playing with Gilbert sets (1971: xviii). In my way of thinking, Goffman was therefore traveling down the same road as his colleague-to-be, Philip Rieff, who also understood sociology as a moral discipline whose role was to preserve both a social and sacred order. Both Goffman and Rieff also emerged at a time when Freud's star was at its zenith, and unsurprisingly both wrote against the backdrop of psychoanalysis.

In my retelling of this story, Goffman's genius was to see a vital connection between the comparative, classificatory, conceptually innovative work of an earlier outcast, William Sumner, and the ethnographic approach of one of his former teachers, Everett Hughes. Goffman therefore separated himself from the more introspective tradition associated with Cooley. Cooley's most psychoanalytic book, *Life and the Student* (1927), has been overlooked and lost to the canon. Ironically, both the classificatory, observational approach of Sumner and the introspective approach of Cooley can be found in Mead's seminal statements in *Mind, Self and Society* (1962 [1934]) and, arguably, it is the "plasticity" or malleability of Mead's ideas which has allowed them to have an enduring appeal.

In separating himself from this introspective tradition, Goffman also severed all ties with a psychoanalytic view of the social world. Although he had a deep knowledge of both Freud's work and psychoanalysis in general, he was not conciliatory at all: he considered the psychoanalytic perspective to be speculative and the work of psychoanalytically minded psychiatrists to be ineffective at best. The thread that ties Cooley to Freud (that was brilliantly analyzed by Rieff) was therefore of no interest to Goffman. As a result, Goffman accepted that the internal worlds of the people who populate the "interaction order" could not be studied sociologically. In Jonathan Glover's telling phrase, Goffman's sociology treated people as having no "inner story" (1988: 175). Goffman's antipathy to psychoanalysis left him no choice. Nevertheless, Goffman's achievements were extraordinary, one of which was to fuse the theories of Sumner and Hughes and demonstrate the empirical power of the union.

Goffman needed but couldn't find a version of psychoanalysis that had an elective affinity with the qualitative, loosely symbolic interactionist, Sumner/Hughes work that he had mastered. Surprisingly, Talcott Parsons, hardly the sociologist associated with symbolic interactionism, found the key to unlock the door to psychoanalysis for sociology. However, Parsons' curse was his inability to walk through it. The key was Parsons' realization that sociology needed a stripped-down version of psychoanalysis. Parsons realized that an "object-relations" approach in psychoanalysis could jettison mechanistic and deterministic aspects of some other versions of psychoanalysis. Further, sociologists as sociologists had no stake in debates about the clinical efficacy or scientific standing of psychoanalysis. After all, sociologists who obtain a license to practice psychoanalysis and then do so are no longer acting as sociologists.

This led Parsons to treat Freud as heading down the road of convergence that took him to Parsons' own unified action theory. By de-emphasizing Freud's developmental schemata and assumption of sexual etiology, Parsons' Freud became, as Parsons himself recognized, a version of Cooley and Mead. This realization, as Jonathan Turner (1974) suggested in a seminal paper, brought both Freud and Parsons into the purview of symbolic interactionism. Blumer (1975), of course, was both angered and genuinely mystified by the suggestion that both his (former) nemeses were now his bedfellows.

The key that Goffman didn't find was therefore the realization that sociology could get what it needed from psychoanalysis without accepting the baggage of mechanistic and/or deterministic schemata.

This left sociologists free to use the powerful psychoanalytic ideas concerning transference, counter-transference, projection and introjection, and the ambivalence that accompanies the construction of internal worlds. This was the path back to the inner stories that Glover had correctly seen as missing from Goffman's work. Parsons, unfortunately, could open but not walk through the door, in part because he was, by his own admission, an "incurable theorist" and in part because he retained ambitions for an amoral, scientific sociology. As a result, he could not produce the empirical study that would accomplish for him what *Asylums* accomplished for Goffman. In the last decade of his life, Parsons made one last effort, producing a fascinating but poorly received study, *The American University*, co-authored by Gerald Platt (1973). Despite many appealing qualities, the book failed to incorporate psychoanalysis meaningfully and produced instead an increasingly confusing array of two-by-two boxes that incorporated themselves in an infinite regress. Parsons needed to revert back to the ethnographic work he had tried in the early 1940s when he studied Boston hospitals. But in truth, as he recognized himself, his talents lay elsewhere. Further, Parsons could not accept that sociology is inevitably a form of moral critique. This is one of the lessons that we are taught by Philip Rieff. Parsons preferred to hold onto the idea he obtained (independently) from Durkheim and Henderson; namely, that sociology has much in common with biology. The flukish coincidence that his own AGIL schema bore a surface resemblance to Crick and Watson's four building blocks of DNA (the AGCT "schema"), and hence to the birth of molecular biology, simply led Parsons further astray.

In the 25 years since Parsons died, sociologists such as Nancy Chodorow and Jeffrey Prager have trained as psychoanalysts and continued the project of paring down psychoanalysis to its key elements. Although they both recognize that this project is compatible with sociology, they have both developed clinical careers, and their insights have been largely clinically oriented. The logic of the position they develop demonstrates that the transference and counter-transference seen routinely in clinical settings is in fact endemic to all social relationships. As a result, the counter-transference experienced by the ethnographer or symbolic interactionist can be a viable, empirical, non-clinical guide to the internal world – or inner story – of the people who populate Goffman's interaction order.

To date, neither Chodorow nor Prager has produced a psychoanalytic, reflexive anthropology or sociology, but they both recognize that this project, though difficult, is possible. Symbolic interactionists identify this work as "auto-ethnography," a phrase coined by David Hayano (1982) to describe his own investigation of the social world of poker players. With no sense of his research as a psychoanalytic project, and lacking the confidence that he was doing anything more than playing poker and pretending that it was research, Hayano stepped back from the radical implication that his own counter-transference to the world of poker was the most interesting thing that he had to say about that world. Very recently, Loic Wacquant (2004), who shows none of Hayano's inhibitions, has investigated the world of boxing, drawing heavily on his own counter-transference to the sport. Nevertheless, like Hayano, Wacquant does not conceive of his project as an extension of the thread that runs from Cooley to Freud, to Rieff, to Prager, and beyond.

It is critical to recognize that the endpoint of my own studies is not a stark choice between the Sumner-Hughes-Goffman tradition and the Cooley-Freud-Rieff tradition. The critical task, as I see it, is to recognize, as Mead and Parsons did but could not demonstrate empirically, that the comparative ethnography of concepts that Goffman developed is in fact compatible with the counter-transferential work of contemporary auto-ethnographers. This new fusion promises exciting yields. The problem is that it will take someone of the caliber of Goffman to produce it, not just someone of the caliber of Parsons to recognize it.

The Intellectual Background

In the last decades of the nineteenth century and the early part of the twentieth century, American sociologists had to clarify where they stood in relation to other, already established, cognate sciences. The space they chose to occupy in part covered the territory of social psychology, along with ecology and social organization. Therefore, insofar as psychoanalysis was understood as a kind of social psychology, sociologists were at least initially receptive to Freudian ideas. In the two decades following Freud's visit to the United States in 1909, sociologists responded to Freud in different ways, ranging from a hostile dismissal to a receptive embrace. What is striking during this time is that Freudian ideas were not considered to be particularly revolutionary (by admirers and critics alike), and as a result they could be readily assimilated into sociological thinking and presented as a coherent, established theory. Thus, psychoanalysis was presented as a version of preexisting American sociological social psychology. Freud was understood therefore for the most part – and at best – as a contributor to and not the founder of an intellectual approach.

It is also important to recognize that the American reception of Freud was complicated by – and was also subservient to – political, moral and methodological debates in Chicago and elsewhere about the appropriate form for sociology to take. These debates concerned three issues. The first was the extent to which sociology could, even in principle, justify political matters. This is hardly surprising, given that American sociology emerged following the Civil War and at a time of tremendous political and economic turmoil. Sociologists themselves had divided loyalties: some advocated socialist, some Progressive and some free-market principles. In some cases, sociologists changed their minds or just dithered, as in the case of Albion Small, who flirted with socialism for many years (Smith, 1988: 76). Second, sociologists debated whether their discipline could be a non-religious moral science of society, as many of its early proponents wanted it to be. Notably at the University of Chicago, but elsewhere also, sociology emerged as a discipline with a distinctive agenda. It was, in Abbot's (1999) telling description, part academic discipline, part outreach effort. The third concern was more focused and technical: it was a debate about the specific role of positivism, quantification, and the role of qualitative research in sociological investigations.

The initial reception of psychoanalytic ideas in the first half of the twentieth century has to be understood against this intellectual background. For example: initially, sociologists who favored an engagement with psychoanalysis could not identify a way of collecting psycho-analytic data. That is, they could not answer the question of what a non-clinical version of psychoanalysis would look like. The developing life-history research at Chicago, associated initially with W. I. Thomas in sociology and William Healy in psychiatry, offered an answer to this question, and in the 1930s John Dollard formalized this, first by demonstrating the role psychoanalysis could play in a case study and then by establishing methodological guidelines. Louis Wirth (1931) offered a separate but commensurable argument when he advocated a "clinical sociology."

It is interesting to note that, until the 1930s, American sociologists for the most part presented Freudian ideas as established theory, even though Freud himself continued to be productive – and to publish – until his death in 1939. In the 1930s, émigré psychoanalysts and American converts to psychoanalysis – notably Karen Horney, Eric Fromm, and Harry Stack Sullivan – began to advocate revisions to Freud that both sparked controversy and demonstrated that Freud's work could be interpreted in different ways and with different points of emphasis. At this time, Herbert Blumer, himself an ardent critic of psychoanalysis, attempted to demonstrate that a powerful union of social psychological ideas, sociological research methods, and substantive interests emanating largely from Chicago could be coherently packaged together into the field of "symbolic interactionism." Blumer understood that psychoanalysis was a potential imperialist force that must be resisted, and, in any case, Blumer had his own imperialist ambitions for his symbolic interactionist synthesis. Without particular knowledge of psychoanalysis, Blumer promoted efforts within sociology to resist any movement toward Freud. Blumer's quasi-successor, Erving Goffman, was extremely knowledgeable about psychoanalysis (unlike Blumer), but he too viewed it as an inferior approach to the homespun symbolic interactionism that covered the same ground as psychoanalysis, but in a more convincing way, both theoretically and methodologically.

In the 1940s, the waters were muddied by Talcott Parsons, the American sociologist who was most committed to the integration of sociological and psychoanalytic ideas. In fact, Parsons believed that this integration had to be recognized rather than constructed, because from his vantage point Freud's ideas already "converged" with those of leading sociologists. Unlike the majority of American sociologists before him, Parsons believed that the way forward for the discipline was to draw upon European intellectual ideas. His initial emphasis was on the works of Durkheim, Weber, Pareto, and Marshall. Later, he emphasized Freud's foundational role in sociological theory. It is striking that Parsons did not initially look to the American sociologists favored by Blumer, but instead imported European elements of sociological theory that were largely unknown and not translated.

Extending the arguments of the cultural revisionists, Parsons pursued a reading of Freud that was quite different from both conventional psychoanalytic and sociological interpretations. The purpose of this reading was initially to make Freud fit into a general theory of the social sciences, and to this extent Parsons emphasized the importance of the internalization of norms in both Freud's account of the super-ego and in his own account of the "personality system." Later, Parsons realized that his version of Freud made Freud readily compatible with the symbolic interactionist alternative to Freud that Blumer had promoted. When Jonathan Turner (1974) pointed this out publicly, Parsons acknowledged the similarity. By contrast, Blumer (1975) steadfastly rejected any invasion onto symbolic interactionist territory.

At about the same time, Philip Rieff initiated a project in which he analyzed the moral implications of Freud's thought. His study *Freud: The Mind of the Moralist* was published in 1959. In this book he demonstrated the richness and nuances of Freud's writings while distancing himself from Parsons, who had ambitions for a unified, general theory. By also ignoring the question of the clinical efficacy of psychoanalysis, Rieff sidestepped many of the debates that began in the 1950s and continue to the present day. Instead he reinstated a question that was very important to the first generation of American sociologists; namely, is it possible to have a moral science of society? Rieff's continuing investigation of this question has resulted in a compelling and as yet unfinished sociology of culture that seeks to explore the bases of both social and sacred order.

The Freudian Mirror

Many of the arguments that follow are guided by a metaphor: that Freud's work can be understood as a mirror which was used by American sociologists to get a better image of themselves. In looking at Freud they caught glimpses of themselves and, in a rather narcissistic way, often discovered that they liked what they saw.

The metaphor of the mirror is of course very familiar. It has also played a role in the development of both American sociology and post-Freud psychoanalysis, the former through Charles Horton Cooley, the latter through Jacques Lacan. Cooley's lucid prose outlined a three-part process involving the realization that we appear to others in a certain way, a judgment concerning that appearance, and then an assessment that produces a "self-feeling" such as "pride or mortification" (1964 [1902]: 184). Unfortunately, Cooley's looking glass doesn't quite work in the same way that I think the Freudian mirror works. In the latter case, American sociologists looked at something that was "foreign," judged it to be either lacking or a lesser version of themselves, and then felt self-satisfaction. Thus, in my telling of the mirror metaphor, American sociologists made a favorable comparison, whereas, in Cooley's, the person makes a re-evaluation.

Lacan presents us with a rather different story from Cooley's, although, as Wiley (2003) has recently shown, there are interesting connections between them. Lacan's mirror stage, like his prose, is much more destabilizing than Cooley's. For Lacan, the mirror stage is a "minimal paraphrase of the nascent ego" and, in Bowie's retelling of the tale, what stands in front of the mirror is "something derisory." In its first telling, Lacan had distinguished between a monkey's and a child's reaction to a mirror, arguing that the monkey actually understood things better than the child. This is because the monkey "is able to recognize that the mirror-image is an epistemological void, and to turn his attention elsewhere, [whereas] the child has a perverse will to remain deluded" (Bowie, 1991: 22–3). Anthony Elliott's recent description of Lacan's mirror stage turns out to be very useful for the argument I want to pursue:

> According to Lacan, a profound sense of jubilation arises when the small infant sees itself in a reflecting surface. He [Lacan] argues that the mirror provides an image of corporeal wholeness, of oneness and unity. This sense of wholeness or unity is what Freud was trying to get at when he explored the concept of narcissism in his theoretical papers, and Lacan allows us to grasp the importance of the visual or optic genesis of narcissism as a condition of the self. The problem is, however, that the unity reflected in the mirror is not at all what it appears. (2001: 53–4)

Lacan's mirror stage, as I understand it, is actually a good description of the process I'm trying to describe. Put indulgently, the "child" is the newborn of the American university: the discipline of sociology, which sees itself in the mirror and is "jubilant" in a narcissistic way. Further, sociologists imagine their discipline to have a wholeness and unity that in reality it does not possess. It also easily imagines itself growing up into adulthood and maturity, all the while remaining true to the likeness it sees now in the mirror. However, it's all a lie and the child is in jeopardy.

In fact, I think the American sociologists' mirror view of themselves involved a double lie. The first lie is the one revealed by Lacanian psychoanalysis, namely, that the reflected image had a discrete coherence, whereas in fact it did not – and does not now. Rather, as Abbot (2001) has shown, by the mid-1920s American sociology was already fragmented and arguably irreparably ruptured by substantive, methodological, disciplinary, and even political debates that, at best, suggest the image reflected back in the mirror was actually of many children, some of whom were bastards – certainly they were not all of one family. The second lie is that American sociologists falsely attributed to both Freud and psychoanalysis what they falsely attributed to themselves, namely, a singular unity. In a strange way, for very unclear reasons, the overwhelming majority of American sociologists from Robert Park onwards interpreted Freud as having a coherent, singular theory. They then often compounded the error by assuming that psychoanalysts themselves were mirror images of the original Freudian mirror, which they clearly were not. That is, American sociologists writing before 1930 could not detect any significant divisions in Freud's own writings. Put dramatically, they seem to have assumed that his followers were all paid-up members of the Wednesday Night Club (Gay, 1988: 173–9) and hence born-again keepers of the faith.

By the 1930s all this changed, as American sociologists were able to watch the prominent Freudian revisionists challenge many of the tenets of Freudianism, and diverse and competing schools became apparent. It was at about this time in England that these competing schools became competing psychoanalytic training programs, a development that did not occur in the same way in the United States, primarily because the medicalization of psychoanalysis ensured a relatively safe haven for the discipline, loosely within psychiatry, a state of affairs that stumbled on until legal action in 1988 established that psychoanalysis had no medical component and hence could be taught to people without medical training (Hale, 1995; Gay, 1989).

Freud's 1909 Visit to the United States

In order to establish what American sociologists knew about Freud, it is reasonable to consider his five lectures at Clark University in 1909, given each evening from September 6 to 10, as a starting point. Ernest Burgess chose 1909 as the "date of the official introduction of psychoanalysis into the United States" (1939: 356). It is doubtful whether many people in the United States knew much about Freud before then. Writing to Freud on February 7, 1909, Ernest Jones commented that there is "colossal ignorance" of his work in the United States and that the only American he knew who had read *The Interpretation of Dreams* was Freud's translator, A. A. Brill (Paskauskas, 1993: 13). While Jones over-stated the point, it is useful to remember that in 1909 Freud was still struggling to establish psychoanalysis as a legitimate field with an insti-tutional home. Further, the then 53-year-old pioneer of psychoanalysis was, unbeknownst even to himself, a long way from finishing his life's work. In fact, many of the ideas that are readily associated with him were developed after his visit to the United States.

Obviously, Freud's Clark lectures were not designed to impress soci-ologists specifically; rather they were intended to present psychoanaly-sis to a wide audience in a manner that would disarm the criticisms Freud expected to receive. Curiously, Freud was invited to lecture at Clark University by Stanley Hall, a well-known psychologist, to an audience containing prominent neurologists. William James was also present for one day, an event remembered because the two men went for a walk together, during which James bravely managed the painful heart condition that killed him the following year, and then announced that he believed that the future belonged to Freud and psychoanalysis. How much of this was his belief and how much his charm is unclear;

nevertheless, James's presence at Clark University guaranteed an airing for psychoanalytic ideas among the different American disciplines interested in pragmatism. E. B. Holt, one of James's students, gave proof of this, when in 1915 he published *The Freudian Wish*, a book that influenced W. I. Thomas, Robert Park, and other sociologists, especially in Chicago.

Freud's lectures were constructed to appeal to an American rather than a European audience. For Freud, this obliged him to pander to views that he thought were rather outmoded or irrelevant. To this end, the five lectures attempted to at least appease a more or less puritan view of human affairs. Peter Gay quoted Freud as disparagingly describing America as "prudish" (1989: 207). Freud was sufficiently keen to impress his audience that he was even prepared to justify psychoanalytic findings using quantitative measures, drawing on those developed by Sanford Bell, an American psychologist, a professor at Clark University, and the future translator of the *Five Essays*. Although he was often gracious enough to pay flattering compliments to his American hosts, in private Freud commented that "America is a mistake; a gigantic mistake, it is true, but nonetheless a mistake" (quoted by Jones, vol. 2, 1955: 60).

From correspondence in the months leading up to Freud's visit, it is clear that Freud considered different ways of introducing Americans to psychoanalysis. Jung advised him to devote all five lectures to dream analysis – advice Freud wisely chose to ignore – although he did comment in passing in one of the lectures that he could have focused exclusively on dreams. In his biography of Freud, Ernest Jones took the credit for steering Freud away from a focus on dream analysis in the Clark lectures, persuading Freud that this might seem a frivolous topic to an American audience (Jones, vol. 2, 1955: 56).

Freud understood that his lectures had to be more than infomercials. Rather, they were seeds planted on foreign soil in the hope of cross-fertilization. For this to have any chance of success, Freud understood that significant political concessions would have to be made and that it would also be necessary for him to be somewhat economic with the truth as he actually believed it to be. Nathan Hale has even gone so far as to suggest (1971: 5) that these lectures "condensed to the point of caricature" his major theories. By contrast, Freud's authorized translators described the five lectures as providing "an admirable preliminary picture which calls for little correction" (*SE*, XI: 5). Despite this difference of opinion, the lectures clearly provide a plausible, defensible, inviting, and upbeat exposition of psychoanalysis. They were also a widely and easily available version of psychoanalysis that had the added cachet of carrying the authority – the signature – of Freud himself. More than merely an elementary introduction to psycho-analysis, they edited psychoanalysis into a form that he thought would be acceptable to his newly acquired American audience. With no one present who was both capable and willing to dispute the story of psychoanalysis as Freud told it, Freud's gift as a remarkable expositor carried the day.

Although given in German, the lectures were published almost immediately in translation in several newspapers. However, the more significant immediate form of dissemination occurred because Freud impressed several of the members of the distinguished audience at Clark University. In particular, William James, Franz Boas, Alfred Meyer, Edwin Holt, and James Jackson Putnam became American advocates of psychoanalysis, to differing degrees. In addition, Freud strengthened his already strong ties to his existing American supporters, Ernest Jones, A. A. Brill, and Stanley Hall himself, all of whom became key pathways, connecting Freud to diverse American institutions and audiences.

Freud's five lectures were masterfully constructed: they were at once both enthralling and relatively uncontroversial. Freud began the lectures by praising Joseph Breuer as the true founder of psychoanalysis, dating its discovery to 1880–2. In his disarming way Freud said, "If it is a merit to have brought psycho-analysis into being, that merit is not mine. I had no share in its earliest beginnings" (*SE*, XI: 9). In one sense, this was a clever strategy, as Breuer was a highly respected Viennese neurologist with impeccable credentials. However, it was a display of modesty that Freud later regretted, and he altered the 1924 edition of *Five Lectures* (*SE*, XI: 3–25), reclaiming the discovery of psychoanalysis for himself. As is well known, Freud's relationship with Breuer was one of extremes. At the beginning, Breuer was a mentor to Freud, taking an active interest in the development of his career, finding him patients and lending him substantial sums of money. Later, as often happened between Freud and his male friends and colleagues, they parted company, each unhappy with the other. By 1895, Breuer was unsupportive of Freud's emerging "cathartic" method and prepared to use his contribution to their jointly authored *Studies on Hysteria* (*SE*, XI: 3–25) to say so. Bearing this in mind, we can see a glimpse of the depth of Freud's strategic thinking, since by 1909 he must surely have had to grate his teeth and cross his fingers to give Breuer the credit for the discovery of psychoanalysis, a tribute that he absolutely believed was his alone.

After emphasizing that a medical background is not needed to understand psychoanalysis, Freud began the first lecture by discussing what is sometimes thought of as the first psychoanalytic case study: the case of Anna O. Anna was described as an intelligent and attractive young woman, 21 years old, who had been ill and a patient of Breuer's for two years. She suffered from a rigid paralysis and loss of sensation, had trouble with her eyes and head and a nervous cough. She avoided eating and couldn't drink despite being very thirsty. For a while she could not understand her native tongue. She also suffered sporadically from what the French call "absences" (*SE*, XI: 10) or what we might think of today as prolonged daydreaming. Anna herself called each absence "time-missing." Given that there was no evidence of organic disease, Breuer explored what Anna thought about during absences, discovering that she had "melancholy phantasies." This led Breuer to a serendipitous discovery: Anna felt better as soon as she spoke about these phantasies, leading him to speculate that her mental state had been brought on by the stimulation they produced (*SE*, XI: 13). Anna was said to be thrilled by her own improvement, referring to the method that became psychoanalysis as "chimney-sweeping" and the "talking cure."

The details of Anna's apparent recovery outlined the making of a method. In one of the most famous phrases in psychoanalysis, Freud declared that "our hysterical patients suffer from reminiscences" (*SE*, XI: 16). Each reminiscence is a "residue" from a traumatic experience that is released once it is consciously recalled and brought out into the open. Each of the patient's symptoms is associated with a specific reminiscence; therefore a thorough treatment involves a thorough examination, symptom by symptom, memory by memory. In this way, a cathartic resolution is possible and the patient can "get free of the past" (*SE*, XI: 17).

Not all but certainly some of the details of Anna's treatment were useful to Freud in his efforts to conquer his American audience. Freud was aware that many of his critics viewed psychoanalysis as an immoral pastime. For example, Oscar Cargill and Richard La Pierre had argued that Freud advocated primitivism, sexual liberation, pessimistic determinism, permissiveness, and decadence (see Hale, 1971: xi). To counter these rumors, Freud was able to present Anna, a gifted woman from a well-to-do family, whose traumatic memories actually concerned the death of her father. It was a noble riposte to Freud's imagined or real critics. The only scandalous component of Anna's memories, and this only a slight moral failure, was that she found the behavior of her English lady companion distasteful. Specifically, she allowed a pet dog to drink from a glass used by the family. Out of politeness Anna said nothing, but the unpleasant memory of it festered until it surfaced as a symptom: a refusal to drink even when very thirsty. Thus with only the most superficial criticism of Anna's character, Freud was able to introduce the importance of what he then called "suppression" (i.e. repression), the division between the conscious and the unconscious, the talking cure, and even a happy ending.

Anna was therefore a landmark case for Freud because she was both demonstrably ill, with a varied set of physical symptoms that had proved unresponsive to traditional medical approaches, and was demonstrably cured, since after Freud's intervention these symptoms (at least apparently) evaporated. The illness and its treatment are both shown by Freud to be rather mechanistic: one repressed memory for each symptom, each of which was removed using a cathartic, hypnosis-induced, "talking cure." Further, although she suffered from "reminiscences" (as Freud thought all hysterics did), she did not suffer from explicitly sexual memories – as did nearly all of Freud's other, to this point unmentioned, patients. At least, this was Freud's argument in the official version of the case. Anna O. could therefore be presented as a benign and uncontroversial success story with which Freud could initiate psychoanalytic discussion. However, the case of Anna was clearly more interesting but also more problematic than Freud's lecture suggested, at least until the final paragraph, at which point he acknowledged that aspects of the method are "impeding and unnecessary" and the findings are "incomplete" and "unsatisfying" (SE, XI: 20). However, here, Freud did not clarify these rather striking criticisms of what was to that point an apparent success story for psychoanalysis.

As is now known, this case study was in fact far more complicated than Freud presented in any of his public lectures or published papers. Two of the aspects of the Anna case that Freud chose not to share with his American audience are important correctives to the otherwise wholesome success story. First, there was in fact a sexual component to the case: Anna at one point had a phantom pregnancy in which she announced privately to Breuer that she had stomach pains associated in her mind with the birth of their baby. Breuer was, no doubt for complicated, contradictory reasons, astonished and frightened of the possible scandal that might ensue, and withdrew from the case. As we see in his correspondence, Freud understood the intellectual significance of Anna's new symptom almost immediately, and it ushered in the analysis of transference that became central to all forms of psychoanalysis thereafter.

In fact, Breuer's reaction to Anna was also of intellectual interest, since he had developed strong feelings for Anna that were also revealing. In fact, his near obsession with Anna came to the attention of his wife, who became acutely jealous. Thus, whereas Breuer inadvertently discovered transference, he actually embodied counter-transference, to a degree that might explain his overwhelming embarrassment about the case. After Anna's announcement of the phantom pregnancy, Breuer left Vienna for Venice with his wife. There, the Breuers had their second honeymoon, which resulted in the conception of a daughter. Freud's first biographer retells this story, adding that Breuer's daughter committed suicide in New York 60 years later (Jones, 1953, vol. 1: 224–5).

Freud's second omission concerned Breuer's later assessment of their joint work on hysteria. By 1895, he was not only unmoved by Freud's own exuberance over their newly found cathartic method, but was ready to throw in the towel. In a letter to Fleiss dated December 18, 1892, Freud reported that publishing with Breuer was possible only after a "long battle" (reported by the editors in *SE*, II: xiv, but the letter is not reproduced in Masson, 1985). In closing his contribution to *Studies on Hysteria*, Breuer invoked Theseus from *A Midsummer Night's Dream*, who declares that "The best in this kind are but shadows" (*SE*, II: 250–1). Thus their cathartic treatment of hysteria was a shadow for Breuer but the light for Freud, even if it was only the light pointing the way forward, since clearly psychoanalysis had still to emerge from catharsis.

In the second lecture Freud introduced Jean Michel Charcot and Pierre Janet (who had at one point been dismissive of Freud and who also had the distinction of being Durkheim's classmate at the École Normale Supérieure). Freud suggested that both Breuer and himself were under the "spell" of Charcot, covering over what were probably already significant differences between them. Freud's break with Charcot, Janet, and Breuer is introduced in this lecture, and linked conceptually to his realization of the therapeutic importance of "resistance." This was explored using a second case study of Elizabeth von R., one of Freud's own patients. The role of resistance complicates the case a little, but in other regards Elizabeth is a replica of Anna: both are young, accomplished women, and both have hysterical symptoms that responded cathartically to efforts to restore their repressed memories.

Freud had earlier discussed the case of Elizabeth von R. in detail as the fifth case study in *Studies in Hysteria*. Once again he was able to show that a damaging, shaming thought had become lodged in her unconscious where it festered, producing debilitating symptoms. For Elizabeth, her unspeakable shame was to have silently delighted in the death of her sister, whose husband she desired. He was now available to her. Once Elizabeth recognized and accepted this repressed thought, her symptoms evaporated. At Clark University, Freud edited his account of this case carefully. For example, he did not tell his American audience that, somewhat like Breuer with Anna, he had a mild form of counter-transference himself, evidenced by his later action to procure tickets to a Viennese ball – so that he could secretly admire Elizabeth's dancing. Nor did he share with his American audience that he had, on his own initiative, approached Elizabeth's mother to see whether the family might actually sanction the strange second marriage Elizabeth desired. Nor did he reveal that Elizabeth's mother told him that both she and the family had always known about Elizabeth's infatuation with her sister's husband. These omissions are significant, particularly the last. Together, they undermine Freud's claim to have discovered something about Elizabeth that was not already well known by her family, and they shed light about the relationship between the unconscious and repression that became central to Freud's later (1923) structural model.

Freud delayed the material about which he anticipated the greatest controversy – dream analysis and child sexuality – until the third and fourth lectures. Again, he went to great pains to introduce them without antagonizing his audience. In the third lecture on dreams, Freud began by discussing jokes and slips of the tongue, probably because he thought that his views on these topics would be acceptable to his audience, as the existence of unconscious thoughts "behind" slips or, as Freud called them, "parapraxes" can be demonstrated persuasively. Even audiences that are hostile to psychoanalytic ideas usually find these examples easy to accept. For example, suggesting that a man who says to his neighbor, "that's the breast haircut you've ever had" has more than one thought in his head is hardly controversial. In the third lecture Freud did risk criticism by signaling the centrality of the interpretation of dreams in psychoanalysis. Perhaps as a gesture to Jung, he admitted that he could have devoted all five lectures to dreams because they are, in one of his most famous phrases, the "royal road to the unconscious." Nevertheless, Freud did not offer a detailed analysis of a particular dream, presumably fearing an icy reception.

In introducing the topic of child sexuality in the fourth lecture, Freud was even more circumspect. To this end, he began by citing Sanford Bell's quantitative findings, who, Freud claimed, had anticipated many of his own ideas about the sexual behavior of children. This is one of the few occasions in which Freud found quantification valuable. Freud also acknowledged that neurotic illnesses could almost always be traced back to impressions from erotic life, leaving his audience, perhaps, to connect the dots back to his discussion of Anna O. so that a truer general picture of her could emerge, albeit without explicit details. Freud introduced the importance of sexuality in a wonderful passage:

> People are in general not candid over sexual matters. They do not show their sexuality freely, but to conceal it they wear a heavy overcoat woven of a tissue

of lies, as though the weather were bad in the world of sexuality. Nor are they mistaken. It is a fact that sun and wind are not favorable to sexual activity in this civilized world of ours; none of us can reveal his eroticism freely to others. (*SE*, XI: 41)

Then, in a remarkably economic way, Freud extended his argument from the observation that "sexual etiology was of decisive importance" to the role of resistance in the creation of neurotic symptoms, to the "almost invariably forgotten memory-traces" from childhood that can only be relieved through cathartic recall. Unlike the safe decorum of the first lecture, the fourth appears to have been chosen strategically as the place to introduce the most controversial material, which Freud did with impressive speed and verve.

The fourth lecture also outlined the basic idea of the Oedipus complex without using the term directly, referring instead to the "nuclear complex." He did mention King Oedipus, whose fate to kill his father and marry his mother he saw as a guide to a universal infantile wish. Freud also suggested that Hamlet's "incest-complex" is another example of this phenomenon (*SE*, XI: 47). Soon after returning to Vienna, Freud wrote explicitly about the Oedipus complex and abandoned the term used in the Clark lectures.

In the fifth lecture, Freud completed his introduction to psychoanalysis by quite general observations about neurosis, treatment, transference, and role of sublimation in civilized life. He reiterated that people become neurotic when their erotic needs are frustrated. In fact, the patient's neurosis is an alternative source of satisfaction; it is therefore not the patient's problem but the patient's solution to his or her problem. Resistance occurs because the patient does not want to give up the neurosis that has become an important source of satisfaction.

In a passage that invited interdisciplinary cooperation, Freud suggested that the neurotic and the non-neurotic are different only by a matter of the degree of suffering. As he put it, it is a quantitative and not a qualitative difference. Freud suggested that since we are all leading more or less unsatisfying lives, we all create fantasies to fill a real void. Some people manage to turn the fantasy into reality; others turn their fantasies into artistic creations. Productive people manage to sublimate their impulses into socially approved behavior. Psychoanalysts use the window offered by transference to penetrate repression, but they do so knowing that the discovery of the object of repression may or may not make the patient happier (*SE*, XI: 52–3). This was the observation that he had chosen as the ending to *Studies on Hysteria*, in which he claimed that "much will be gained if we succeed in transforming . . . hysterical misery into common unhappiness" (*SE*, II: 305). In the Clark lectures, he chose to conclude his exposition differently, with a joke that played on connotations of the word "oats" in a tale about horses (an animal which elsewhere in his work symbolized the id). Thus, he left his audience to contemplate a weakly coded message about the positive role of sexuality in the life of neurosis-free individuals.

After spending several days with the prominent Harvard neurologist James Putnam at his retreat in the Adirondacks, Freud returned to Europe with his traveling companions, Jung and Ferenczi, in September 1909, never to visit the United States again. It took Freud several months to write up the Clark lectures. This was necessary because he had given them extempore. Despite the delay that inevitably followed, and despite the need for translation, they were available the following year, in 1910. For our purposes, the obvious questions are whether they reached an audience of sociologists and with what effect, or whether Freud's elegant, albeit economic, account of psychoanalysis fell on deaf ears. Given that sociologists were writing about Freud by 1915, they must have found out about psychoanalysis somehow. If the Clark lectures were not the source, what was? As we shall see, sociologists were initially cagey regarding their sources of information about Freud, and it is not at all straightforward to say where their ideas came from.

Freud among American Sociologists

Many of the first American sociologists spoke fluent German and had in fact studied in Germany. There was therefore no language barrier to reading Freud in the original, and in principle his work was available to them as soon as it was published. However, given the general agreement that it was Freud's visit to the United States that sparked (rather than renewed) interest in psychoanalysis, it is worth thinking about what publications either by or about Freud were available at the time of the Clark lectures or soon after. That is, what were American sociologists reading as they formed their opinions about Freud? It is possible to answer this question by looking at what was being said about Freud in the leading journal in the field, the *American Journal of Sociology*, which reigned over the discipline until the emergence of a competitor in 1935, the *American Sociological Review*. By this account, sociologists only began discussing Freud in print in 1917, about seven years after Freud's visit. However, in 1915, the prominent Chicago sociologist Robert Park published a supportive account of psychoanalysis. This publication confirms that by this time Freud's thought was part of the agenda of American sociology. However, neither Freud nor psychoanalysis was a large part of the agenda at this time, or indeed for some time.

So, in one sense Robert Park can be credited with introducing Freud to American sociology, in 1915, in a short book called *The Principles of Human Behavior*, published in a series edited by W. I. Thomas. At the very least, he was positioned to introduce Freud: he was one of a number of people (including presumably, his mentor at that time, Thomas) who knew something about psychoanalysis and wanted its voice to be heard by sociologists.

Park's Freud is a medical psychologist who studied the emotional conflicts that derive from the suppression of a "single instinct – the sexual impulse" (1915: 30). This suppression produces a range of "psycho-neuroses" that have their origin in memories from childhood. These memories are of events that predate the fully formed version of the sexual impulse found in adults. The resulting conflicts are stored in suppressed memories in a person's "sub-conscious," from which they emerge as symptoms of hysteria. Park gave different examples: tics, twitchings, stammering, and muscular convulsions, in addition to "all forms of fanaticism, fixed ideas, phobias, ideals and cherished illusions" that he claimed Freud viewed as the by-products of the suppressed complexes. They may become so strong as to have a "controlling place in the life of the individual" (1915: 31). Then, in a statement intended to cover both the suppressed and the "normal" complexes, Park gave a striking recommendation outlining the potential importance of psychoanalysis for sociology:

> We are invariably moved to act by motives of which we are only partially conscious or wholly unaware. Not only is this true but accounts we give to ourselves and others of the motives upon which we acted are often wholly fictitious, although they were made in perfect good faith. (1915: 32)

In this passage Park emphasizes that it is insufficient and perhaps useless to ask people to explain their motives for what they do because they may be "wholly unaware" of them. This seems potentially to be a rather damning confession for a sociologist committed to a model of the sociologist as investigative reporter, for whom asking questions is a way of life.

However, what Park doesn't say here and in his general discussion of Freud is also revealing; specifically he does not indicate how a sociologist might go about discovering hidden motives. There is also the issue of how and why Park simplified psychoanalysis. Even writing in 1915, long before Freud's structural model, there was still a lot of psychoanalytic theory that could have been but wasn't included in his account.

This leads to the biggest hurdle in assessing Park's 1915 description of Freud's work: he did not reference anything explicitly. Unlike the other sections of his book, where ideas are linked firmly to published sources, Park referenced nothing in the section on Freud. However, the bibliography lists A. A. Brill's 1914 exposition of psychoanalysis, and that, rather than Freud's Clark lectures, is presumably the origin of Park's view. If this is the case, there is inevitably a dilution of Freud's views as it passes from Brill's to Park's commentary. Park's reliance on a secondary source may indicate that he was reluctant to invest a lot of time in the matter, perhaps because he did not consider it central to his concerns.

Freud's Initial Reception in the *American Journal of Sociology* and the *American Sociological Review*

Alan Robert Jones (1974) has investigated Freud's impact on American sociology by looking at published articles on psychoanalysis in the *American Journal of Sociology* (AJS) and the *American Sociological Review* (ASR) between 1909 and 1949. Taking a narrower time frame between Freud's arrival in 1909 and the publication of AJS's rival sociology journal, the ASR, in 1935, 29 articles were published in this 27-year span of time (Jones, 1974: 22–4). After 1935, the number of articles on psychoanalytic topics increased significantly, as both AJS and ASR published relevant papers every year until 1949. Combining AJS and ASR, the 14 years between 1936 and 1949 saw the publication of a further 146 papers. This number is somewhat misleading, as both journals published several "special issues" on the topic of psychoanalysis. Nevertheless, the fact that both journals were prepared to host a special issue on psychoanalysis suggests that the topic was of interest to their constituencies.

The existence of these papers demonstrates that American sociologists knew about Freud and psychoanalysis and were increasingly interested in papers about them. However, the sheer number of papers alone does not reveal the nature of their interest. To what extent were American sociologists genuinely interested in Freudian ideas? Was Freud seen as a threat, a failure, an under-laborer, a competitor, a collaborator, or an intellectual imperialist? To varying degrees, American sociologists in the first half of the twentieth century portrayed Freud in each of these ways. Consider some noteworthy examples. Most famously, Talcott Parsons understood Freud as an important contributor to a unified theory of the social sciences, but this understanding relegated Freud to under-laborer status in the face of Parsons' sociological imperialism. By contrast, Herbert Blumer, while critical of psychoanalysis, understood it as an imperialistic threat to sociology. Ellsworth Faris viewed psychoanalysis as a scientific failure. Ernest Burgess also described psychoanalysis as a failure, but as one that was both promising and salvageable. Kimball Young, John Dollard, and Louis Wirth, each in his own way, anticipated collaborative research between psychoanalysts and sociologists through clinical research and shared methods. Robert Park and W. I. Thomas arrived at the same conclusion by different routes; namely, that what Freud has to offer American sociologists is inferior to what American sociologists already have. They were, then, home-team supporters. In the case of Park, even his widely recognized debt to his former teacher Georg Simmel has to be put in context, as Park himself saw the influence of his Yale colleague William Sumner as a far greater force in his intellectual development.

Two years after Park's 1915 description of psychoanalysis, Ernest Groves published the first refereed paper about Freud in the leading journal of the day, *AJS*, in 1917. This paper had initially been blocked by Albion Small, the editor of *AJS* and Chair of the Department of Sociology at the University of Chicago. Whether he questioned the quality of the paper or its message is not clear. What is clear is that Groves described Freud in glowing terms. More specifically, Groves emphasized that one of Freud's books – *The Psychopathology of Everyday Life* – was an important sociological resource. Groves argued that in this book Freud demonstrated that "normal mind states are revealed through abnormal experiences" (1917; *SE*, VI: 108) and hence the division of labor between sociologist and the "alienist" should be rethought. Groves' Freud is not simply a physician who confronts medical problems, but is also an investigator of the "field of human experience" that stretches far beyond the world of the neurotic (1917: 108–9). Groves was careful to separate the importance of Freudian ideas from their future scientific verification, arguing that whether this occurs or not, they are of value to the sociologist. Nevertheless, the great prize promised by Freud was the discovery of "causal relations within the realm of mind experience" and the "laws that govern these relations" (1917: 110). For Groves, the logical extension of the argument that psychoanalysis has discovered causal laws concerning mental phenomena among both the normal and the neurotic is that Freud is in a position to reveal the "governing motives" of human conduct (1917: 112). Thus, Groves effectively anticipated the more celebrated argument made by Talcott Parsons about 30 years later.

Still relying on *The Psychopathology of Everyday Life*, Groves furthered Freud's cause by crediting him with a profound theory of instinctual sublimation. Although this had in fact been the topic of Freud's fifth and final lecture at Clark University in 1909, Groves appears not to have known this. The introduction and celebration of Freud's theory of sublimation was a coup for Groves, who could then demonstrate that Freud was in fact working a topic central to American sociology at that time; namely, the social psychological theory of social control pioneered by Edward Alsworth Ross, whose study *Social Control* (1901) captured the imagination of America's intellectual class. Clearly, then, if Groves could establish a connection between Freud's theory of sublimation and the sociological study of social control, the case was made immediately for the importance of psychoanalysis for American sociology. Groves' argument was that human society was only possible because sublimation allowed individuals to manage the conflict between internal, instinctual gratification and external, normative regulation (1917: 113). Groves told his readers that Freud's discovery of the unconscious allowed accomplished psychoanalysts to connect their patients' present misery to disturbed childhoods.

Groves' discussion up to this point has said little or nothing about Freud's theories of sexuality. However, he was evidently aware that readers of *AJS* may well not be predisposed toward Freud because they perceived him to overstate the role of the "sex instinct" in everyday life. Groves therefore chose to address this apparent criticism, even though it was not pertinent to the description of Freud he had given himself. Drawing upon W. I. Thomas's early work of 1907 to support his claim, Groves' defense of Freud was that he provided a necessary corrective to sociology's underappreciation of the sex instinct. Given Thomas's later troubles – the allegations of sexual misconduct and his reputation for scandalous living – at the University of Chicago, the first of which occurred at roughly the time Groves' paper was published, this was perhaps unfortunate. Groves ended his discussion by describing Freud's "theory of progress" as a kind of puritan renunciation of frivolous activities in order to achieve mastery of the "real world." Again, Freud is presented as a sympathetic figure confronting and solving social problems in ways that resonated with the beliefs and practices of American sociologists of the day.

However, it would be quite wrong to represent Groves as someone who had persuaded American sociologists of the relevance of Freudian ideas for sociological investigation. Although he presented a sympathetic version of psychoanalysis to an audience who in all likelihood already knew something about the field, it does not appear that he was able to kindle much interest. Indeed, it is probably more accurate to say that Groves' paper was the highpoint of interest, and the psychoanalytic flame, though not extinguished, was thereafter reduced to a flicker for quite some time. As evidence for this, consider the number of psycho-analytic papers published in *AJS* between 1918 and 1923 (the five years following Groves' paper). During this time, only five papers appeared, none of which built on Groves' arguments. In January 1918, Joseph Folsom published a very long paper on "The Social Psychology of Morality and Its Bearing on Moral Education." Although Folsom mentioned several of the Freudian themes highlighted by Groves, notably the sublimation of instincts, what is striking about the paper is that Freud appears as a very marginal character in a drama where American sociologists such as Edward Ross play all the major roles and American psychologists, such as G. Stanley Hall, are the supporting actors. Thus there is absolutely no sense of an emerging "Freudian school of American Sociology" in Folsom's paper. In fact, I suspect that Folsom's paper, which is long forgotten, actually offers an important key to understanding the initial reaction of American sociologists to Freud. Perhaps they were suspicious about Freud's alleged over-emphasis on the "sex instinct," as Groves suspected. They may also have doubted the scientific status of psychoanalysis. However, Folsom's contribution to this debate may have been to show us – albeit unintentionally – that American sociologists were not particularly impressed by Freud, not because they rejected his ideas but because they thought they already had a superior, homegrown version of Freud that came without the unwanted baggage associated with psychoanalysis.

The idea that American sociologists did not reject Freud, but rather preferred their own homegrown version of psychoanalysis, is a theme that will be developed throughout this project and which can be provisionally dated to Folsom's paper. Consider his preference for Ross over Freud. In 1901, several years before Freud visited the United States to deliver the Clark lectures, Edward Ross published his hugely influential study, *Social Control*. Like Groves before him, Folsom was anxious to show the intellectual links between his paper and Ross's work. Since Ross is now largely forgotten, it is important to emphasize the extraordinary sway his ideas once had. Louis Menand, in his engaging intellectual history, *The Metaphysical Club* (2001: 383), points out that Ross's books sold more than 300,000 copies – a staggering number even today and truly remarkable then. Freud's *The Interpretation of Dreams* (*SE*, IV–V), for example, sold only a few hundred copies in the first 10 years after it was published. To put Ross's success in perspective, consider the fact that American universities awarded 14 Ph.D.s in 1920, 25 in 1925, and 40 in 1930. Although these numbers seem paltry, in 1934 Ellworth Faris and Stuart Chapin debated whether the "oversupply" of American Ph.D.s in sociology now constituted a problem, to be solved by identifying career paths for future doctoral students outside of the university (see Turner and Turner, 1990: 62–3). Given this background, it is clear that Edward Ross was a publishing phenomenon whose influence may have begun in sociology, but eventually stretched across the entire American intellectual life. Whatever else we learn from Groves and Folsom, we discover that by the end of World War I American sociologists considered Freud as a secondary figure to their own concerns, a lightweight in the ring with intellectual giants. It is of course a contemporary judgment made by us and unknowable to anyone then that Ross, and arguably an entire generation of American sociologists, would be forgotten even by their own discipline, and Freud would become a household name whose recognition was comparable to that of Karl Marx, or, perhaps more aptly, to Pepsi-Cola or McDonald's.

In 1919, Carol Aronovici published "Organized Leisure as a Factor in Conservation" in *AJS*. Although the title does not suggest a concern for psychoanalysis, Aronovici drew upon Freud in order to bolster her Progressive political agenda for labor reform. Thus, although her substantive interests were quite different from Folsom's, her use and understanding of Freud were similar. Aronovici's primary interest was the exploration of Progressivism, an interest she shared with many and probably the majority of sociologists at that time. Freud was interesting to her insofar as he contributed to this American debate. In one sense, Aronovici did an admirable job of transforming the European, medical discourse of psychoanalysis into a strand of political theorizing, but of course in so doing she too downgraded Freud's role in the formation of American sociology.

Among Chicago sociologists, Freud's first committed follower was arguably the statistician, William Ogburn, whom Franz Boas had introduced to psychoanalysis in 1910 while Ogburn was still a student at Columbia. There is therefore a direct link between Freud's 1909 visit to the United States, Boas (who attended Freud's Clark lectures), and Ogburn, who later became one of the leading advocates of Freudian ideas in Chicago. By 1915, Ogburn had incorporated psychoanalytic ideas into his lectures, and so participated in the transfer of psychoanalytic knowledge to students – first at Reed College (1912–17), then at Columbia (1919–27), and finally at the University of Chicago, where Ogburn was a professor from 1927 to 1951 (Laslett, 1990: 417–20). In 1918, Ogburn even underwent a brief training analysis with Trigant Burrow and later became President of the Chicago Psychoanalytic Society (Hinkle, 1957: 582). Interestingly, Trigant Burrow also contributed to *AJS* and helped build a disciplinary bridge (see Burrow, 1926: 80–7). However, since Ogburn was also one of the pioneers of a positivistic, quantitative approach in sociology, he remains a curious, contradictory, figure in the early investigation of Freudian ideas by American sociologists.

Ogburn's fascination with and commitment to psychoanalysis certainly made Freud a continuing topic for debate among Chicago sociologists. However, Freud does not seem to have influenced Ogburn's academic work at all: he remained committed to a quantitative, observational model of science that left sociology with no opportunity to incorporate Freudian ideas. The worlds of subjective experience and internal representations neither interested Ogburn professionally nor were topics about which he thought that sociologists as sociologists could have scientific opinions. In a strange sense, then, his sociological practice (although not his non-sociological beliefs) led to an entrenched and rigid separation between sociology and psychoanalysis. Ogburn was very much a sociologist in his office and a psychoanalyst in private discussion, a sociologist by day and a psychoanalyst at night and by inclination.

Impressed by Ogburn's advocacy of psychoanalysis, Thomas Eliot published a paper in *AJS*, in 1920, in which he attempted to show that psychoanalytic ideas could strengthen the sociological understanding of the complex and often contradictory motivations for group membership. Using several hypothetical cases and elaborate, hand-drawn figures, with a classification of the different (more or less) unconscious motivations for a variety of church members explaining their church attendance, Eliot proposed an ambitious revision to economic theory. This paper inadvertently reveals that by 1920 a psychoanalytic vocabulary was sufficiently commonplace to be used without either definition or citation. Rather, the language of sublimation, wish fulfillment, fantasy, libido, the unconscious, and so on was presented as common knowledge. Eliot argued that Freud's ideas can be used to show that, in his example, a bachelor may attend church because he was "thwarted in love long ago" and a "mystic" may do so because of an "introverted libido" (1920: 343). Further, Eliot speculated that all group affiliation can be understood as sometimes conscious, sometimes unconscious, forms of wish fulfillment – which he attempted to portray in a remarkable graphic (1920: 340). He concluded by arguing that beneath the rational basis of economics lay an irrational stratum of unconscious impulses (1920: 352). Eliot did not identify the methodology by which sociologists might study these unconscious impulses; rather he left this as a problem for future research. Thus, although Eliot was as supportive of psychoanalysis as Ogburn before him, he did not establish the existence of a method by which the theoretical and speculative claims he presented could be tested – or even pursued. Ironically, then, the belief that the bachelor attended church because he was thwarted in love remains as speculative as the more conventional belief that he attended church because he believed in God. In fact, Eliot's hypothetical examples are arguably as speculative as belief in God. As I will argue later, American sociologists were at this time establishing a social psychology that was also an empirical plan of action, which, in effect, gave sociologists something to do as well as a set of beliefs to have.

Empirical doubts about Freudian claims were in fact aired almost as soon as sociologists began to discuss Freud. Early papers were certainly not uniformly supportive of Freud. For example, in 1921, Ellsworth Faris published the first of four papers in *AJS* in which he outlined the reasons to oppose the infiltration of psychoanalysis into sociology. This critique was also made in 1922 by L. L. Bernard, writing in the *Psychological Review* (28: 96–119). Faris argued that Freud's analysis of instincts was far weaker than sociologists' analyses of habits and customs. He drew a contrast between the intellectual strength of William Graham Sumner's *Folkways* (1906), holding this study up as a model of excellence in social science, and Freud's intellectually questionable and unscientific, outmoded discussion of instincts. Curiously, then, for Faris, Freud is "old news" and Sumner is the pioneer. Although targeting John Dewey, William McDougall's paper, "Can Sociology and Social Psychology Dispense with Instincts?" (1924) considered many versions of social psychology as "obscurantist" (1924: 657). McDougall singled out Freud for criticism as someone who "seized upon some one instinctive tendency" and "worked it for all and far more than it was worth, seeking to make it the spring of all human activity and the master-key to the understanding of all social phenomena" (1924: 664).

Thus, sociological critics of Freud detected two interwoven empirical problems that had to be solved if psychoanalysis were to be of practical use. The first was whether any of Freud's ideas were actually true; the second was whether any of Freud's ideas could be translated into a research agenda. What, critics wondered, would sociologists do when engaging in sociological research that was informed by psychoanalysis? What were the sociological equivalents of the couch and free association? Kimball Young (1927: 959–61) addressed some of these concerns in a paper published in 1927. This paper is important because it suggests that psychoanalysis and sociology can benefit from each other. Young used Freud's analysis of the life of Leonardo da Vinci as an example of how insightful psychoanalysis can be in revealing how aspects of childhood influence adult life. However, he then suggested that psychoanalytic findings remain overly speculative unless they are confirmed by other means. Young singled out Healy, the prominent psychiatrist who was central to delinquency studies in Chicago, as someone employing an imaginative and productive mixture of psychoanalytic ideas and sociological measures. Young argued that the use of personal documents, interviews, and observational data by Chicago sociologists such as Thomas, Znaniecki, Faris, Park, Burgess, and others lent itself to psychoanalysis.

Kimball Young proposed that collaboration between psychoanalysts and sociologists would be beneficial. Louis Wirth (1931: 49–66) tried to make this proposal concrete, using the example of child guidance clinics. Drawing in part on his own experiences in clinics and in part on his wife's experiences as a social worker, Wirth suggested that sociologists could make a valuable contribution to the treatment of delinquents undertaken by psychiatrists and social workers. To this end he invented a new field: "clinical sociology." Without referring to Young, Wirth made use of a similar argument, to the effect that the case method favored by clinicians is readily compatible with sociological research. Thus, the sociologist can cooperate in a team approach to case management. Wirth argued that some psychiatrists have themselves concluded that in order to treat their patients they need the knowledge of their "social situation" – knowledge that sociologists are ideally placed to offer.

This has led to the creation of "sociological clinics" in which psychiatrists, social workers, sociologists, and psychologists collaborate in assessing the "total situation." The sociological contribution to these clinics is to present a "cultural" analysis. This consists of studying status hierarchies, roles, group behavior, and the context of perceived delinquency. Thus, Wirth argued, the perception that a child is behaving problematically only makes sense in the context of his or her life. As an example, he pointed out that being lazy is a moral failing in some groups but an expectation in others. Rather than automatically seeing poor behavior as a symptom of an underlying disease, Wirth suggested that "Behavior problems turn out to be those forms of conduct which the person himself or others with whom he comes into contact regard as problems" (1931: 60). Echoing the social constructionist position of W. I. Thomas, who had earlier claimed that "if men define situations as real, they are real in their consequences," Wirth added, "a child's world is real if he can get the people who are significant in his life to accept it as real" (1931: 60). The proto-labeling argument advanced here is a compelling statement about the importance of understanding the individual's point of view in the context of his or her group life. Wirth added that the methods used by psychoanalysts and sociologists are often similar, as both collect life histories, the former as part of the therapy, and the latter as data.

Wirth's invention of clinical sociology was an impressive statement outlining one of the practical roles sociologists could play in social reform. He urged sociologists to be modest about their skills, and to take their time adapting to their new quasi-medical environment. However, this paper also contains a subtle critique of psychoanalysis. Although the overall tenor of the paper is one of collaboration, on closer inspection the sociologist's role is to correct the individualist bias of psychoanalysis. Before accepting internal explanations for a person's misconduct, Wirth wanted the clinical sociologist to make sure that any perceived misconduct really was unusual, and not simply expected conduct when judged by the standards of a person's milieu. In some ways, then, Wirth anticipated arguments concerning both the internalization of norms and the relativity of standards of conduct.

Sociologists learned to write about Freud and psychoanalysis with increasing subtlety and hesitation. Certainly, by 1936, sociologists appreciated that both the specification of Freud's ideas and the delineation of the different and sometimes competing types of psychoanalysis were complicated, often contradictory, projects. The early ease with which Park and others had characterized Freud was gone by the 1930s and their situation then remains our situation now. In one of the first papers published in the new journal, *American Sociological Review*, Read Bain (1936) – a student of Cooley's – wrote about the intersection of sociology and psychoanalysis with a new sophistication and textual awareness that had been until then largely absent. Bain showed an impressive grasp of the broad range of Freud's writings, the eclectic contributions of warring schools within psychoanalysis, and the broad literature within sociology and psychology. If he achieved nothing else, Bain initiated an elaborately referenced and detailed engagement with Freud.

The tone of Bain's paper was contradictory, making his assessment easy to miss. He began by suggesting that psychoanalysis resembles a "religious cult" and that the "internecine warfare" of the Adlerians, Jungians, and Freudians is reminiscent of religious bigotry (1936: 203). Bain then joked that there are "perhaps 57 varieties of psychoanalysis" (1936: 204). However, the bulk of the paper is committed to a specification of the conditions that psychoanalysis must meet if it is to be useful to sociologists. This suggests that at least one of psychoanalysis' 57 versions has something going for it. To clinch the deal, Bain then cited Holt and Jastrow's support of Freud, quoting the latter saying that Freud has so transformed our thinking that we cannot return to a pre-Freudian world again.

Nevertheless, Bain identified several key weaknesses in Freud's work. Bain found Freud to be a mechanical determinist who overemphasized the role of sexuality in the creation of neuroses. He was also critical of both Freud's separation of the mental and the physiological and his failure to incorporate behaviorist ideas into his theory. However, according to Bain, Freud's major mistake was to underestimate the importance of group life. As he put it, psychoanalysis "fails to envisage the human personality as a culture-product as well as a culture-producer" (1936: 206).

What must psychoanalysts do in order to receive an audience among sociologists? Bain wanted American psychoanalysts to be what they often thought they were: namely, natural scientists who rely on objective data. If they could meet this standard and incorporate a sociological understanding of the constitutive role of group life, then Bain thought that psychoanalysis could become a valuable, complementary field. What this shows is that Bain thought that it was reasonable to make the initiation fee to join the sociology club very high for psychoanalysis. And if the price became too steep, Bain was confident that sociology would thrive without any help from either Freud or his followers.

Writing in *AJS* in 1939, the year of Freud's death, Ernest Burgess identified discrete periods in the American sociological reception of Freud. Perhaps rather simplistically, he described the first period, 1909–19, as one in which American sociologists resisted Freud's ideas (see Burgess, 1939: 356–4). While it is true, as Burgess pointed out, that during this time sociologists were suspicious of Freud's emphasis on the "sex instinct" both substantively and methodologically, viewing it as a particularistic fallacy, and that sociologists were then, following Ogburn, seeking out positivistic approaches to which psychoanalysis seemed antithetical, it is also true that there were admiring voices who were given an audience. Gisela Hinkle's assessment of the first period of engagement between American sociologists and psychoanalysis is more revealing than Burgess's. She argues that, from 1905 to 1918, American sociologists gradually adopted the view that social problems were the result of the "maladjustment of individuals to the complexities of modern civilization" and that this focus allowed several Freudian notions, especially those concerning wish fulfillment, repression, and sublimation to slip into sociological discourse (1957: 577).

There are three striking features about the support that Freud initially received from American sociologists. First, they seemed to be quite comfortable with a Freudian vocabulary, they assumed that the readers of academic journals were equally comfortable, and they rarely made detailed references to Freud's then incomplete corpus. Second, sociologists writing between 1915 and 1924 did not appear to find Freud's ideas revolutionary; instead, they are portrayed as variations or at best extensions of already existing ideas. For example, Burgess criticized Freud for not integrating his work into the existing social psychological literature (1939: 358–9). Third, even those sociologists who were sympathetic to Freud considered the work of American sociologists to be more praiseworthy, and it was relatively commonplace to compare Freud rather unfavorably with either Ross or Sumner.

There are also two different kinds of observation that can be made about the initial reception. First, American sociologists wrote in the years around 1920 as if the understanding of Freud's work were unproblematic. This is more than an assumption by them that American intellectual culture was familiar with Freud's work; it is an almost arrogant presumption that, although Freud was then still alive and still writing, it was nevertheless possible to "close the book" on psychoanalysis and investigate it as a finished product. Arguably, the cultural revisionists of Freud in the 1930s, of whom Karen Horney was probably most significant for sociologists, were initially important because they effectively reopened the book on Freud, so that his ideas could be discussed anew. These efforts paved the way for the two truly revolutionary, sociological, reinterpretations of Freud in the 1950s, first by Talcott Parsons and then by Philip Rieff. And what is so extraordinary and inspiring about these two revolutionary readings is that they were so very different from each other. Indeed, it could be argued that Parsons and Rieff approached Freud from different worlds.

The second observation that can be made about Freud's initial reception among American sociologists is that, even when that reception was positive, Freud's supporters had little sense of how they could use psychoanalysis. Although they were initially drawn to Freud in part because he demonstrated that the demarcation between medical and social problems was often arbitrary, this did not clarify how sociologists could practice psychoanalysis without becoming psychoanalysts. It was, from their point of view, a theory in search not just of a method of verification but of any method at all. The next generation of sociologists who emerged in the 1930s, notably Louis Wirth and John Dollard, articulated answers to this question, but these answers had been conspicuously absent earlier. The reliance on hypothetical cases by Eliot (1920) is a good statement of this frustration: how can psychoanalysis be incorporated into empirical, sociological research?

For Burgess, the second period of the American reception of Freud was 1920–39, and was marked by increasing interest in his ideas. There were five "levels of influence" during this time. There were sociologists who rejected psychoanalysis but who were nevertheless indirectly influenced, and who adopted a hodgepodge of psychoanalytic terms in their work. Second, there were sociologists who uncritically accepted psychoanalysis. Third, some sociologists, among whom Burgess included himself, attempted to test Freud's theories using the methods of the natural sciences. Fourth, Burgess claimed that after 1920 many sociologists used psychoanalytic concepts when analyzing the behavior of individuals in groups, adapting terms to meet their own needs. Finally, some sociologists, notably Folsom, Waller, and Dollard, attempted to integrate the theories and methods of sociology and psychoanalysis.

Burgess frequently praised Karen Horney, seeing her as someone from the psychoanalytic side who was aware of both the limitations of psychoanalysis as a practice and of the need for theoretical revision so as to include "cultural factors." However, despite limitations and weaknesses, Burgess maintained that psychoanalysis made three important contributions to sociology. The first is Freud's recognition of the importance of the unconscious. Like Groves 25 years earlier, Burgess singled out *The Psychopathology of Everyday Life* as a study that extended the insights of Sumner and others into irrational behavior. Burgess credited Freud with both substantive and methodological advances over Sumner's arguments in *Folkways*. Second, Burgess argued that Freud offered an analysis of wish fulfillment that was compatible with existing sociological research by Thomas, Mead, and others. Third, Burgess believed that Freud demonstrated that not all behavior can be explained as the by-product of culture, and that experiences during childhood play an important role in human development that have been underappreciated by sociologists.

Burgess's conclusion was that the future of sociology lay in the synthesis of the discipline with cognate fields, including psychoanalysis. Coming from the very different vantage point of European sociological theory, Talcott Parsons reached the same conclusion just a few years later.

Assessment

The pre-Parsonsian engagement by American sociologists with Freud has a number of interesting elements. First, despite Freud's careful and somewhat manipulative portrayal of psychoanalysis in the 1909 Clark lectures, they had no tangible effect on American sociology. Sociologists rarely if ever referred to these lectures in their published work. However, despite this, I believe that they did have an informal bearing on sociologists, who quietly became aware of Freud from a dissemination of his ideas through multiple interdisciplinary channels. What sociologists thought about Freud until around 1920 was based on three things: a general grasp of "what people know about Freud' that did not require scholarly documentation, the view of Freud provided by his first translator, A. A. Brill, and a reading of what was for a long time Freud's best-known and accessible work, *The Pyschopathology of Everyday Life* (*SE*, VI). Rather like the ideas of Michel Foucault in the 1980s and 1990s, Freud's ideas were "in the air" after the Clark lectures.

Second, pre-Parsonsian American sociologists often interpreted Freud not as a radical, imperialist, intellectual threat, but as a flawed contributor to an existing set of ideas. However, the flaws that sociologists detected in Freud were often the same flaws they detected in their own work: difficulties of operationalization, unclear concepts, insufficient data, and questionable science. Therefore, Freud's perceived flaws did not lead to his immediate dismissal. Rather, they demonstrated to his American sociological audience that he was struggling with the same issues that affected them.

Further, although some of Freud's ideas seemed fanciful and methodologically suspect, others were quite familiar. For example, the concept of the unconscious was certainly not new to American sociologists. On the contrary, Sumner had analyzed unconscious actions at length in his widely read and highly regarded study, *Folkways* (1906). Similarly, although there was without doubt a puritan streak in early American culture and in sociology – as Freud himself feared – sociologists did not react simply against Freud's analysis of sexuality. Instead, they reacted against what they perceived to be the particularistic fallacy in Freud's handling of the topic. After all, W. I. Thomas and others had written about sex and gender before Freud – and Thomas was perhaps the dominant figure in early American sociology – and so the study of sexuality predated Freud's visit.

Third, American sociologists valued theory that was reasonably close to empirical investigations. To use Robert Merton's felicitous phrase, they wanted the "systematics" of sociological theory that could be put to use, having proved itself in existing research. Pre-1920 writing about Freud airs the suspicion that there is no non-clinical application of psychoanalysis and hence the theory is useless for sociology. The life-history movement was a solution to the "systematics" problem, but it emerged slowly, in part because William Healy left Chicago in 1915 and in part because W. I. Thomas was at best ambivalent about psychoanalysis.

In Park and Burgess's "Green Bible" (1921), sociology was characterized as the science of collective behavior. It was composed of three core areas: social psychology, ecology, and social organization. Freud had a space earmarked for him there if sociologists could be persuaded that his work was as worthy as that of Sumner, Thomas, or even Park and Burgess. However, by the 1930s, by which time Freud had published a lot more work, and distinct and perhaps incompatible schools of psychoanalysis had emerged, it was clear that "Freud and psychoanalysis" was no longer a discrete entity but a maze of possibilities. Cooley's student, Read Bain, demonstrated the new sophistication needed to engage in Freudian discourse. The topical question was no longer whether Freud could contribute to American sociology. The new questions were "Which Freud?" and "Which school of psychoanalysis?" By the mid to late 1920s, theoretical, methodological, and even political divisions were also very evident in American sociology itself, and some of the discipline's initial cockiness had also been eroded. In short, the intellectual map had become very complicated indeed.

2

From Sumnerology to Cooley's Social Self: Proto-Symbolic Interactionism

Introduction

The ideas of both William Graham Sumner (1840–1910) and Charles Horton Cooley (1864–1929) continue to exist for us today, but they do so for the most part only as echoes. It is not easy to establish the moment when they ceased to be the authors of books and became the owners of key concepts, but it has certainly occurred. Perhaps Sumner was still read until World War II. Writing in 1968, Philip Rieff noted that Cooley had been lost to his generation, whose faith in its own "radical contemporaneity" made Cooley appear hopelessly "out of date." He was in danger of becoming the latest recruit in the army of the "distinguished but ignored" – along with Albion Small and others (in Rieff, 1990: 310–11). Sumner is now remembered as the sociologist who distinguished folkways, mores, and taboos; Cooley is the person who coined the terms "primary group" and "looking glass self." The downward mobility implied by this transformation makes it hard for us to recognize now the excitement once generated by their books. In fact, there is a double problem: to recognize their importance then and to realize that they can still speak to us now.

I want to propose that despite their many differences – political and temperamental, among others – at least aspects of the work of Sumner and Cooley outlined a viable sociological social psychology. Thus, although Sumner and Cooley were antithetical political figures, they were nevertheless convergent sociological theorists. However, it was a strange convergence. To use part of Sumner's own vocabulary, although Cooley was an absentee in-group member of Chicago sociology, Sumner was definitely part of the out-group, an outcast, a pariah whose perceived pro-business, laissez-faire politics was completely out of step with the Progressivism favored by Cooley, Ward, Ross, Small, and most of the sociologists in the United States at the beginning of the twentieth century. Dorothy Ross has characterized this political impasse very well:

> Cooley was the Progressive Era complement of the Gilded Age William Graham Sumner; together they frame the liberal political spectrum that emerged from the crisis in American exceptionalism. Drawing round them traditional strands of republican political theory and exceptionalist history, Sumner spelled out the tenets of possessive individualism, as Cooley articulated the new liberal organicism. Cooley was as bold in revealing the sanguine premises of his organic creed as Sumner was in articulating the harsh bases of his competitive doctrine. . . . Just as Sumner has remained a repository for libertarians in their battle against the new liberalism, Cooley's work has equally proven a resource for new liberal defenders of an idealized American democracy. (1991: 247)

Ross's assessment allows us to understand the intellectual challenge – and risk – involved in separating out parts of Sumner's work and recognizing their relevance to parts of Cooley's sociology. This is not an easy step for anyone to take. Writing in the 1960s, Blumer showed that he was still unwilling to take this step – and so he included Cooley in the list of contributors to symbolic interactionism, but not Sumner. Perhaps Robert Park – along of course with Cooley – deserves credit for trying to ensure that Sumner is given his intellectual due. This required Park to recognize that Sumner's politics could be separated from his sociology.

Once this separation was achieved, the combination of Sumner and Cooley could be seen as part of what Parsons called "proto-sociology" (1964: 349). I would like to appropriate Parsons' term and alter it to "proto-symbolic interactionism," in order to stress the extent to which Sumner and Cooley contributed to a perspective which their colleagues could view as the standard against which Freud's ideas should be judged.

From Sumnerology to the Second Sumner

William Graham Sumner was a brilliant, erudite, impassioned, and personally difficult man, and American sociology largely developed in the early part of the twentieth century as a response to his ideas.

Sumner taught the first university course in sociology in the United States at Yale in 1879, assigning Herbert Spencer's *Study of Sociology* to seniors. Almost immediately, Yale's President Porter objected, informing Sumner that both Spencer and the fledgling field of sociology had no place in Yale's curriculum (Curtis, 1981: 61–4). It is instructive to note the difference between Yale's hostile attitudes to sociology in 1880 and the University of Chicago's welcoming embrace a little more than a decade later, as it reveals an important difference in the two universities' understanding of themselves. Yale still saw itself as a traditional, religious bastion, whereas Chicago anticipated its place in the rapidly changing twentieth century.

Although some students found Sumner's manner to be both abrasive and overly confident, most admired him as someone who could be gentlemanly, scholarly, and masculine at the same time (Curtis, 1981: 47–8). Perhaps Sumner had some of Herbert Blumer's panache, as Blumer too was a formidable scholar who also proved himself in other fields – in his case by playing professional football for the Chicago Cardinals. At any rate, those who revered Sumner did so with a passion, and at Yale there was a "Sumner Club" run by graduate students. Their goal was to promote and disseminate "Sumnerology" – the science of Sumner's ideas (Keller, 1927: xxxi).

Sumner was clearly someone about whom everyone had strong opinions. For the most part, he antagonized his fellow sociologists as much if not more than he antagonized college administrators. This is because Sumner was loosely associated with Social Darwinism and this lent itself to free-market principles and laissez-faire social policies. In a phrase which he first thought was very clever but later came to regret, Sumner announced that the alternative to the "survival of the fittest" was the "survival of the unfittest." By contrast, the key sociologists at the turn of the twentieth century – Albion Small, Edward Ross, and Lester Ward – were at least sympathetic to socialism and in favor of Progressivist social policies. Thus, what Small and others saw as their justifiable interventionism in social affairs, Sumner saw, in his curmudgeonly way, as inefficient meddling.

There is no doubt that it is difficult both to assess the value of Sumner's work today and to understand the controversies it inspired in its day. This is because although most of his contemporaries responded to the economic and political writings that he published around the 1880s, most sociologists thereafter identified Sumner as the author of *Folkways* (1959 [1906]), the book he published toward the end of his life. Unlike his confrontational, populist work on economic and political topics, *Folkways* is thoroughly sociological and scholarly. Indeed, it could be argued that Sumner laid the cornerstone of the approach that became associated with the Chicago sociology of Thomas, Park, and others. Thus, it is useful to think of not one but two Sumners. Robert Bannister has made this argument in order to show that Sumner is not easily understood as a Social Darwinist. Bannister (1979: 98–9) described Sumner as follows:

> A defender of property, he was not a 'business hireling' but a spokesman of an older middle class threatened by a variety of developments in American life. Accepting relativism and naturalism, he never relinquished his faith in individualism and democracy. By the end of his life, there were in effect two Sumners: the one a defender of an orthodoxy that most of his own middle class had deserted for progressive reform, and the other a pioneering sociologist whose *Folkways* never seemed quite reconciled with the rest of his thought.

An alternative characterization of the two Sumners is that the first was an anti-socialist elitist, whereas the second was a proto-symbolic interactionist. The second Sumner could easily be overlooked by sociologists used to and tired of his free-market rhetoric, just as later sociologists found it easy and convenient to forget the first Sumner, whom they often considered to be politically suspect.

It is this second Sumner, then, who initiated a distinctively American sociological tradition that many of his successors viewed as an explanation of human conduct that covered similar ground to Freud but in a more compelling way. Further, Sumner's proto-symbolic interactionism was grounded in empirical work that other sociologists could adapt and apply in their own research. Understood in this way, then, it seems that American sociologists did not resist Freud's ideas after his 1909 lectures; rather they compared Freud's work unfavorably with a homegrown product. However, for them to even make this comparison required them to distinguish the political and economic bravado of Sumernology from the inspired analysis in *Folkways*.

Sumner's Background

In 1836, four years before he was born, Sumner's father, Thomas, and his wife Sarah, moved 3,000 miles from the small village of Walton-le-Dale near Preston in Lancashire to the industrial center of Hartford, Connecticut, where Thomas Sumner obtained work as a mechanic. The Sumner family fled Lancashire for Hartford to escape poverty, believing, as did millions of other immigrants, that America was a land of prosperity. Although many immigrants became disillusioned with American life and subsequently returned to Europe, Thomas fought through many setbacks. Ambitious, he worked hard both to take care of his family and to pursue his own education, which he did at night either through personal study or through classes in public institutes. Later in life he managed property and saved enough money to build houses for sale. However, Thomas Sumner's life was not a success story of the American dream, and despite his best efforts and work ethic he ultimately died poor. Much earlier Sumner's mother, Sarah, died when he was eight years old, leaving Thomas to care for their three children. Thomas remarried Eliza Van Alstein. Apparently, Sumner and his younger brother so hated her that they plotted her murder. However, it was Eliza's financial planning that later made it possible for him to have a college education, at a cost of about $1,000 (equal to about a year of Thomas's salary as a railroad mechanic). Eliza died in 1859, when Thomas remarried, this time to Catherine Dix, who outlived him and saw Sumner's career prosper (Curtis, 1981: 14–15).

In 1859 Sumner attended Yale College, and thrived in an intellectual environment that emphasized classical training and traditional values. He participated enthusiastically in college clubs and debating societies and became a member of the secretive "Skull and Bones" society. Through these various activities, the abrasive Sumner made influential and affluent friends who became important for his advancement (Curtis, 1981: 17). Sumner graduated from Yale in 1863 and traveled to Europe to further his education, first in Geneva and then in Göttingen, where he continued his classical and biblical studies. Surprisingly, given his later suspicions of theology, he remembered his biblical teachers with great admiration, commenting that, "They taught me rigorous and pitiless methods of investigation and deduction . . . their method of study was nobly scientific, and was worthy to rank, both for its results and its discipline, with the best of the natural science methods" (Sumner, quoted in Davie, 1963: 1).

Sumner's study in Europe coincided with the American Civil War. Since he did not wish to serve himself, a substitute had to be found and paid for. The financial cost of this was very significant, well beyond his family's resources. It was covered by his new Yale friends, initially as loans and later as gifts (Curtis, 1981: 18). This made his European graduate study possible and may have saved his life. The moral cost of sending someone to war in your place must be heavy in a quite different way, but what it meant to Sumner himself is unknown.

In 1866 Sumner attended Oxford University, ostensibly to study theology, although he was far more interested in the informal study of political science. Two books were particularly important for him during this time. The first was Richard Hooker's *Laws of Ecclesiastical Polity*, from which Sumner received confirmation of his view that social change occurs in a slow, orderly way. The second key text for him was Henry Thomas Buckle's *History of Civilization in England*, which raised the related issues of whether a science of society was possible and, if so, whether it would be able to discover law-like phenomena. Sumner later traced his initiation into the social sciences to his brief period of study at Oxford (see Curtis, 1981: 19–20).

Back in the United States the following year, he was ordained deacon and then priest in 1869. He served in the Church until 1872, when, aged 32, he resigned to take up the appointment of Professor of Political and Social Science at Yale, where he stayed until 1909, shortly before his death (Davie, 1963: 2).

The First Sumner

Although not central to the argument that I want to pursue – that the second Sumner outlined a sociological social psychology that American sociologists saw as preferable to the part of Freud's thought that they knew – it is worth pausing to consider the intellectual ideas that impassioned Sumner in his first two decades at Yale.

There are two very different components to the first Sumner and one glowing contradiction. The first component is the enduring respect in which he held his father, whose work ethic and ambition became his own. Sumner's economic and political views were an attempt to preserve the equality of opportunity that allows people to pull themselves up by their own bootstraps. Sumner more or less consistently opposed any restriction or price put on the free pursuit of self-interest. That his father failed as an entrepreneur and died poor was not the lesson Sumner took from his life. Rather, he felt enduring gratitude to a country that gave his father simply the chance to succeed. With this perspective in mind, Sumner investigated different restrictions placed on individuals and found nearly all of them inappropriate. From his vantage point, tariffs on foreign goods, limitations on immigration, and wage demands by trade unions were all inefficient devices that were ultimately intended to benefit one group of people at the expense of everyone else. Sumner's perspective was hard to classify in party political terms: his opposition to import tariffs made Sumner unpopular with some Yale alumni, who sought his dismissal, whereas his suspicions concerning trade unions alienated him from Progressives, as did his opposition to any government intervention that he considered excessive, i.e. most government interventions. Sumner also wrote presciently about the damaging impact of monopolies and of the evils of very large businesses in general, some of which, in his day, of course, were run by the wealthy alumni of the Skull and Bones Society. These were also the alumni who were transforming Yale College from an under-funded small school into a world-class university.

Sumner described the person he sought to defend as the "Forgotten Man." He also referred to the "Forgotten Woman" in equally sympathetic terms. It is not too sentimental to suggest that the Forgotten Man is an idealization of his father, someone who worked hard, took care of his family, voted, invested his money, bought property if possible, and strove to better himself intellectually, economically, and socially. Sumner's mission was to devise a world in which the Forgotten Man and Woman had the maximum chance to prosper with the minimum number of constraints placed on their lives. Whether in fact they did prosper was a completely separate matter, about which he seemed indifferent. Years later, Robert Park made a similar but independent argument about the role of the "Marginal Man" in urban America in the early twentieth century.

The second component of the first Sumner is intellectual. As stated earlier, his brief stay at Oxford had convinced him of the importance of a science of society that is built out of a combination of laws and facts. From this experience, Sumner became an implicit and sometimes an explicit disciple of Adam Smith, whom he thought had established a law concerning the role of self-interest in the efficient organization of economic markets. As have many others before and after him, Sumner therefore separated the Smith of *The Wealth of Nations* from the Smith who wrote *A Theory of Moral Sentiments*. This took Sumner down a path leading to economic and moral individualism, where interventions in the lives of people who could take care of themselves, but somehow failed to do so, was a form of harmful meddling that helped neither the recipients of the help nor the society at large. This argument is not quite a version of the "survival of the fittest" but it is close enough to explain why Sumner was viewed by many as a Social Darwinist.

A useful way of grasping Sumner's political and economic position is to follow his argument in *What Social Classes Owe to Each Other* (1883). The first chapter of this book is discouragingly entitled, "On a New Philosophy: That Poverty is the Best Policy." On closer inspection, Sumner's worrying title was an attention-getting way of introducing his less threatening Durkheimian thesis that contractual arrangements are the best way of organizing a modern society. The inference he took from this was that in a free democracy there couldn't be a requirement to help others (1883: 26–7). In general, Sumner grasped fully the contradictory, competing aims of freedom and equality – and opted for the former at the expense of the latter. The book ends with the following assessment:

> Every improvement in education, science, art, or government expands the chances of man on earth. Such expansion is no guarantee of equality. On the contrary, if there be liberty, some will profit by the chances eagerly and some will neglect them altogether. Therefore, the greater the chances the more unequal will be the fortune of these two sets of men. So it ought to be, in all justice and right passion. The yearning after equality is the offspring of envy and covetousness, and there is no possible plan for satisfying that yearning which can do aught else than rob A to give to B; consequently all such plans nourish some of the meanest vices of human nature, waste capital and over-throw civilization. But if we can expand the chances we can count on a steady growth of civilization and advancement of society by and through its best members. In the prosecution of these chances we all owe to each other good-will, mutual respect, and mutual guarantees of liberty and security. Beyond this nothing can be affirmed as a duty of one group to another in a free state. (1883: 168–9)

This was the position that many of Sumner's colleagues in sociology could not accept. Rather, in keeping with the Progressive politics they favored, they looked forward to increasing interventions by different institutions in the day-to-day running of American society. Although there is certainly truth to Sumner's main claim – that freedom and equality are antithetical – the way he presented the case was clearly tilted in favor of the wealthy. Thus, when he complained that liberal interventions rob A to give to B he didn't consider the counter-argument that B may already be the victim in his example, having first been robbed by A. If A is a factory owner and B an assembly-line worker, it seems churlish to complain that costly welfare programs funded by Progressive taxation are a way of robbing A, since A's wealth was garnered from B's labor. Sumner's justification here is that the As of this world are the "best members" but that seems more hopeful than demonstrable.

But the curious part of Sumner's assessment is also a part of the title of his book. The book ends by stating that beyond good will, respect, liberty, and security one group owes another group nothing, just as the book's title singles out the question of what classes owe each other, not what people owe each other. Is it that people within groups or classes owe each other something that classes do not?

Sumner's answer to this question can be gleaned from his reaction to the role of trade unions in labor–management disputes. He recognized that "to say that employers and employed are partners in an enterprise is only a delusive figure of speech" (1883: 85). Their relationship is rather one of "antagonistic cooperation," to use one of Sumner's favorite terms. Despite the inherent conflict between management and labor, Sumner was suspicious of efforts by trade unions to increase the wages of their members. He believed that often strikes simply made things worse, since workers and business owners alike lose money during them. Believing in market forces to set the price for labor, Sumner was content to argue strongly against monopolies and then leave well enough alone. He believed that capitalist competition within industries for profits and workers alike will set pay scales at or above those obtainable by organized strikes. Understood less formally, Sumner suggested, strikes take place all the time: workers quit their jobs and work for other companies, consumers refuse to buy commodities unless their price is reduced, tenants seek new lodgings when rents are set too high, and so on. These "strikes," Sumner argued, are legitimate and useful (1883: 89–92). The valid role of trade unions, in his view, was simply to ensure that companies adhered to government regulations concerning safety and the general welfare of workers.

With his disconcerting ability to barge in where angels and everyone else fear to tread, Sumner drew upon the experiences of African Americans following the Civil War. He argued that they and many Northern abolitionists assumed correctly that the life of a free man or woman had to be better than the life of a slave. What they did not understand, he thought, is that free men and women are free in the sense that "they now work and hold their own products, and are assured of nothing but what they earn" (1883: 65). Emancipation guaranteed formal equality and hence (the prospect of) equality of opportunity; freedom in the marketplace, however, guaranteed inequalities and hardships. Interestingly, later in *Folkways* he returned to the same issue, drawing a very different conclusion from it. Where the first Sumner focused on the unrelenting hardness of the market, which made no concessions for past events, the second Sumner revisited what historians now call the Age of Reconstruction and learned that folkways and mores have a hard, thing-like quality. They are not impervious to change, but they are hard to change, and, as Sumner pointed out, Southern racist attitudes were not dissolved or even weakened by the Civil War. On the contrary, they grew stronger. The second Sumner's assessment turned out to be prescient (see, generally, Foner, 1989, 1998).

In retrospect, some of Sumner's failings seem as striking as his ideas. The glaring contradiction in the political and economic theories of the first Sumner is, then, ironically, Sumner himself. As an extremely intelligent man, he must have recognized that his own success owed more to the interventions of his friends than to his own sought-after talents in the marketplace. Although it is true that his initial academic success was bought and paid for by the labor of his Forgotten Man and Woman parents, it is also true that many of his later troubles were taken care of by fellow members of the Yale Skull and Bones society. If ever there was an example of protectionism, it is shown in the allegiance of these wealthy capitalists to their poor relation, known fondly by them as Billy Sumner. It was their generosity that kept him out of the Civil War, allowed him to travel to Europe, and later in life to take leaves of absence from Yale. It's not too much of a stretch to assume that these friends also played a role in his initial appointment to Yale. Ironically, then, Sumner himself turned out to be a Darwinian loser who was allowed to survive by the misplaced sentiment of well-meaning friends, who allowed him to survive by placing an invisible "pro-Sumner" tax on the goods they sold in the marketplace. Had Sumner given equal weight to the moral writings of his hero Adam Smith, he might have acknowledged what both Smith and his colleague-of-sorts Charles Horton Cooley recognized – namely, that the sympathetic ability to put yourself in someone else's position is as important as the market's invisible hand.

The Second Sumner

Unlike most of Sumner's earlier writings, which are brief, polemical pieces, *Folkways* is a long, scholarly book that presents a framework. The two introductory chapters of *Folkways* are, for example, longer than the entire *What Social Classes Owe to Each Other*. In keeping with the scholarly model Sumner had formulated at Oxford, *Folkways* fused conceptual innovation and empirical research in the manner later associated with symbolic interactionism. Arguably, then, the second Sumner was a proto-symbolic interactionist. Since he drew heavily on secondary, anthropological data, which he used comparatively, Sumner also implicitly gave a supportive nod to a qualitative science of society. At least until the publication of Thomas and Znaniecki's *The Polish Peasant in Europe and America* (1958 [1917]), the second Sumner occupied pride of place in American sociology. Even as late as 1927, Charles Horton Cooley described *Folkways* as probably "the most successful work of research that American sociology has produced" (1927: 325).

In *Folkways*, Sumner does not elucidate a political position, except perhaps the conservative notion that social change is best pursued slowly. Instead he established the "normative approach to social phenomena by viewing behavior as patterned by cultural norms or social codes which contain the notion of what ought to be and which exert moral pressure on the individual to conform to them" (Davie, 1963: 44). The full title of the book is *Folkways: A Study of the Sociological Importance of Usages, Manners, Customs, Mores and Morals*. As is often the case, what follows the colon in the title of the book is a better guide to its content than what comes before it. In the preface, Sumner defined the folkways as the "habits of the individual and customs of the society which arise from efforts to satisfy needs." They are learned during childhood through tradition, imitation, and authority. In a phrase that could have been written by either Simmel or Goffman, Sumner suggested that although folkways are "carried out in small ways" they are done by many people and as a result become very important. They become the means by which a society "is made to be what it is" (1906: 3). The habits and customs of a society regulate behavior and are "made unconsciously" (1906: 3). They must form a consistent system and satisfy our needs by modifying pleasure and pain. Folkways operate within "in-groups" or "we-groups." Insiders are mutually supportive, recognizing each other in contradistinction to members of "out-groups." In-group membership leads easily to "ethnocentrism", Sumner's term for the belief that "one's own group is the center of everything and all others are scaled and rated with reference to it" (1906: 13). In-group loyalty was something positive, a form of patriotism, not to be confused with chauvinism, a degenerative form of patriotism in which "watchwords" replaced reasoned argument and conscience and the whole group is imperiled by a small clique within it (1906: 15).

Sumner viewed chauvinistic behavior as the denial of the need for the "antagonistic cooperation" that is necessary for a group to succeed in the "struggle for existence and the competition of life." It is tempting to see chauvinism as a denial of what Parsons later described as "adaptation:" the functional prerequisite of a social system to adapt to its environment. Sumner argued that antagonistic cooperation is a very productive way for groups to coexist insofar as they are able to suppress trivial differences in order to combine for mutual gain. In a phrase reminiscent of Max Weber's description of politics as the slow boring of hard wood, Sumner suggested that, at their best, political parties cooperate antagonistically in statesman-like acts that suppress dogmatic factions in order to introduce meaningful social policies (1906: 18).

Generally acknowledged rights that preserve peaceful coexistence regulate the behavior of in-group members. Sumner drew on an eclectic anthropological set of studies to show that the rights of in-group members are relative and in no sense natural. In-group morality is preserved through taboos and prescriptions that constitute appropriate group conduct. This morality is historical, institutional, and empirical, and sociology, as Sumner came to understand it, was the study of the moral code of one's own culture (1906: 29). Since this could be undertaken empirically, presumably by qualitative investigation (although Sumner did not say this explicitly), the "science of society is the study of folkways" (1906: 34). This formulation was reworded a decade later by Robert Park when he described sociology as the study of collective behavior.

Rather speculatively, Sumner declared that folkways are a response to the "four great motives" of human action: hunger, sexual passion, vanity, and fear (1906: 18). Folkways respond to these four motives in ways that are "unconscious, spontaneous, uncoordinated" (1906: 19).

It is instructive to pause here for a moment in order to imagine the intellectual position of American sociologists in 1920, familiar on the one hand with some of Freud's work, his American lectures, and Park's précis of his ideas, and on the other hand equally or better acquainted with Sumner's *Folkways*. If we sympathetically put ourselves in their shoes, it is possible to understand why the "topographic" Freud of the Clark lectures, who had not yet distinguished between the id, ego, and super-ego, did not seem to offer them anything radical or even new. Rather, their own first sociologist, forgiven for his Social Darwinist sins, seemed to them to have already offered a model of group behavior that accounted for unconscious actions and sexual drives. In addition, Sumner seemed clear of the particularistic fallacy that was widely attributed to Freud. And, as the icing on the cake, sociologists found in Sumner a method they could use, something they could not discern in Freud. It is small wonder that they were therefore suspicious of psychoanalysis.

Sumner's account of the folkways was only part of a wider scheme of interpretation. As has been immortalized in successive editions of introductory sociology textbooks, Sumner distinguished between folkways, mores, and taboos. The last of these proved easy to define. Taboos are things not to be done: they are the accumulated wisdom of the ages that protect group life. Some taboos protect social practices; others destroy harmful practices (1906: 31).

By contrast, Sumner's convoluted although ultimately clear definitions of folkways and mores have troubled sociologists ever since. Little did he understand that his failure to firmly distinguish between folkways and mores would be the source of endless grade disputes in multiple-choice tests across America for decades to follow. After his death, his student Albert Galloway Keller, helped financially by the Sumner Club, published and co-wrote (with Sumner) the first of four volumes called *The Science of Society* (1927). Anticipating classificatory problems, Keller suggested the following:

> After practicing certain folkways for an extended time, people acquire the conviction that they are indispensable to the welfare of society. They come to believe that their own ways are the only right ones, and that departure from them will involve calamity. It is with the addition of the welfare-element that folkways become mores. To illustrate: the removal of the hat when a civilian meets a woman on the street is in our folkways, while the practice of monogamy belongs to our mores. We do not regard neglect of the former usage as dangerous to society, though it is discreditable to the individual; but we are so convinced as to the expediency of the latter that we will promptly and severely repress the polygamist, and that in the interests of society. There is a real distinction in analysis between a folkway and a more, but it is a discrimination for the laboratory rather than for actual practice. . . . Anyone who uses the two terms very much finds it in any case unprofitable if not impracticable to insist upon consistency in discriminating between them. (1927: 33)

Etymological dictionaries suggest that the term "mores" came into being around 1907, suggesting that the term is Sumner's, although Alexis de Tocqueville used a similar French expression in *Democracy in America* (2002 [1835]). Sumner defined mores as "folkways thought to be true and right – and hence necessary for common welfare" (1906: 30). Drawing on his extensive classical education, he distinguished "ethics" as that which pertains to the "ethos" from the "moral" as that which pertains to the customs. For the Greeks, ethos referred to the characteristic ideas, standards, and codes of a group. For the Romans, the mores are the "customs that are general and serve general welfare" (1906: 36–7). This suggests that ethics are, in Sumner's terms, in-group specific, whereas mores regulate the behavior of all groups in a given society. Thus, mores, though unconscious and involuntary, cover an "immense and undefined domain" that pave the way for new formal regulations and laws (1906: 56–7). This discussion led Sumner to suggest at various times that his field of inquiry could be thought of as "ethology," although he feared that his new word was much more off-putting than the familiar-sounding folkways. This in turn suggests that if Park was the immediate successor to Sumner, arguably Goffman was the key later figure to pursue the ethological investigation of everyday interaction.

Like Goffman 50 years later, Sumner recognized the ethological importance of ritual. Sumner viewed it as the unconscious embodiment of ideas that serve a group's interests. Rituals are militaristic in that they regulate habits learned through repeated and perfected drills. Prescribed behavior is thereby internalized. Rituals are at their most powerful when they are "most perfunctory" and unquestioned. They cover innumerable cases, allowing rapid decisions to be made in circumstances where the active consideration of each case is not just inefficient but impractical. The mores that comprise our social rituals are therefore doubly necessary, as they both root group interests in the unconscious of each group member and they facilitate potentially troubling exchanges in day-to-day life (see Sumner, 1906: 60–72).

For Sumner, mores must be institutionalized; that is, they need a structure that will sustain them over time. The institutionalization of the mores occurs in one of two ways: it is either "crescive" (i.e. growing) or "enacted." Crescive institutionalization is a slow, gradual process whereby folkways become customs and then mores before being formalized into rules and laws. Sumner used the normative regulation of marriage as an example of crescive institutionalization. By contrast, enacted institutions are brought about by "rational invention and intention." Clearly, given his cultural and political conservatism, Sumner assumed that enacted institutionalization occurs infrequently because "it is too difficult to invent and create an institution, for a purpose, out of nothing." Nevertheless, they exist. Sumner proposed that norms concerning the role of credit in modern banks are realizations of enacted institutionalization (see Sumner, 1906: 53–5). Crescive institutionalization, he concluded, is an unconscious process, whereas enacted institutionalization is conscious (1906: 56–7).

The Manifest and Latent Second Sumner

In my view, the manifest second Sumner was a proto-symbolic interactionist. His later work was championed by many prominent American sociologists, perhaps most notably Robert Park and Charles Horton Cooley. *Folkways* was a genuine contribution to the systematics of sociological theory. It presented an elegant conceptual schema with which to analyze the moral codes of in- and out-groups. Its extensive use of comparative anthropological data also demonstrated an emerging qualitative methodology that could easily be applied to the analysis of contemporary American society.

The latent messages of the second Sumner are also powerful, if controversial. The position set forth in *Folkways* is such that sociologists can dispense with an account of motivation. The answers that Sumner exhorted sociologists to find were located in the structures of group life and not in individual actions. In fact, the latter were of interest to Sumner only insofar as they exhibited the former. Whether Sumner thought that the delineation of folkways and mores was the ultimate explanation of human conduct is unclear. What is clear is that, to adopt a Wittgensteinian phrase, Sumner believed that once sociologists have grasped the ethology of the social situation, their "spades are turned."

The second latent feature of the second Sumner is his avowed relativism. Comparative anthropological data had convinced him that normative organization is not natural; on the contrary, folkways and mores are richly divergent. It is not, he thought, for sociologists to provide a ranking order for normative variations but only to study and understand them. The second, but clearly not the first, Sumner believed that neither his own rather idiosyncratic politics nor the broad Progressive politics of many of his sociological colleagues had any role to play in the practice of sociology. Sumner's later view was that societies change gradually through crescive institutionalization and therefore the proposed interventions by sociologists – or politicians – are just delusions of grandeur. At best they are simply inefficient interventions in market forces.

The third manifest feature concerned the presentation of sociological research. Given the logic of crescive institutionalization, it was reasonable for Sumner's sociology to be atemporal, since whatever changes were taking place were for the most part occurring very slowly. This led Sumner to propose (implicitly) a non-narrative view of sociological analysis that stressed not the unfolding of events over time but the normative, ritualistic structuring of group life at one moment in time. To the extent that the next generation of sociologists – many of whom were trained at Chicago – took investigative reporting as a template for sociology, a non-narrative form of sociology was counterintuitive. Their role model was Robert Park, and perhaps also the exposé novels of Upton Sinclair and Theodore Dreiser. Chicago-trained, second-generation followers of the second Sumner had to confront the narrative question. Theoretically, a move to narrative implied a move away from crescive institutionalization and toward enacted institutionalization. Politically, the move toward the second Sumner seemed to suggest – although it certainly did not have to – a move away from the Progressive politics that was a stable feature of early twentieth-century sociology, especially at Chicago.

Anti-Sumnerology and the Institutionalization of American Sociology

Although sociology was taught in the United States in different places for much of the nineteenth century, the discipline took an institutionalized form when Albion Small resigned as President of Colby College to accept the newly formed position of Chair of the Department of Sociology at the University of Chicago in 1892. The department began graduate instruction in 1895, thereby transforming sociology into a profession and ensuring the dispersal of sociological ideas, whatever they turned out to be. Sociology found a congenial home in Chicago. Committed Baptists, anxious to establish a new kind of educational institution, had saved the almost bankrupt university after decades of insolvency following the Civil War. The new university president, William Rainey Harper, had a vision of the University of Chicago as the "Harvard of the Midwest." However, unlike Harvard, which combined research excellence with class elitism, Chicago was recast by Harper as a new kind of university. To this extent, the University of Chicago had the heady goal of beating Harvard at the research game, even if it could not compete with Harvard as a finishing school for America's elite. Harper appreciated that sociology was a new discipline that could contribute to his vision of a new kind of university, and even though sociology did not expand very much as a department until much later, Harper supported it throughout his tenure.

Harper therefore gave Small at Chicago what Yale's President Porter was unwilling to give to Sumner: an institutional base from which the discipline could emerge. Sumner's place and ideas at Yale could have been solidified into a research tradition, at which point the phrase "Sumnerology" might have actually taken hold. Instead it became just an insider's joke. Sumner's place and ideas at Chicago were obviously quite different. He had no physical presence there, no former students were there to continue his work, and not many scholars in Chicago were sympathetic. Further, Sumner died about five years before his biggest supporter, Robert Park, arrived on campus. The mood at Chicago was pro-Progressive and therefore it was also anti-Sumner. By contrast, although Cooley was a quasi-outsider, in that he spent his academic career at the University of Michigan rather than Chicago, in other respects his personal connections to Dewey and Mead, his Progressive politics, and his general sociological outlook made him part of the Chicago fold.

Three Strands of Cooley's Sociology

Charles Horton Cooley (1864–1929) was a complex, reticent, and modest character, in style a far cry from Sumner. He never boasted of his academic accomplishments, although, almost apologetically, he would from time to time remind people that he was not just an academic but also a capable carpenter. He was proud of both the log cabin he built for his family as a vacation home and of the desk and bookcases he built for his office at home in Ann Arbor. Adopting the style of Emerson, Thoreau, and Whitman, he spoke in glowing terms about the outdoor life, physical hardships, and the commune with nature. And yet in the same breath, Cooley could also applaud the very different cultural, urban commentaries of Henry James and Theodore Dreiser (see, for example, 1927: 58–9).

In the manner of many of his heroes, Cooley kept a journal in which he recorded his thoughts and musings, as well as drafts of ideas and commentaries on books. He began this journal in 1890 and a complete record still exists from 1895 to 1929. Thus, this journal provides an interior map to Cooley's world from the age of about 25 until the last few weeks of his life. Two years before he died, Cooley began teaching a young graduate student, Edward Jandy, who attended his seminars at his house every Friday afternoon. After Cooley died, and with the encouragement of Mrs Cooley and faculty members at the University of Michigan, Jandy used the journals and other personal documents to reconstruct Cooley's life and work (Jandy, 1969 [1942]).

Charles Horton Cooley was the fifth of six children born to Thomas and Mary Elizabeth Horton Cooley. He grew up in an affluent, congenial, and academic family. His mother played a role in the local community, reared the family, and supported her husband's successful legal career. Cooley's father set a standard that was hard for him to reach. As a prominent member of the legal community, a law professor at the University of Michigan and a Supreme Court judge in Michigan, he was an impressive figure. Cooley himself initially sought a career as an economist, obtaining a doctorate in the field before working as a statistician in Washington, DC.

Cooley was a sickly child, who, according to Jandy, built "fortresses" to protect himself from the outside world (1969: 15). His health and temperament improved following a long trip to Europe when he was 20, but this was not enough to rid him of the thought that he had endured an unhappy childhood. His ill health continued during his college education at the University of Michigan, and his undergraduate degree took him seven years to complete. In 1890, he married Elsie Jones, a very intelligent young woman who appears to have been a perfect match for the bookish and often sick Cooley. They had three children who were later memorialized in Cooley's books through his detailed observations of their behavior. They were: Rutger (born 1893), Margaret (born 1897), and Mary (born 1904). In 1894 Cooley completed his academic training, earning a Ph.D. in economics with a minor in sociology. He immediately accepted an academic position at the University of Michigan, where he stayed until his death in 1929 (see, generally, Jandy, 1969, Part 1). Cooley's life – like his books – was introspective, quiet, and private, but at the same time engaging and vibrant. It is as if the shell were a protective, deceptive cover for the interior.

Cooley's work is the by-product of his attempt first to absorb a broad intellectual culture and then to cultivate a constructive dialog between the disparate voices of past generations. In his intellectual world, Marcus Aurelius speaks to Henry James and Nietzsche argues with Whitman. With Cooley's help, we are flies on the wall as all this takes place. Cooley digested these exchanges very slowly, documenting his reflections in many journals, portions of which were published toward the end of his life in a remarkable book called *Life and the Student* (1927). This book provides us with a glimpse of Cooley's private thoughts about his life and work, and a little about his personal life. *Life and the Student* is, then, Cooley's contribution to the tradition of writing diaries, journals, and autobiographies – a tradition he admired very much. The book is, perhaps, loosely comparable to Freud's *The Interpretation of Dreams* (*SE*, IV–V), in that both are revealing interior monologs – they are what Philip Rieff likes to call (rather mischievously) "interior decorating."

In reading Cooley, it is clear that three themes dominate his thinking (and especially the first two of these). They are: (1) a sociology of culture as a political assessment of Progressivism; (2) a proto-symbolic interactionism; and (3) methodological inquiries. Perhaps the dominant theme of Cooley's work was the critique of contemporary American culture. Like Freud, Cooley took a cultural turn, although unlike Freud he did so early in his career. Interestingly, Cooley is not always thought of as a cultural theorist; instead he is now usually thought of as a theorist of identity and the social self. This too was an important part of his sociology, as he tried to demonstrate that there was not a coherent way of thinking about the individual and society as separate entities. Rather, he thought, they are two sides of the same coin, two vantage points from which to observe the same phenomenon. Cooley was also interested in political analysis, and a large amount of his published work is an exploration of the prospects for the Progressive political movement of his day, and the implications of this for American culture. Finally, almost despite himself, Cooley had an interest in methodological issues. He did not consider his own mathematical training to be particularly useful for sociology; rather, he favored a sympathetic approach in the manner of David Hume and Adam Smith. The cultivation of sympathy was, Cooley thought, brought about in part through self-knowledge, and in part through detailed observations of the day-to-day practices employed by members of social groups. Thus, in an understated way, Cooley hinted at the kind of ethnographic work later associated with Chicago sociology, all the while showing little interest in employing it himself. An adequate understanding of Cooley's work has to show that these three strands are interwoven.

Cooley's Cultural Theory

Cooley's cultural and political theory – like his sociology in general – is written in straightforward prose that leaves the reader ill-prepared for the subtlety of his arguments. Cooley's style was a feigned casualness, belying the fact that he must have worked extremely hard to distill his ideas into such a concentrated but accessible form. Cooley's preferred medium was not the book or even the academic paper, but rather the paragraph. The result was something more than an aphorism but less than a well-formed argument. His books emerged out of the personal journals that he kept throughout his academic tenure at Michigan. In them he "stitched" together and developed the paragraphs of his journals as he explored the limits and plasticity of plain-speaking. For example, in a series of almost off-hand observations about university life, he made the following comment:

> One of the most depressing things I do is to go to faculty meeting[s]. How much more edifying are students than professors!
>
> The true reason, no doubt, is that I do not shine on these occasions. (1927: 169)

The first part of this comment expresses a charming and, in its day, probably unusual commentary on college life. However, it is a sentiment that now seems rather familiar. What is striking is the second part of his comment, in which he questioned his own honesty. In an almost psychoanalytic riposte to his own thought, Cooley undermined his own claims by suggesting that his views about faculty and students were actually defenses against his own failures. But then, curiously, Cooley added the phrase, "no doubt," perversely implying that there might actually be doubt about whether the fact that he didn't shine in faculty meetings really was the "true reason" for his preference for the edification of his students over that of his colleagues. Perhaps, then, Cooley's intention here is to leave us with the same lingering doubts and hesitations that he felt himself – about himself.

Cooley's politics are not easy to characterize, in part because it is often necessary to establish what he opposed in order to infer what he supported. Cooley certainly did not like political extremes, and wrote negatively about what he perceived to be the extremes of the political left and right. Thus, although he was often sympathetic to socialist ideals, he also condemned revolutionary efforts: "Violent revolutions are made by people who have had no chance to try out their ideas. Inexperienced minds think in formulas, and the formulas of a suppressed class are – what you might expect" (1927: 16).

Cooley was equally dismissive of a crude form of political conservatism: "Dr. Johnson, protagonist of loyalty and conservatism, observed that patriotism was the last refuge of a scoundrel. In any time of national excitement it becomes the first. Every base passion, every mean scheme, wraps itself in the flag" (1927: 22).

What was the middle ground that Cooley favored between revolutionary change and ill-conceived patriotism? Again, it is easier to characterize his opposition, and, in this case, his ambivalence about the existing political positions of his day. Living through the post-Civil War reconstruction, witnessing extraordinary industrial development, massive immigration, the expansion of urban life, and the emergence of modern forms of travel and communication, Cooley was forced to consider the merits of the prevalent Social Darwinist views that had many supporters in both corporate and academic worlds. He had to take a position vis-à-vis Social Darwinism because this theory was both an explanation of and justification for the widespread changes that Cooley witnessed. On the face of it, Cooley rejected Social Darwinism outright, viewing it as merely a form of pro-big-business ideology:

> Any theory which makes it appear that the class on top have a natural right to be there is eagerly accepted by that class. As, for example, that the process of making money is a 'survival of the fittest'; that opportunity is equal to all; that it does more harm than good to try to help the poor; that the successful belong to a distinct and superior race; that 'intelligence tests' in which the children of the well-to-do generally excel those of the poorer classes, are tests of native ability alone and not also of social advantage. (1927: 49–50)

In this passage Cooley appears to be almost working his way through Sumner's earlier work, dismissing each claim as simply bread to be soaked up in the soup of the upper class. However, Cooley could not imagine a version of America without a dominant class and so held onto the rather slim hope that enlightened public opinion, aided by new communications technology, might curb the worst excesses brought about by class inequality. For those on the left, even for his contemporary sociological colleagues on the left, such as Ross, Veblen, and Small, Cooley's anticipation of a mass-mediated control of inequality through the power of political opinion, must have seemed weak, if not simply naive.

In fact, Cooley's position with regard to Social Darwinism was far less clear than suggested here. Elsewhere Cooley proposed that Social Darwinism is simply one "aspect" among many that should be "harmonized:"

> Competition and the survival of the fittest are as righteous as kindness and cooperation, and not necessarily opposed to them: an adequate view will embrace and harmonize these diverse aspects . . . the normal self is moulded in primary groups to be a social self whose ambitions are formed by the common thought of the group. (1916: 35–6)

Here Cooley appears to advocate "relativistic pluralism." What I mean by this is that Cooley saw competition and cooperation as two aspects of the same social and political world, both of which contribute to each citizen's identity through the internalization that occurs in primary groups. The sting in the tail is that the fact that (normative) internalization does occur in primary groups does not make those norms "natural" or "right." In this regard, Cooley and Sumner concurred. Rieff understood very well that Cooley leaned despite himself toward a kind of relativistic faith in the healing power of primary groups. Rieff showed this by recalling a question that Cooley had earlier asked himself: "The group disciplines its members but who will discipline the group?" Rieff noted that in asking this question Cooley showed that he "still hankers after some authority larger than in his own group" that can give content to a life worth living (see Rieff, 1990: 300).

Before turning to the importance of the primary group in Cooley's thinking, it is instructive to understand the full scope of the pluralism he proposed for the United States. For such pluralism to endure, a healthy democratic system is required. In particular, it requires free speech, partly because this is the best way of diffusing dangerous ideas, partly because it is the best way of mobilizing opposition to such ideas, and partly because, sometimes at least, these dangerous ideas will actually be right and should be adopted (1927: 21–2). Pluralism further requires not just that ethnic groups should be accepted but that they should be welcomed. Cooley commented: "How poor American life would be without the immigrants – strangely colored threads from the fabric of the old world come to enliven our texture!" (1927: 25). He further envisaged the end of all formal and informal sanctions based on race. Racial hatred, he thought, was part of the irrational unconscious of people suffering from diffuse feelings of inferiority; it was a way of re-establishing self-respect (1927: 29). He put the matter forcefully in *Human Nature and Social Order*:

> The immigrant has for the most part been treated purely as a source of labor, with little or no regard to the fact that he is a human being, with a self like the rest of us. There is nothing less to our credit than our neglect of the foreigner and his children, unless it be the arrogance most of us betray when we set out to 'americanize' him. (1922: 262)

This sentiment is one that is captured in the fiction of Sinclair and Dreiser, both of whom present a devastating critique of American industrialization at the turn of the twentieth century. Sinclair's widely influential "muckraking" account of the meat-packing industry in *The Jungle*, and Dreiser's more subtle but equally telling account of the personal conflicts surrounding a young woman's attempt to find any work in Chicago in a time of changing sexual mores, in *Sister Carrie*, convey in detail Cooley's condemnation. What is interesting about Cooley's statement above is that he recognized in himself some of the disturbing tendencies to want to Americanize the many men and women who arrived in the United States in the nineteenth and early twentieth centuries.

Cooley viewed class conflict from both a shorter-term and a longer-term perspective. In the shorter term, he considered it inevitable and indispensable. This is because unions are effective both in securing material benefits for their members and in functioning as a version of a primary group. Without them, Cooley feared for the survival of democratic institutions. Where they were weak, he thought, was in their limited understanding of their mission. Rather than fight for the rights of all workers, unions tended to be sectarian and hence divisive. Cooley was less clear about what he thought of a non-revolutionary form of socialism, although he appeared to be at least sympathetic to its cause (see 1916: chapter XXV). Where unions failed to stave off poverty, Cooley placed the blame firmly on the shoulders of capitalists, who both benefit from existing economic conditions and have the power to change them (1927: 297–8).

However, the longer term is different. At some point Cooley believed that the inefficiency of class conflict outweighed its usefulness. He advocated – and weakly anticipated – widespread government intervention into educational, political, economic, and health spheres, resulting in dramatically improved life-chances for the families of working men and women (1916: 294–300; 1927: 50).

Cooley thought of the harmonization of sectional interests as a vital part of the democratic process in which people strive "somewhat blindly, for freedom and cooperation" (1922: 23). He hoped that American democracy could reduce economic inequality, while increasing the "spiritual" differences between people. What he feared was a kind of mass cultural homogeneity that produced mediocrity (1927: 40). Part out of optimism, part out of naivety, Cooley anticipated a revival of democratic principles and artistic achievement – brought about by the expansion of industrialization and mass communication. Rieff in particular has been dismissive of Cooley's "paradoxical hope" that something organic can emerge from something mechanical. Rather, Rieff notes, "television in the bedroom helps the members of even that sticky primary group ignore each other" (1990: 299). For Rieff, Cooley's worst fears have come true in the mass culture of celebrity-ridden Hollywood, pop videos, and cable television. The contemporary supporter of Cooley is the person who admires the Internet for its capacity to bring together people whose interests fall outside of the mainstream. The contemporary critic of Cooley is the person who reminds him that the Internet is a massive depository of pornography, pointless diversions, and online gambling.

As Cooley himself later realized, the concept of the primary group is far more than merely a descriptive category. He defined the primary group as one characterized by "intimate face-to-face interaction and cooperation" which form the shared ideals of its members (1922: 23). It is not a stretch to say that the primary group functions for Cooley rather as the super-ego functions for Freud. In keeping with a Freudian motif, Cooley described primary groups as the "nursery of human nature," giving three examples: the family, the child's playgroup, and the neighborhood (1916: 26). These are critical because they mold each child's understanding of the world, providing a complete sense of "social unity." This social unity was also a moral unity that Cooley described, rather revealingly, as the "mother" of all social ideals (1916: 35). Like Freud, Cooley also recognized that childhood was an "open and plastic time," in which the internalization of norms and values left a permanent mark that affected each child's understanding of both self and the world. Subsequent primary groups were

judged against the benchmark of family, playgroup, and neighborhood (1916: 26–7).

The concept of the primary group is central to his explanation of
and the justification for a democratic society: this is the core of his
sociology because the principles of the primary group are of the principles of the good life for both the individual and the wider society.
The sociological problem becomes one of translation: how can the
ideals of the primary group become the ideals of industrialized,
urban society?

Put charitably, Cooley was cautiously optimistic about the possibility of this translation, as he envisaged a new industrial and techno-
logical order, in which the benefits of life in primary groups could exist
in environments where families are no longer central to collective life,
where adults routinely relocate in order to further their careers, and
children live privatized existences away from the solidifying effects of
playgroups and neighborhoods. Put less charitably, Cooley was very
naive. He misunderstood the role of the mass media, confusing the dissemination of ideas with the manipulation of political agendas and
crass entertainment. For his critics, the primary group has not sur-
vived modernization. As his most astute interpreter, Rieff commented
that Cooley wanted to overcome the "discontinuous life" that we now
experience. To do so, he made the transformed but continuing presence of the primary group in twentieth-century America a "God-
term," an image of hope, if not a description of reality itself (see Rieff,
1990: 299).

Cooley as Proto-Symbolic Interactionist

Cooley, of course, never called himself – or even thought of himself –
as a symbolic interactionist of any kind. That term is a famous and
enduring partial reconstruction of the history of American sociology
made by Blumer in 1937, about eight years after Cooley's death. What
has become significant is not Cooley's assessment of himself, but
rather Blumer's later judgment that Cooley was a de facto symbolic
interactionist. Thus, with Blumer's blessing, Cooley became a legitimate contributor to a distinctively American school of sociology and an
honorary but absent member of Chicago sociology. Clearly, the theme
of this chapter is that Blumer made an inspired choice in including
Cooley, but a mistake in excluding Sumner. With Cooley, he overlooked the absence of empirical work and emphasized the importance
of his social theory. With Sumner, Blumer overlooked the importance

of both his social theory and his qualitative methodology, apparently because of his anti-Progressivist politics.

What I am calling Cooley's proto-symbolic interactionism is the end product of an amalgam of two projects. The end product is one of the master keys of his work: his theory of sympathy. The two prior projects are, first, his attempt to incorporate instinct theory (and biology in general) into sociology and, second, his attempt to replace utilitarianism (and individualistic theories in general) with an account of the interdependence of self and society.

Reacting both to the Social Darwinism of his time and to the then fluid disciplinary boundaries between the natural and social sciences, Cooley attempted to theorize the relationship between heredity and culture as two distinct forms of transmission. He referred to the former as a "stream" and the latter as the "road" that runs "along the bank" of the stream (1922: 4). Sometimes the stream and road are parallel, sometimes not, as when an adopted child is brought up in a new and different culture (1922: 6).

Cooley was troubled by the notion of instinct because it did not fall squarely into either of these two modes of transmission. He rejected the claim that instincts are part of our "germ-plasm" because this suggested that we have no choice in our actions, and that we act "instinctively" without will or control. However, Cooley could not find a way of making instincts cultural either, because there is clearly a physicality to them. His solution was to create a new term, an "instinctive emotion," and to then identify five basic types. They are: anger, fear, maternal love, sex drive, and a self-assertive drive for power (1922: 25). Cooley believed that these five types are all instinctive because they are universal, associated with physical reactions, and found in both humans and animals. Nevertheless, they are also emotions because they are adapted according to circumstances and experienced differently in different social situations. In the second (but not the first) edition of *Human Nature and Social Order*, Cooley added that psychoanalysts, among others, are at fault for trying to separate instincts from the social processes in which they are found and by which they are transformed. In overemphasizing the instinctive component of human behavior, Cooley believed that psychoanalysts were relying on old-fashioned, mechanistic ideas that displayed the fallacy of particularism (1922: 29).

Cooley's alternative conception of the instinctive emotion allowed us, he thought, to recognize that we all have the capacity to monitor and hence control our instinctive drives. He suggested that we use reason as the "team-work of the mind." Reason "takes the energy of the instinctive dispositions, as an officer takes his raw recruits, instructing and training them until they can work together" (1922: 30). Ironically, then, Cooley's formulation, which he explicitly thought was in complete opposition to what he saw as an outmoded psychoanalytic view, turned out to be readily compatible with the structural model of the id, ego, and super-ego that Freud published the year after Cooley's revised edition of *Human Nature and Social Order* in 1922. Cooley's claim here that reason is a "principle of higher organization" that controls and transforms instinctive energies covers, at least provisionally, the same territory as Freud's concept of sublimation. Cooley also gave an approximate account of the Freudian concept of transference (in its object-relations form), when he argued that, in order to study the social world, sociologists must investigate the "imaginations" people have of one another, recognizing how significant and consequential these may be (1922: 121–2). Thus, as Parsons (1968) argued much later, there were certainly signs of an unintended convergence between the emerging theories of Freud and Cooley.

The culmination of Cooley's discussion of the two lines of transmission was his definition of human nature, which he understood to be simultaneously hereditary, a social product of primary-group identification, and an umbrella term for our various personal strengths and weaknesses (1922: 31–4). Thus, as with his account of instinct, he attempted to incorporate the apparent physicality of human nature into a broad sociological view of the world.

So, Cooley's first mission was to reconcile what he knew of biology, heredity, and instinct with social theory. His second mission was to promote the idea that the individual and society are interconnected, to the point that we cannot meaningfully discuss one without the other. Cooley expressed this in a typically concise way when he argued that society and individuals "do not denote separate phenomena but are simply collective and distributive aspects of the same thing" (1922: 37). This idea was implicit in his political, anti-Sumnerian, Progressivist commentary, which railed against any defense of instrumental action that benefited the individual and harmed the group. However, it was also a necessary prerequisite for the kind of sociology he wanted to practice, since it assumed (as did Durkheimian sociology in France at about the same time) that there was an accessible, discrete social reality that stood apart from the individual. This was what he wanted to study by "sympathetic introspection." This was also the social reality that Sumner had at the end of his life found a productive way to conceptualize and classify. So, curiously, by circuitous means, their different paths had led them both to the same new intellectual territory. But how to study this new territory?

Cooley's Methodology

The implicit instruction accompanying most of Cooley's methodological work is "do what I say, not what I do." That is, Cooley did not often practice what he preached. His preferred way of practicing sociology for himself was the hermeneutic investigation of texts, and this was in keeping with his withdrawn, private, scholarly manner. His readings aimed to capture the "feeling" of each work rather than to characterize arguments or assess evidence:

> An intelligent reader goes slowly when he feels that each word has its peculiar and essential force. He watches the author. We *want* to make out personality, and if there is the least trace of it imagination is excited and puts forth guesses, we become clairvoyant. We want the author himself, as an explanation, a guaranty, a vehicle for the thought. And we find him in his choice of words, in the movement of his sentences, in the attitudes and habits of feeling implicit in what he says, in a hundred signs not less telling, to the sensitive reader, than the visible and audible man. (1927: 57)

However, Cooley thought of sociologists as more than just "intelligent readers" – they are also empirical researchers. This is where Cooley's prescriptions no longer matched his practices, in that he rarely gathered data, and when he did so it was usually in the form of haphazard personal observations, often of his three children. This was not what he encouraged others to do. Much as David Hume, Adam Smith, and, closer to home, Sumner, had advocated, Cooley considered "sympathetic introspection" to be the "principal method of the social psychologist" (1916: 7). The term is somewhat misleading, as it could be taken to suggest that research can be carried out from an armchair in a study. In fact, Cooley actually thought of sympathetic introspection as something sociologists do in the field by putting themselves into "intimate contact with various sorts of persons and allowing them to awake in [them] a life similar to their own" that can later be described and analyzed (1916: 7). Thus, Cooley's methodology for himself was hermeneutic interpretation and appreciation; his methodology for other sociologists was active participant observation. This preference for qualitative, ethnographic work was in keeping with his disdain for quantification, overtly moralistic or mechanistic, systematic approaches. Cooley practiced a kind of intellectual history, but preached a kind of ethnographic research that only became commonplace toward the end of his life.

His methodological preference for ethnography as the realization of sympathetic introspection was, as stated earlier, very consistent with his starting theoretical premise – that self and society "go together, as phases of the common goal" (1916: 8–9). If this is indeed true, then there must be the possibility of intersubjective access to the individual through the normative conventions of the group. Attacked from the other direction, Cooley also realized that autobiography could be a powerful tool of group analysis, since the experiences of the individual can be a window to the experiences of the group. Thus, his journals, like Freud's self-analysis, are simultaneously a form of introspection and a group-oriented, social commentary.

Proto-Symbolic Interactionism and Freud

Cooley understood that the existence of a social self that could be studied by sympathetic introspection meant that emotions were properly part of the subject matter of sociology. Emotions are not individualized, physical reactions to events, but rather internalized group standards. Both positive and negative physical feelings – such as the red face of someone who is embarrassed or the glow of someone who is proud of an accomplishment – are the residues of these internalized group standards, and as such they can be learned. Cooley pointed out that each of us must gain public mastery of these emotions in order to function in the adult world. Just as children must grasp the meaning of "I," "you," and "me" early in life, so too must we all grasp the meaning of abstract qualities such as disgust and hope. Not unlike Freud, then, Cooley initiated what might now be called a deconstruction of emotion. It is a deconstruction in the sense that emotions are usually composites of both good and bad elements. This facet of emotions is captured in the many everyday expressions to the effect that a person's greatest strength is also his or her greatest weakness. Cooley demonstrated this using two examples: pride and honor. Pride is a display of consistency and hence is a strength; however, pride's weakness is that it also tends to make people inflexible, to prevent change (and therefore growth), and to antagonize others. Honor functions in a different way, in that it contains contradictory elements, since honor is simultaneously a form of self-respect and a recognition of the overriding importance that the opinions of others play in the life of the honorable person (1922: 238).

It is tempting to see Cooley's deconstruction of emotions as the first step in a theory of ambivalence as a symptom of modernity. This ambivalence is not simply the by-product of disenchantment, instrumentality, and secularization. It occurs – it is felt – because what we now set out to achieve seems necessarily and inevitably modest, and even these achievements involve mixtures of good and evil. Cooley wrote about this in his journals and a summary of this was published in *Life and the Student*: "Life as it is is in great part confined, stagnant, futile. We have constructive energy, but it works in narrow channels, for a small class and to rather low ends" (1927: 53). The tone – and even the wording – is eerily like Freud's cultural analysis of the discontents of modern life. For Cooley, much of what we do is futile; for Freud, successful psychoanalysis returns the neurotic patient to a normal state of unhappiness. The strains are felt in the person but they reside in the contradictions of modern life, to be managed by defenses, sublimations, and various transferences. For Cooley, this management was achieved by a quiet, reserved life of contemplation, interrupted by physical work and the admiration of nature in the manner of his American heroes, Emerson and Thoreau. For Freud, this management was achieved by a psychoanalytic intervention to strengthen the ego. Perhaps, then, just as Cooley and Sumner found circuitous paths to the same point, so too did Cooley and Freud. The difference is that Cooley and Sumner converged on an understanding of what sociology could be and how it could be studied empirically, whereas Cooley and Freud converged on an understanding of the self and the contradictions that inevitably emerge because of the ambivalence of our times.

3

Symbolic Interactionism and Psychoanalysis: Blumer's and Goffman's Extension of Mead

Introduction

After the institutionalization of sociology at the University of Chicago in the mid-1890s, there was a protracted effort to establish theoretical and methodological bases for the discipline, that would preserve its autonomy from cognate fields (Bulmer, 1984; Smith, 1998). The formulation of a credible sociological social psychology was a major component of this effort, identified primarily but not exclusively through the work of George Herbert Mead. Although disconnected from methodological concerns, Mead's theory of social behaviorism resonated with the efforts of contemporary sociologists to understand the ecology and social organization of urban life. Mead's theory was therefore one that could be used (if not exactly tested) in the University of Chicago's sociological "laboratory" – the city of Chicago itself. In formulating a sociological social psychology, Mead was certainly aware of Freud but was not intimidated by him. Rather, he saw Freud as someone who had overstated a general observation about the sexual etiology of neurotic disorders. Mead understood his own work as a corrective to and extension of this approach. Blumer's subsequent incorporation of Mead's social behaviorism into a broad theoretical and methodological approach produced "symbolic interactionism," a term he first coined in 1937. Blumer pared down Mead's social behaviorism to those elements that he thought were compatible with the qualitative methodology that emerged from

Chicago sociology. Despite his antipathy to the label, later it became apparent that Erving Goffman's sociology was a powerful theoretical, methodological, and substantive display of the symbolic interactionist approach.

In this chapter I use both Blumer and Goffman's opposition to psychiatry and psychoanalysis as a way of understanding their quite different contributions to symbolic interactionism. The traditional reading of Blumer has judged him by the standard of faithfulness to his mentor, George Herbert Mead. Thus, a major concern for many commentators has been to assess the degree of similarity between Mead's initial description of social behaviorism and Blumer's later, reconstructive, symbolic interactionism. Although I will comment on Blumer's "translation" of Mead, for the most part I want to consider Blumer's contribution quite differently, as a theory composed in opposition both to Freud and psychoanalysis and to Parsons and functionalism.

Blumer's opposition to Freud and psychiatry is somewhat hidden. By contrast, Goffman's antipathy to psychiatry as a profession is well known. His most explicit assault on psychiatry as a scientific pursuit and as a medical practice is in the concluding essay of *Asylums*. This antipathy led him to the claim that psychiatric knowledge was frequently less credible than his own ethnographic observations of the behavior of the mentally ill. I present this as an example of "ontological gerrymandering" and therefore as something illegitimate and in fact unnecessary for Goffman's cause, namely, the ethological investigation of the interaction order. His project involved the rejection of the kind of intrasubjective inquiry that, at its most general, is the core of psychoanalytic inquiry. Nevertheless, in *Asylums* he was sometimes drawn into introspective inquiry, where his work was closer to Cooley and Freud than to his more obvious predecessor, Sumner.

Most of Goffman's various sociological investigations – the ethnographic, the ethological, the taxonomic, the strategic, and later the conversation analytic – shared an indifference to speculation about subjective states, preferring instead to use observable interaction. The advantage of his approach is that his findings remain open to further empirical investigation. The disadvantage, as many of his critics point out in one form or another, is that there are no "plot lines" in Goffman's account of the social world. Instead, we are portrayed as individuals with highly developed "generalized others."

Mead's Social Behaviorism and Assessment of Psychoanalysis

Although it is wrong to consider George Herbert Mead as simply the inventor of social behaviorism, I wish to limit the discussion here to this element of Mead's overall work because it is both closest to psychoanalysis and also most familiar to sociologists. Other commentators (including Cook, 1993; Joas, 1997; Maines, 2001; and Habermas, 1987) have indicated the richness of Mead's contributions to our understanding of pragmatism, time, philosophical topics, evolutionism, and educational reform, thereby revealing the breadth of his overall thought. Instead, I only consider Mead's social behaviorism, which he contrasted with the then prevailing behaviorism of John Watson. Mead understood and supported a broad version of behaviorism that he defined as: "an approach to the study of experience of the individual from the point of view of his conduct, particularly, but not exclusively, the conduct as it is observable by others" (1962: 2). The hedge "but not exclusively" is in fact very consequential, since it made the domain of social behaviorism much wider than Watsonian behaviorism. Watson's attitude to internal states, Mead suggested rather drolly, was comparable to that of the Queen in *Alice in Wonderland*, namely: "Off with their heads!" (Mead, 1962: 2–3). By contrast, like Cooley, Mead wanted a broader approach that could include the field of introspection, even though this was not directly observable. With the inclusion of a few words, then, Mead had opened sociology's door to the investigation of internal states and internal worlds, and made the relationship between sociological and psychoanalytic investigation a live issue.

The focus of sociological interest in Mead has been the second section of his masterpiece, *Mind, Self and Society* (1962 [1934]) that contains a sustained investigation of the dynamic interplay between the self and the social group. Mead's intention is to show that a person's sense of self is significantly (but not completely) formed through the internalization of the norms and values of the different groups to which he or she belongs. These group standards are internalized rather than simply learned, indicating that they are fused into the person's sense of self. Whereas a knowledgeable outsider might simply understand that group members will probably feel, for example, anger in response to a certain event, insiders both understand that this is the likely response and actually feel anger themselves. Their blood boils, or at least their blood pressure goes up. Thus, the Meadian self has discursive, emotional, and even visceral reactions that are simultaneously the "property" of the person and the group.

A person's self is not and cannot be present at birth. Rather, Mead suggests, it emerges during "social experience and activity" (1962: 135, and again: 136). These experiences and activities take place in groups, and the socialization and later internalization of group standards is a prerequisite for group membership. Mead outlined a developmental schema that children pass through as they master socialization and internalization skills. This involves a critical passage from a "play stage" to a "game stage." During the former, children take on the roles of "significant others" that have a concrete existence for them, such as their own parents, or perhaps the roles of specific comic-book figures, such as Spiderman or Superman. Later, they enter a game stage where they understand the different roles played by members of the group. This allows children to play the roles of "generalized others" that exist only in the abstract, such as police officers or bank robbers. During the game stage, children's activities become structured by rules and bounded in space and time, thereby preparing them for the practical constraints of adult life (1962: 150–64).

Since we qualify for membership of multiple groups, it follows that we also have multiple personalities, a state of affairs that Mead considers to be "normal" (1962: 142–3). As part of the creation of multiple personalities, we internalize the requirements for membership of each group. In Mead's vocabulary, we adopt the "morale" of each group and this gives us a sense of belonging (1962: 160). It is much more powerful than the morale we have when we belong to a large, undifferentiated group, such as a town, to which we may feel only a slight attachment.

In order to conceptualize the process of forming a normal multiple personality, Mead introduced a famous distinction between the "I" and the "me." The "me" characterizes the attitudes of the group and as such contains community standards: "The 'me' represents a definite organization of the community there in our own attitudes" (1962: 178). Since we simultaneously belong to multiple groups, we must also have more than one "me." The "me" "is the organized set of attitudes of others which one . . . assumes" (1962: 175). By assuming these attitudes, the person internalizes them. The "me" is therefore the attitude of the generalized other that the child learned to adopt repeatedly during the game stage.

A person with an over-developed "me" is a hyper-conformist whose "ideas are exactly the same as those of his neighbors," with only limited and "unconscious" adjustments (1962: 200). To counteract the mechanical behavior that results from this, Mead argued that we also have an "I" that is each person's (that is, each organism's) response to attitudes of the generalized other contained in each me (1962: 175).

The self is formed out of the "conversation" between the "I" and the "me" (1962: 179). This conceptualization of identity is complicated by the fact that each person has a multiple personality and is therefore composed of more than one "I" and "me." As a result, we are all therefore composed through multiple internal conversations.

Although not of immediate interest to Mead himself, it is not difficult to see that sociologists could understand Mead's delineation of the "me" as something that could be empirically investigated. Mead inadvertently positioned himself as the inventor of a set of ideas crying out for a qualitative method of inquiry to ascertain the content of the "me" that is formed in and by specific social groups. Since the "me" is the property of both the person and the group, it can be studied, in the manner of Durkheim, without recourse to the psychological investigation of the individual. This is because the "me" imposes an external constraint on the individual (what Searle called a "regulative rule") that exists *sui generis*. The "me" can therefore be understood as a Durkheimian social fact.

The "I" in Mead's theory is harder to pin down, and, as Lewis (1979) has shown, Mead used the term in different ways. However, at a minimum, the "I" is the response made by the person to the dictates of the generalized other. It is a repository of impulses that are regulated, in fact censored, by the "me."

This conceptualization of the "I" has generated more concern than that of the "me" and, with this, more controversy. Lewis (1979) has argued that commentators on Mead have often falsely reduced the concept of the "I" to either a remedial or a residual status. He suggests that both approaches fail because they separate Mead's conceptualization of the "I" from his overarching account of social behaviorism. Understood as a remedy, Mead's "I" is interpreted as a way of avoiding a deterministic conception of self. Understood as a residue, it is a way of accounting for the unpredictability of human conduct. In effect, these two interpretations are two sides of the same coin. These problems occurred in part because Mead used the term "I" "equivocally" (1979: 266). Habermas made a similar observation when he suggested that Mead "vacillates in his use of the expression 'I' " (1987: 41). For Habermas, the Meadian "I" referred both to spontaneous emotional responses and to the self's capacity to find creative solutions to problems of self-realization (1987: 41).

Habermas assumes (1987: 40–2) that the vocabularies of social behaviorism and psychoanalysis are readily compatible. He therefore presents the "me" as a super-ego and the "I" as an id-ego composite. In a statement that is important for the argument that I want to pursue, Habermas then equates the "me" with the external world and the "I" with the internal world, arguing that Mead made the boundary between them increasingly clear (1987: 42). In my retelling of this argument, the inference is that he stepped back from the investigation of the non-observable part of the social world that can only be reached through introspection. Had Mead stepped back even further and then initiated an empirical research program, he would have anticipated, in my view, the work of his greatest successor, Erving Goffman.

However, Habermas (rather like Shibutani before him) assumed but did not discuss the compatibility of social behaviorist and psychoanalytic vocabularies. By contrast, Lewis considers this assumption to be grossly incorrect (1979: 273) because it overstates the extent to which the "I" should be characterized as a depository of impulsive animal drives. However, Mead himself recognized (1962: 210) that the "I" and the "me" bore a resemblance to Freud's id, ego, and super-ego. Mead accepted what we can now think of as Habermas's position, since he agreed that his notion of the "me" played the same censorious role as Freud's super-ego, thereby functioning to control the impulsive conduct of the "I" or the ego. Lewis is aware of Mead's view but downplays its importance. As will become clear, this was also Blumer's approach.

Blumer's Opposition to Freud and Parsons

Blumer's own specification of symbolic interactionism is, roughly, that Mead laid the conceptual foundation in his formulation of social behaviorism, and two generations of Chicago sociologists developed the methodological tools with which to build the house. Thus, metaphorically, Mead was the architect, Chicago sociologists were the builders, and Blumer himself was the general contractor who brought everything together. Presented thus, Blumer really claims little for himself, other than the capacity to see the overall project clearly, and, perhaps, to facilitate its completion.

Although there is truth to this view, I want to propose a second way of understanding Blumer's explication of symbolic interactionism. This involves thinking of Blumer's contributions as being inherently oppositional. Clearly, this is evident in his methodological work, in which qualitative sociology emerges from the ashes of experimental and quantitative sociology. However, theoretically, Blumer characterized symbolic interactionism not only as a continuation of Mead, but also in opposition to both the Freudian psychoanalysis and Parsonsian functionalism of his day. Moreover, Blumer's symbolic interactionism is silently oppositional in the sense that his (and its) adversaries are rarely named. Rather, their existence is just hinted at, described only vaguely or mentioned elliptically through code words. Blumer's decision to proceed by silent opposition is unfortunate because the overlaps between at least some of his ideas and concerns and those of Parsons and Freud is revealing, as Jonathan Turner (1974) has demonstrated.

In a celebrated paper, Blumer identified what he proposed were Mead's five central concerns (1969: 62): (1) the self, (2) the act, (3) social interaction, (4) objects, and (5) joint action. As suggested above, this respecification and paring down of Mead's social behaviorism has been controversial, but it does at a minimum identify the central concerns from Blumer's perspective.

In characterizing the self in Mead's work, Blumer emphasized that it is a process of self-interaction. This draws upon Mead's reflexive definition of the self from *Mind, Self and Society* as that which can be "an object to itself" (1962: 136). Blumer did not name Freud and Parsons explicitly here, but he came close when he stridently distinguished Mead's characterization from the faulty view of the self as either an ego with an "organized body of needs" or as a "structure of internalized norms and values" (1969: 62–3).

Blumer emphasized that Mead's understanding of acts assumed that people act after an internal conversation and in the light of their interpretations of events. People do not, Blumer says elliptically, resemble Freudian or Parsonsian constructions of them. That is, they are not determined by, among other things, unconscious motives or social-system requirements (1969: 65). It is important to remember that Freud and Parsons are not discussed explicitly here and so they cannot be cited. In fact, no one, including Mead himself, is cited in this paper.

Blumer distinguished between non-symbolic and symbolic interaction. The former occurs when a person makes a direct response to another's actions; the latter occurs when people interpret those actions. The meaning and significance of acts is therefore the by-product of the common task of mutually interpreting and defining acts in ways that facilitate communication. Unusually, Blumer mentioned (without citing) Parsons by name at this point in his discussion, suggesting that his work fails because it is parochial in that it imposes its own interpretations of acts, rather than seeking out the interpretations of the participants themselves (1969: 67).

In outlining Mead's account of objects, Blumer emphasized that an object does not have an intrinsic meaning but only the meanings that are given to it. This is affected by prior expectations but may change over time. To understand group life, Blumer claimed, requires the sociologist to understand how group members identify and think about the objects in their world.

Finally, Blumer proposed the term "joint action" as a replacement for Mead's "social act." This is the fundamental unit of sociological analysis because it characterizes the way people fit their lives together rather than live alone. It is plausible that Blumer does not want to preserve Mead's concept of the social act because it contained an account of both attitudes and impulses (see Cook, 1993: 58), both of which were an anathema to Blumer, as they were tainted by the triple sins of psychoanalysis, functionalism, and quantification.

Despite his opposition to Freud and Parsons, Blumer's "translation" of Mead emphasized three issues that suggest an overlap to their ideas. They concern (1) the nature of the self; (2) the role of interpretation; and (3) the use of objects as discussed above. Blumer often downplayed Mead's designation of the self as a conversation between the "I" and the "me," perhaps because the primacy of the "me" for Mead gave a constitutive role to the attitude of the generalized other. Blumer may have reacted against this because the resulting analysis is rather static: the generalized other is in a sense imposed on the self. Instead, Blumer favored Mead's definition of the self as that which can be "an object to itself." This definition emphasized the reflexive, continuing, self-constituting aspects of identity. Secondly, Blumer emphasized that symbolic interactionism is centrally concerned with interpretation and definition, that is, with "ascertaining the meaning of the actions or remarks of the other person" and with "conveying indications to another person as to how he is to act" (1969: 66). Third, Blumer emphasized that symbolic interactionism involves the study of objects, that is, the study of the meanings, even fantasies, people have about "anything that can be designated or referred to" (1969: 68). Objects are social products that we respond to subjectively (often in accordance with a general plan of action).

Blumer intended his portrait of symbolic interactionism to represent the state of sociological theory after Mead, and, in conjunction with the qualitative practices of Chicago sociologists, to characterize the core of the most viable version of sociology. He also envisaged a kind of imperialistic rule for symbolic interactionism over and above both other sociological approaches and cognate disciplines, including psychoanalysis. However, the fault line running through his argument concerns the relevance of internal states and the viability of a sociological study of them. In opposing Freud and Parsons he ruled out these inquiries, but in refining Mead's thought he inadvertently brought them back in. This is because the "I" and "me" formulation in Mead appeared to favor the "me" and drew social behaviorism toward a Parsonsian account of internalization. Blumer's reaction to this – to favor a reflexive definition of the self – raised the prospect of introspection, and drew him toward Freud instead. He was, therefore, caught between a rock and a hard place.

Goffman's Understanding of Mental Illness

Erving Goffman is widely recognized as one of the most influential critics of the institutional treatment of the mentally ill. Based in part on his observations of St Elizabeth's Hospital in Washington, DC, in 1955–6, Goffman's *Asylums* (1961a) documented the oppressive and threatening conditions of one mental hospital, and, by extension, of all closed organizations, which he referred to as "total institutions." Everett Hughes had first proposed this suggestive phrase in lectures at the University of Chicago (Burns 1992: 142).

Goffman recognized the comparative power of this idea, although it is doubtful that he understood how pervasive it would become; indeed it is now a central concept in the vocabulary of twentieth-century social science. The success of *Asylums* crossed academic disciplines and national borders. It is assigned reading for many university courses and has been widely translated. The second chapter of *Asylums*, which was initially published in *Psychiatry*, has since been reprinted 33 times, ironically, more than any other paper in the history of that journal (Weinstein 1994: 349). Goffman's arguments have also been used as evidence in legal proceedings (Weinstein 1994: 349).

The wide audience for *Asylums* has led some commentators to suggest that it had some definite impact on the plight of the institutionalized mentally ill. Specifically, it has been suggested that his work helped initiate the program of deinstitutionalization that reduced the inmate population of American mental hospitals from a high of 559,000 in 1955 to their present levels of around 110,000 (Mechanic and Rochefort 1990: 301).

However, to attribute a direct connection between Goffman's *Asylums* and the social policy of deinstitutionalization is, as has been forcefully argued elsewhere, far too strong a claim (Mechanic and Rochefort 1990; Scull, 1984, 1989; Weinstein, 1994). As has been demonstrated statistically, the process of deinstitutionalization began at about the same time as Goffman first started his research, and hence he could not be held responsible for a chain of events that had already been initiated. As Mechanic put it (1989: 148), "Goffman's work had only a subsidiary role in the massive changes in mental health policy," although he immediately added that *Asylums* was "as influential as any theoretical statement or study can hope to be."

It is also important to consider that there were powerful groups whose interests were well served by the deinstitutionalization of the mentally ill, and for them Goffman was simply ammunition in a battle that had already begun (Scull, 1984, 1989). Scull has argued persuasively that the driving force behind deinstitutionalization was fiscal constraint: "For the mentally ill, at least, states have been only too willing to grant the negative right to be left alone, to be free from the obvious coercion that involuntary hospitalization represents. Neglect, after all, is cheaper than care" (1989: 265).

According to Scull's account, Goffman's ideas did not bring about a social policy of deinstitutionalization; rather, they were used to justify and defend such a policy. Used in this way, Goffman's significance was not as an innovative thinker but as a quasi-member of the "anti-psychiatry" school, and his ideas were thought to be in line with those of Laing, Szasz, or Foucault, among others (an observation also made by Weinstein, 1994: 349; and Sedgwick, 1982). As Mechanic and Rochefort put it (1990: 304), Goffman was seen as an advocate of community mental health and as such a defender of federal policy. Clearly, when seen as just a representative of a school, the singularity of Goffman's thought is lost.

In assessing Goffman's account of mental illness, it is important to recognize that his work primarily addressed four interwoven issues. These were an account of the nature of mental illness, criticisms of psychiatry, criticisms of the institutional treatment of the mentally ill, and an assessment of the merits of deinstitutionalization. In addition, he offered reflections on the career trajectories of psychiatrists and a more sustained investigation of the psychiatrist–client relationship. With the exception of the last of these issues, Goffman rarely treated them as discrete topics of inquiry, with the result that the apparent lightness of his prose often disguised a dense thicket of observations, reflections, analyses, and complaints with several intended targets.

There are other reasons for being cautious in assessing Goffman's account of mental illness. Part of the difficulty in clarifying his views is that mental illness was of recurring interest to him, with the result that he wrote about various aspects of it throughout his career. The result of this is that any attempt to reconstruct his "general understanding" of the problem requires disparate materials written at different points in his career to be integrated into a single account, and this can violate the content or probable intention of particular texts. Secondly, as mentioned above, Goffman often conflated ideas that would have been clearer if allowed to stand separately. Thus, many important passages contain references to, among other things, his understanding of the nature of mental illness, criticisms of psychiatry, ironic commentary about psychiatrists, and hints at his overall sociological intentions. The result is that the relevant passages in Goffman's work successfully convey a tone of dissatisfaction but they rarely provide a concise, discrete, reasoned position. This has allowed a plethora of commentators to respond to Goffman in quite different ways. Finally, despite Goffman's general willingness to footnote every twist and turn of his sociological arguments (in fact his references make fascinating reading by themselves, and offer a glimpse of his modus operandi), Goffman rarely footnoted key claims concerning his understanding of psychiatry and mental illness. As a result, it can be difficult to substantiate or clarify some of the positions that he presented elliptically.

Nevertheless, a coherent position regarding mental illness does emerge from his work. Goffman stated quite clearly that he believed that some specific mental illnesses were caused by biological problems (1961a: 313–16, 1963: 235–6, 1971: 335–6). He routinely referred to these as "organic" mental illnesses, and he believed them to be the proper domain of medicine. After having determined that a particular episode involved organic mental illness, he rarely if ever continued to discuss it. It is as if he considered these cases to be protected from sociological commentary (for example, see Goffman, 1961a: 316). His willingness to provide such protection has been the subject of a critical commentary by Sedgwick (1982).

It is also clear that Goffman thought that the majority of cases seen by psychiatrists – perhaps the overwhelming majority of cases – did not involve a diagnosis of organic mental illness. Instead, he believed that they involved "functional" mental illness that was not diagnosed by medical test but by the disclosure of inappropriate behavior. Early in his career Goffman began referring to different types of inappropriate behavior as "situational improprieties" (1963: 23–4, 1967: 142). It is unclear if Goffman thought that some kinds of situational impropriety might be symptoms of an underlying organic disease, or whether the situational impropriety was the problem itself.

Whether or not a class of situational improprieties betrays an underlying disease, Goffman did acknowledge that there was a distinction, albeit a conceptually difficult one, between "symptomatic situational improprieties" and "non-symptomatic situational improprieties." The latter are easier to identify than the former. Clearly, there are various kinds of situational improprieties that do not suggest that the person performing them is mentally ill. Rather, there is an available public explanation for the behavior: perhaps the person does not understand what he or she is expected to do, is tired, drunk, joking, arrogant, selfish, and so on. In each case, the situational impropriety can be recognized as inappropriate behavior without an accompanying attribution of mental illness. By contrast, a person exhibiting a symptomatic situational impropriety both acts in an inappropriate way and does so such that other observers, both lay and professional, cannot supply an accompanying explanation that condemns the misconduct but affirms the sanity of the norm-violator. Goffman made this point in *Asylums* with regard to the construction of medical case histories:

> The events recorded in the case history are, then, just the sort that a layman would consider scandalous, defamatory, and discrediting. I think it is fair to say that all levels of mental hospital staff fail, in general, to deal with this material with the moral neutrality claimed for medical statements and psychiatric diagnosis, but instead participate, by intonation and gesture if by no other means, in the lay reaction to these acts. (1961a: 145)

Goffman tried at different times to explain the strangeness of behavior through the metaphor of language, suggesting that everyday behavior has a "grammar and a syntax," whereas the behavior of the mentally ill is "ungrammatical." Symptomatic situational improprieties defeat all efforts at interpretation until designated as symptoms of mental illness. For example, in *Asylums* he noted that "self-insulation [from the symbolic implications of the hospital settings] may be so difficult that patients have to employ devices for this which staff [presumably falsely] interpret as psychotic symptoms" (1961a: 139, n.30).

In one of his last papers (1983a), Goffman returned to this issue, invoking the work of the Oxford philosopher John Austin, to suggest that the actions of the mentally ill fail to meet "Felicity's Condition." The connection Goffman made here to ordinary language philosophy ties into his earlier ideas about the grammaticality of behavior, as Austin's (1961) work on speech acts used the notion of the felicitous condition to explain how people make sense of what other people say. Related to this, Felicity's Condition describes those circumstances where no sense can be made of a person's actions. Thus, anyone who does not demonstrate Felicity's Condition fails to demonstrate his or her sanity.

These ideas framed Goffman's understanding of the legitimacy of psychiatry. Goffman suggested that if psychiatry is to have a scientific understanding of functional mental illness, psychiatrists must explain how they are able to distinguish symptomatic and non-symptomatic situational improprieties. He believed that, as of the mid-1960s, psychiatrists were not even close to being able to do this. Instead, he suggested, psychiatrists appealed to their clinical experience, and by so doing merely invoked lay standards of mental illness:

> while psychiatric knowledge often cannot place the psychiatrist in a position to predict the patient's conduct correctly, the same nescience provides the psychiatrist with interpretive leeway: by adding post hoc qualifications and adumbrations of his analyses, the psychiatrist can provide a picture of what has been happening with the patient that can no more be disproved than proved. . . . To this authority that cannot be discredited, the psychiatrist can add a force derived from tradition, "clinical experience". Through this magical quality, the formally qualified person of longest experience with the type of case in question is accorded the final word when there is doubt or ambiguity, this person also being apt to be the ranking practitioner present. (1961a: 322)

Goffman is not conciliatory here: psychiatry is a "nescience" that lacks a biological understanding of mental illness, is unable to predict the behavior of patients, and hides behind vague formulations that cannot be disproved. These sins of omission are themselves wrapped in the language of clinical experience that has a "magical quality" rather than a scientific content.

It is interesting to note that much of Goffman's own work about "unremarkable" conduct in public settings was an attempt to provide part of this "technical mapping." It is only by understanding the constraints operating in the "interaction order," that is, in the ordinary circumstances of face-to-face interaction, that the behavior of the mentally ill can be properly understood to be inappropriate. Goffman pointed to this in *Behavior in Public Places*:

> the sociologist might find cause to nibble at the psychiatric hand that feeds him data. For while psychiatry forcibly directs our attention to situational improprieties, there appear to be ways in which psychiatry embodies and rationalizes lay attitudes toward this aspect of conduct, instead of carrying us beyond these conceptions. (1963: 232)

On several occasions, often in the context of a discussion of Garfinkel's ideas, Goffman mentioned that one of the goals of research in this area should be to learn to "program insanity" (for example, see Goffman, 1974: 5). Without this knowledge, psychiatric knowledge about the symptoms of mental illness and lay opinions about mental illness are too closely connected.

This observation relates directly to one of the controversial arguments underlying Goffman's ethnographic study of St Elizabeth's; namely, that most of the situational improprieties exhibited by mental patients in the hospital were non-symptomatic. For the most part, Goffman claimed, the apparently strange actions of patients were understandable "secondary adjustments" to an oppressive and threatening environment. Goffman defined a secondary adjustment as anything people learn to do to get around what the institution thinks they should do and hence what they should be (1961a: 172). If patients were making secondary adjustments, their behavior made sense and hence wasn't symptomatic of mental illness. And, as Goffman argued in the first essay of *Asylums*, many examples of these secondary adjustments could be found in other kinds of total institution as well. In the third essay, Goffman was quite explicit about this, arguing (1961a: 303) that it is "presumptuous" to assume either that the mentally ill are "ill" or that they are even at one end of a continuum of normal behavior. Rather, he suggested, "a community is a community" and the actions of patients are simply examples of "human association." As will be discussed shortly, Goffman implicitly claimed in these passages to have a better understanding of mental illness than that of psychiatrists. This claim places a special burden on ethnographic observation to prove that its understanding of mental illness is superior to that of psychiatry.

In addition, and just as controversially, Goffman claimed that nearly all the behavior exhibited by patients at St Elizabeth's (except that on the back wards) could also be observed in other total institutions, such as military barracks, prisons, monasteries, and boarding schools. In settings other than the mental hospital, inmate behavior is rarely interpreted – that is, diagnosed – as mental illness. This theme recurs throughout Goffman's work on total institutions (1961a: 269). The same line of inquiry is pursued and summarized in the third essay of *Asylums* (1961a: 186).

What is easily recognized as a tone of dissatisfaction in Goffman's writings can now emerge as a reasoned and poignant critique of the work of psychiatrists: Goffman's argument is that, with the exception of organic mental illness, psychiatrists primarily diagnose functional mental illness, that is, they identify situational improprieties. Since it is patently false that all situational improprieties indicate mental illness, psychiatrists must claim to have a way of knowing which improprieties are symptomatic and which aren't. This requires a "technical mapping" of the kind mentioned by Goffman above. In the absence of a technical mapping, or in the absence of a protocol for distinguishing symptomatic and non-symptomatic situational improprieties, psychiatrists are often doing little more than applying a technical vocabulary to lay ideas and opinions. As he put it in *Interaction Ritual*: "Psychiatrists have failed to provide us with a systematic framework for identifying and describing the type of delict represented by psychotic behavior" (1967: 138). Goffman also made this point clearly in *Behavior in Public Places* (1963: 232).

The inadequacy of psychiatric diagnoses – even the perception of inadequacy – threatens psychiatry's disciplinary legitimacy. Perhaps it is not by chance that its knowledge claims are more often debated in courtroom proceedings than in scientific settings. Goffman argued that there was a gaping discrepancy between what psychiatrists and other mental health professionals said about what they did in mental hospitals and what they actually did in mental hospitals. In fact, the existence of discrepancies between accounts and actions is the best and basic justification for all ethnographic research.

According to Goffman, the absence of a formal way of distinguishing symptomatic and non-symptomatic situational improprieties produced three problems: the conflation of custodial and therapeutic roles, the invisibility of secondary adjustments, and the decontextualization of the meaning of the patients' actions. Goffman described the conflation of custodial and therapeutic roles by drawing a distinction between "people-work" and "object-work" (1961a: 73). In *Asylums* he wrote that:

> Many total institutions, most of the time, seem to function merely as storage dumps for inmates, but . . . they usually present themselves to the public as rational organizations designed unconsciously, through and through, as effective machines for producing a few officially avowed and officially approved ends. (1961a: 73)

Writing a decade later, Goffman reaffirmed this thought, suggesting in "The Insanity of Place" that the mental patient's "deal" was "grotesque" (1971: 336), an adjective that he earlier used in *Asylums* (1961a: 321) when analyzing the psychiatrist–patient relationship.

The first essay of *Asylums* contains a tone of moral outrage that is masked by the studied neutrality of its prose. For example, in discussing the impossibility of presenting solitary confinement as a medical treatment, Goffman noted that psychiatrists had renamed this punishment, making it instead "constructive meditation" (1961a: 82). He also noted that, in the interests of administrative efficiency, some mental hospitals "have found it useful to extract the teeth of 'biters,' give hysterectomies to promiscuous female patients, and perform lobotomies on chronic fighters" (1961a: 77). Goffman's outrage is controlled, and his observations of the mistreatment of patients are presented in a flat tone and often as an aside. Cumulatively, they support his description of total institutions as "forcing houses for changing persons; each is a natural experiment on what can be done to the self" (1961a: 22). The experiment reveals what can be done "to the self," as a form of control, and not "for the self," as a form of treatment.

Goffman claimed that psychiatrists had little more than a lay understanding of the difference between symptomatic and non-symptomatic situational improprieties. As a result, any effort by a patient to make a secondary adjustment to St Elizabeth's was likely to be understood symptomatically. As Goffman noted, from "the point of view of psychiatric doctrine, apparently, there are no secondary adjustments possible for inmates . . . everything a patient does on his own can be defined as symptomatic of his disorder" (1961a: 186). From Goffman's sociological point of view, all secondary adjustments are non-symptomatic situational improprieties, since they can be understood as rational attempts to protect oneself from a threatening and humiliating environment, and hence they are not properly the concern of the psychiatrist at all.

However, Goffman's willingness to interpret patients' actions nonsymptomatically sometimes led him either to stretch credibility or to claim special access to a patient's intentions. For example, in *Asylums* Goffman made the very general claim that "the craziness or 'sick behavior' claimed for the mental patient is by and large a product of the claimant's social distance from the situation that the patient is in, and is not primarily a product of mental illness" (1961a: 121). It is reasonable to ask how Goffman knew that this behavior was *not* the product of mental illness, unless he has the kind of knowledge that elsewhere he suggested that psychiatrists lack and need. Similarly, in *Behavior in Public Places*, Goffman noted:

> At Central Hospital I have observed an otherwise well-demeaned (albeit mute) youth walking down the ward halls with a reasonably thoughtful look on his face and two pipes in his mouth . . . another with a ball of paper screwed into his right eye as a monocle. . . . As already suggested, this situational self-sabotage often seems to represent one statement in an equation of defense. It seems that the patient sometimes feels that life on the ward is so degrading, so unjust, and so inhuman that the only self-respecting response is to treat ward life as if it were contemptibly beyond reality and beyond seriousness. . . . In short, the patient may pointedly act crazy in the hospital to make it clear to all decent people that he is obviously sane. (1963: 224–5)

And also:

> The aim, then, of some of these bizarre acts is, no doubt, to demonstrate some kind of distance and insulation from the setting, and behind this, alienation from the establishment. (1963: 225)

In fact, Goffman doesn't have a way to justify his claim to know what these various actions mean without claiming to possess the kind of knowledge that elsewhere he claimed no one has. This means that his inclusion of the phrase "no doubt" above was either ironic self-criticism or misplaced emphasis for an unwarranted claim. It is possible that Goffman's use of irony was not simply a way of portraying his detachment; rather, it allowed him to hint that he possessed a special and superior understanding of mental illness (although for another view of Goffman's use of irony, see Fine and Martin, 1990: 106–9). There is a subtext to much of Goffman's work on mental illness which implicitly suggests that ethnography-based sociology is, to play on one of Wittgenstein's ideas (1958: para. 97), a "super-psychiatry" whose understanding of mental illness is far superior to its poor relation and predecessor, psychiatry. And, ironically, the justification for Goffman's claim to understand what motivates mental patients when they perform bizarre acts is comparable to the justification used by psychiatrists, namely, observation and experience. Goffman is therefore guilty of what Woolgar and Pawluch (1985) refer to as "ontological gerrymandering." At various points, Goffman claimed – albeit implicitly – to speak from a privileged space from which he could see the truth about mental illness. But at no point did he, or could he, justify this claim.

This issue is related to Goffman's frequent complaint that psychiatrists decontextualize their patients' behavior. This is because Goffman's implicit claim to possess a super-psychiatry was based on his ability to recontextualize patients' behavior, an action which he thought transformed our understanding of it: once symptoms have been recontextualized, most hospital-based improprieties can be properly understood as defensive measures, that is, as non-symptomatic actions. However, he also acknowledged that to recontextualize a patient's behavior fully, it would be necessary to consider all aspects of his or her life outside the hospital (1961a: 316).

However, the psychiatrist is influenced by a medical model of mental illness that is itself based on the decontextualization of symptoms. That is, insofar as psychiatrists are first and foremost physicians, it is reasonable to expect them to adhere to a view of symptoms that is common among the broad medical profession. To do otherwise would only accentuate the already pronounced difference between psychiatry and other medical specialities. As Goffman put it:

> The limited applicability of the medical model to mental hospitals brings together a doctor who cannot easily afford to construe his activity in other than medical terms and a patient who may well feel he must fight and hate his keepers

if any sense is to be made of the hardship he is undergoing. Mental hospitals institutionalize a kind of grotesque of the service relationship. (1961a: 321)

It would be easy to interpret the cumulative effect of Goffman's arguments as indicating support for deinstitutionalization. If mental hospitals were or perhaps still are as bad as he made them out to be, how could a community alternative be any worse? At the beginning of "The Insanity of Place" Goffman appeared to subscribe to this point of view: "Given the life still enforced in most mental hospitals and the stigma still placed on mental illness, the philosophy of community containment seems the only desirable one" (1971: 336). Nevertheless, even this endorsement was tempered by his use of the word "seems." It also raises questions about who benefits from deinstitutionalization, what are the kinds of available benefit, and what kinds of community and containment are waiting for ex-patients upon their release.

Goffman had earlier argued that mental hospitals exist mainly to ease everyday life for ordinary citizens who would rather not be bothered by the unpredictable outbursts of the mentally ill, and to assist the various personnel who administer to and process those who disrupt the social order. At the end of *Asylums* Goffman made exactly this observation:

> Nor in citing the limitations of the service model do I mean to claim that I can suggest some better way of handling persons called mental patients. Mental hospitals are not found in our society because supervisors, psychiatrists, and attendants want jobs; mental hospitals are found because there is a market for them. If all the mental hospitals in a given region were emptied and closed down today, tomorrow relatives, police, and judges would raise a clamour for new ones; and these true clients of the mental hospital would demand an institution to satisfy their needs. (1961a: 334)

To which he added: "Mental patients find themselves crushed by the weight of a service ideal that eases life for the rest of us" (1961a: 336).

In *Behavior in Public Places* he continued this thought, suggesting that one goal of psychiatry is to "protect the sanctity of the social occasion and the sentiments of the participants" (1963: 235). In fact this book ended with a similar comment, an oft quoted remark that asylums exist primarily to protect our gatherings and occasions (1963: 248). If, then, the true client of the mental hospital is not the patient but just about everybody else, then community treatment is unlikely to be successful.

Goffman only hinted at the difficulty of implementing community treatment. Research since Goffman's death has presented a fuller picture of the dismal circumstances facing ex-mental patients, both in the United States and elsewhere. Indeed, in a poignant reversal of fortune, the new social movements advocating hospitalization had often been initiated by patients themselves (see Barham, 1992).

Goffman's "The Insanity of Place" is a long essay devoted to an investigation of social interaction in families in which one person is mentally ill. It is now clear (see Winkin, forthcoming) that this essay contains reflections about tensions in his own family. Given the extraordinary detachment of much of his prose, "The Insanity of Place" is striking for its poignant personal insights into these day-to-day familial difficulties. However, as a statement of the general predicament of the ex-patient, it is of only limited interest, because it concerns the situation of an affluent patient returning to a caring family, and clearly most ex-patients are not so fortunate.

The Implications for Goffman's Sociology

Although Goffman's concerns were primarily sociological, it has been possible to reconstruct his account of mental illness because of his stubbornness: Goffman often failed to heed Jon Clausen's initial advice to avoid "junior psychiatry" and stick to sociology (see the preface to *Asylums*, p. 8). Goffman's main concerns were thoroughly sociological, but these were at times obscured by his wide-ranging arguments. It is necessary, then, to fell some trees in order to see the forest.

Undoubtedly, his experiences at St Elizabeth's fueled his suspicions about the inadequate treatment of the mentally ill, and this is responsible for the almost pervasive, if subtle, tone of the text, which varies from moral indignation to outright condemnation. As Fine and Martin put it:

> We read *Asylums* as a political tract, aimed, in part, as unmasking the "fraud" of mental hospitals and psychiatric practice. It does not aim to demean individuals, but it does take on this system and those elements of the outside world that are being convenienced by the existence of the system. (1990: 110)

I want to suggest that Goffman's account of mental illness should be understood to exist at the intersection of two distinct ideas and projects. The first project is the realization of an empirical, comparative program of research based on Hughes's invention of the term "total institution;" the second is the study of the organization of face-to-face interaction. Hughes had initially discussed total institutions in the context of nunneries (see Burns, 1992: 142). It is instructive to keep this in mind, as it clearly separates Goffman's later study from its immediate physical setting at St Elizabeth's, and indeed from the general question of the appropriate characterization of mental illness.

To realize Hughes's embryonic research program, Goffman had to construct a new genre of ethnographic research. It required him to replace the traditional idea of ethnography as case study with a new model in which there are ethnographies of concepts rather than ethnographies of places (see Manning, 1992). In a sense, Goffman was an important contributor to grounded theory, as I have argued elsewhere (Manning, 1998).

A major part of the study of total institutions is (1) an attempt to uncover their underlying structure, (2) the clarification of the typical experiences of a broad array of inmates, and (3) the delineation of a predictable sequence of social psychological hurdles for patients to manage. It is interesting to note that David Rothman saw this comparative analysis of total institutions as Goffman's most enduring contribution, arguing that "historians have confirmed the validity of Erving Goffman's concept of 'total institutions,' which minimizes the differences in formal mission to establish a unity of design and structure" (Rothman, 1990: xxv).

The study of total institutions is also directed to an analysis of the structural elements of power, surveillance, and discipline, a formulation that highlights the similarity between the research programs of Goffman and Foucault, as Giddens (1984), among others, has recognized. Goffman saw that total institutions are "forcing houses for changing persons; each is a natural experiment on what can be done to the self" (1961a: 22). Clearly, the theme here is generalized institutional power, not the diagnostic capabilities of psychiatrists or the peculiarities of the organization of mental hospitals.

Goffman's second sociological project was to investigate ordinary, unremarkable, behavior in public places. He was particularly interested in the management of interaction among the unacquainted. To live in an urban environment is to live in proximity to a large number of other people, about whom we are likely to know only what we can glean from their various presentations of self. Under these circumstances, social life becomes a delicate game in which people must try to show respect for the rights of others while remaining vigilant and aware of possible public dangers. Goffman saw himself as a student of the norms governing human traffic, as a student of the web of practices used in mass society to facilitate and monitor interaction among the unacquainted.

Goffman's analysis of the interaction order permeates all his work, but is clearly set out in *Behavior in Public Places* (1963) and *Relations in Public* (1971). Extended secondary discussions of his account of the interaction order can be found elsewhere (Drew and Wootton, 1988; Burns, 1992; Manning, 1992). What is germane to this discussion is that although Goffman's focus was sociological, the behavior of the mentally ill was significant for him because it revealed by default the unremarkable behavior of ordinary people conducting unremarkable transactions in their daily lives. The mentally ill were interesting to Goffman because, as a group, they bungled the performance of these transactions and hence unintentionally demonstrated the norms and constraints that constitute the interaction order.

In principle, Goffman's project did not require him to have any view about the nature of mental illness. As I have tried to demonstrate, the view that he actually had, but didn't need, was a dubious one, in that it was based on ontological gerrymandering. Goffman exploited an ironic distancing to suggest that he somehow had a superior knowledge of mental illness – a super psychiatry – that superseded conventional psychiatry. But of course Goffman's earlier criticisms of psychiatric knowledge had already cut off the branch that he later wanted to sit on.

Once Goffman's interests are properly located in the sociological investigation of the interaction order, his views about deinstitutionalization can be clarified. Whether in families, as he poignantly analyzed in "The Insanity of Place," or in anonymous social settings, the disruptive and "ungrammatical" behavior of the mentally ill undermines our general capacity to carry on with our day-to-day concerns. It makes the traffic signs of human interaction unreliable; perhaps at its worst it makes us wonder whether there is even a road. Our solution to this problem has not been to broaden our understanding of human association; instead, at least until recently, it has been to sequester these "offenders" in closed hospitals. As Goffman pointed out, psychiatrists, social workers, police officers, and judges are the "true clients" of the asylum, and through them, all of us. Sequestration is therefore a way of preserving the "grammar" of the interaction order. The policy of deinstitutionalization, of restoring the mentally ill to the community, was therefore doomed from the beginning, since it was the community, broadly understood, that first wanted the mentally ill institutionalized. The grim reports by Scull (1984, 1989) and others about the "malign neglect" of the deinstitutionalized mentally ill are depressing but predictable, given Goffman's argument.

Goffman was also a moralist and a critic. His detached tone reminded Marx (1984) of a figure from a Raymond Chandler novel. In some ways this is true. However, Goffman was not so detached as to be indifferent to what he saw as the hypocrisy of institutional psychiatry. He believed that the mental patient was on the wrong end of a "grotesque deal" that required a public rhetoric about the legitimacy of psychiatry and which made life easier for everyone else. Goffman hoped that *Asylums* would show up the gap between what psychiatrists said about what they do and what they actually do. He wanted to air the truth as he saw it from his vantage point as a knowledgeable and unaffiliated insider. However, he wasn't naive enough to think that any manifestation of community care would ease the plight of mentally ill men and women who have the sad distinction of belonging to the most unwanted of social groups.

Goffman's analysis of psychiatry and mental illness made four broad contributions to his overall sociology. First, it is his major published work that uses comparative ethnography. Second, it presents "plot lines" (in his vocabulary, it outlines the patient's "moral career"). Third, it is his most moral-political research. Fourth, despite himself, Goffman considered the internal worlds of his ethnographic subjects at St Elizabeth's. This view of the self is not obviously compatible with taxonomic, ethological analysis of the interaction order, as he himself realized. This is particularly evident in his analysis of secondary adjustments. In order to theorize the role of secondary adjustments in all total institutions, Goffman had to incorporate an elaborate theory of the self that could show how inmates draw upon inner resources to withstand oppressive institutional conditions. The third essay of *Asylums* is a long and often poignant tribute to the many ways through which inmates preserve their sense of worth. Ironically, then, in order to criticize what he saw as the paucity of orthodox psychiatry's account of the self, Goffman had to develop a theory that was more sophisticated than his own analysis of the interaction order could accommodate.

Asylums and related papers are theoretically different from his general analyses of face-to-face interaction, in that they contain a potentially viable theory of the self. Goffman needed this theory so that he could investigate what might be called the inmates' strategies of resistance throughout their moral careers as mental patients. For this, Goffman had to draw upon what he often rejected: namely, a theory of the self's inner core that is expressed in various performances and that stretches between them.

The Interaction Order: Taxonomic Zoology

Like Sumner before him, Goffman's concern was with the classification of the ethological material he collected on the interaction order. He did not want, nor did he believe that he needed, a theory of the self. He made tremendous progress in understanding the resources used by people to preserve or manipulate a shared sense of what is taking place, but he did so at the expense of a viable account of the people themselves who use these resources. In Goffman's role-analytic account, the self is in danger of collapsing into its roles; it becomes, in an infamous phrase, a peg on which something can be put for a while.

Despite the many illustrations, telling examples, and subtle observations, Goffman remained an abstract thinker who sought to expose the most general characteristics of the world of face-to-face interaction. As he put it in his presidential address, the analysis of face-to-face interaction is as much an abstraction as the "behavior" of corporations or New York crime statistics (1983b: 9). Goffman's examples are all used in the service of his classificatory schemes. It is quite possible to strip away his examples, and what is left is an account of the micro-sociological world with a high level of abstraction. This is quite clear in *The Presentation of Self in Everyday Life* (1959), which Goffman himself described as a book that outlines a general framework – with the result that much of it is necessarily abstract (1959: preface). However, it is also true that even his ethnographic studies were abstract and self-consciously theoretical.

Goffman liked to masquerade as someone who knew next to nothing about the abstract world of social theory, which he sometimes portrayed as part of the alien world of European sociology and hence literally and metaphorically miles away from his Canadian and American background. Wrong has tried to warn us against any tendency to minimize Goffman's theoretical sophistication:

> Goffman stories are legion among those who knew him at all well, although mine go back farther than just about anyone else's. I shall confine myself to a few recollections about his intellectual outlook. The widespread notion that Erving was an inspired naif, a novelist manqué with unusual powers of social observation, is utterly wrong. He already had an acute and far-ranging theoretical mind when I met him [in Toronto]. (1990: 9)

Wrong points out here that Goffman was clearly knowledgeable about European social theory before he began his graduate work at Chicago. His (1953) dissertation was written – at least in part – in Paris and contains many references to existential debates of the 1950s. He was similarly knowledgeable about French social theory in general, as writers who found an underlying structuralism in his work discovered, sometimes to their cost.

The most influential contemporary reading of Goffman's social theory portrays him as a theorist of the interaction order, of the ritual accommodation of face-to-face interaction (Giddens, 1984, 1987; Drew and Wootten, 1988). Goffman in fact coined the term "interaction order" in the conclusion to his dissertation (1953) and then highlighted its importance by recycling it as the title for his presidential address. In much the same way that each of Goffman's prefaces serves as a general introduction to a particular book, the presidential address is a preface and introduction to his work as a whole. Clearly, an important part of this is his attempt to analyze the world of face-to-face interaction as a separate domain worthy of independent study. The interaction order consists of "systems of enabling conventions" that render public conduct orderly and predictable, and it is sustained by shared cognitive and normative presuppositions (1983b: 5–9). It can be understood by sociologists in part through empathy and introspection because the normative conventions of our day-to-day lives are anchored in subjective feelings that are not only shared but which have been "worn smooth by constant repetition" (1983b: 9).

It is therefore the very orderliness and interpretive accessibility of the interaction order that suggests its viability as an independent domain for analysis. Many mundane tasks could not be achieved without tacit agreement about the ground rules of the interaction order. Consider some of the multiple and sometimes simultaneous tasks accomplished during face-to-face interaction: the preservation of efficient pedestrian traffic flow, the management of environments populated by strangers, and the achievement of shared understandings. Goffman believed that the accomplishment of these things was made possible by a set of "arrangements which allow a great diversity of projects and intents to be realized through unthinking recourse to procedural forms" (1983b: 6).

This way of reading his work is typical of what I would like to call the "European Goffman" who, as Giddens puts it, is striving to be a "systematic social theorist" (1987). The European Goffman has almost Parsonian ambitions, aiming to be maximally inclusive in his account of the interaction order. Reading Goffman in this way makes his ideas compatible with Parsons' account of socialization and the internalization of norms as forms of social control (see Parsons, 1951: 297–321). This is the Goffman whom Giddens integrated into structuration theory and who plays an important role in his reconceptualization of the relationship between structure and agency (Giddens, 1984). In Giddens' work, the European Goffman emerges as the principal theorist of "practical consciousness," that is, of the taken-for-granted, non-discursive practices whereby much of everyday life gets accomplished without fuss, albeit behind our backs (see particularly Giddens, 1984).

However, I want to suggest that there is also an "American" Goffman who has emerged as a controversial transitional figure between a Hughesian version of Chicago sociology and the emergence of ethnomethodology. The American Goffman had not, as Goffman himself realized, overwhelmed his colleagues by the strength of his arguments (1983b: 2). On the contrary, he had offended different groups in different ways. For Hughes, who had a well-documented strong dislike for social theory (see Fine, 1995), Goffman had drifted into barren theoretical speculation and away from empirical work. Nevertheless, Goffman described himself as a "Hughesian urban ethnographer" (in Verhoeven, 1993: 318), although he later added in the same interview: "I am really on that side, closer to the structural functionalists, like Parsons or Merton" (in Verhoeven, 1993: 324). Arguably, it was this ability to make creative use of the different influences of both symbolic interactionism and structural functionalism that made Goffman's work powerful, and which positioned him as one of the leading post-World War II American sociologists.

By contrast, for many ethnomethodologists, the flaw in Goffman's work was his failure to analyze the complexities of the actual procedures used in day-to-day life. Ethnomethodologists often consider his descriptions to be too general to account for the complexity of naturally occurring social interaction (for example, see Schegloff, 1988).

Although it has limitations, the "European" reading of Goffman as principally a theorist of the interaction order is a very useful way of highlighting part of Goffman's contribution to sociological thinking. By contrast, the "American" reading of Goffman raises a different but also important set of issues concerning his relationship to both symbolic interactionism, and Hughes (see Jaworski, 2000), and to ethnomethodology, and Garfinkel. Giddens' reading of Goffman assumes that his ideas are easily compatible with Garfinkel's. This assumption needs to be looked at very carefully: although both Goffman and Garfinkel are "micro" sociologists (but see Schegloff, 1990, for a discussion of this) their approaches are different. Garfinkel's Wittgensteinian emphasis on the elucidation of social practices as contingent achievements seems to preclude the attempt at systematic social theory that Giddens (1987) identified in Goffman's work.

However, there is a substantive problem with the view that Goffman was primarily a theorist of the interaction order: much of his work was not, directly at least, about the interaction order, trust, or ritual accommodation. Rather, it was an analysis of deception and it signals Goffman's contribution to what Ricoeur (1970: 30) called the "hermeneutics of suspicion." Lyman and Scott (1970: 29–70) have written extensively about the connection between game theory and deception in Goffman's sociology. Goffman's first published papers, "Symbols of Class Status" (1951), which analyzed the ways in which symbols can be misused, and "On Cooling the Mark Out" (1952), which analyzed all social situations as confidence tricks, initiated his long-term interest in deception.

In the "Symbols" paper, Goffman argued that because class symbols represent a "complex of social qualifications" (1951: 296) that are often hard to substantiate, they are particularly vulnerable to misuse. As a result, legitimate holders of status seek to find ways to authenticate and hence protect the symbols they rely on to distinguish bona fide members of their group from imposters. Goffman outlined six devices that are intended to prevent a person from misrepresenting his or her class (1951: 297–301). He also described the role of "curator groups" in the maintenance of the machinery of status. However, as Goffman emphasized, the very devices used to maintain class symbols can be used by imposters. As a result, the "circulation of symbols" (1951: 303) cannot be stopped and "[a] sign which is expressive for the class in which it originates comes to be employed by a different class – a class for which the symbol can signify status but ill express it" (1951: 304).

Deception is also integral, of course, to the world of the confidence trickster, explored by Goffman in "On Cooling the Mark Out" (1952). This paper attempts to take the structure of the confidence trick and show that it can be applied to any situation in which a person suffers a loss of status. In this sense the paper is an introduction to the sociology of failure. The "mark" is robbed of something and in return is given "instruction in the philosophy of taking a loss" (1952: 452).

The theme of deception is at the center of *The Presentation of Self in Everyday Life* (1959), a book that could easily and perhaps more appropriately have been called *The Misrepresentation of Self in Everyday Life*. The dramaturgical vocabulary developed by Goffman concerning "impression management" offers a framework with which to understand the types and components of deception. *The Presentation of Self* is in a sense a textbook of deception. Thus, the chapter on "Performances" describes techniques for the "dramatic realization" of manipulative presentations of self that are built out of impressions and fronts that are designed to mislead. Goffman showed this using, among others, the example of a baseball umpire who must make his decisions immediately in order to give the impression that he is sure of them, thereby forgoing the moment he needs to confirm his judgments to himself (1959: 40).

What is true of the individual performer is also true of the team: "the definition of the situation projected by a particular participant is an integral part of a projection that is fostered and sustained by the intimate cooperation of more than one participant" (1959: 83). This gives every team the "character of a secret society" in which their members all share the "sweet guilt of conspirators" (1959: 108). This conspiracy is confirmed in the back regions away from public view where the team members' front-stage performances are "knowingly contradicted" (1959: 114).

Dramaturgical deception requires more than impression management; it also needs performers to show "dramaturgical discipline:"

> It is crucial for the maintenance of the team's performance that each member of the team possess dramaturgical discipline and exercise it in presenting his own part. I refer to the fact that while the performer is ostensibly immersed and given over to the activity he is performing, and is apparently engrossed in his actions in a spontaneous, uncalculating way, he must none the less be affectively dissociated from his presentation in a way that leaves him free to cope with dramaturgical contingencies as they arise. He must offer a show of intellectual and emotional involvement in the activity he is presenting, but must keep himself from actually being carried away by his own show lest this destroy his involvement in the task of putting on a successful performance. (1959: 210)

In his early work, then, Goffman developed an analysis and a vocabulary of the ways in which people are able to mislead others by manipulating their assumptions about appearance and reality.

Goffman's analysis of deception is also evident in his various analyses of industrial spies, espionage agents, and rational choice dilemmas, all of which are prominent in *Encounters* (1961b) and *Strategic Interaction* (1970). The essay "Expression Games," in the latter of these books, contains what is in effect Goffman's basic theory of deception. The essay ends with a justification for its intensive interest in the espionage world:

> In every social situation we can find a sense in which one participant will be an observer with something to gain from asserting expressions, and another will be a subject with something to gain from manipulating the process. A single structure of contingencies can be found in this regard which renders agents a little like us all and all of us a little like agents. (1970: 81)

This conclusion was drawn out of Goffman's account of the basic moves involved in deception and counter-deception. These basic moves are the unwitting, the naive, the covering, the uncovering, and finally the counter-uncovering move (1970: 11–27). They can be understood as a "set of tricky ways of sympathetically taking the other into consideration as someone who assesses the environment and might profitably be led into a wrong assessment" (1970: 13).

Later, in *Frame Analysis* (1974), Goffman offered a theory of deception that combined these game-theoretic ideas with his dramaturgical perspective. In *Frame Analysis* Goffman defined deception as consisting of the work done to ensure that "incorrect assumptions are initially made" (1974: 440). In a manner reminiscent of *The Presentation of Self*, *Frame Analysis* contains a structural and almost textbook-like account of the resources available to those wishing to deceive.

The key to Goffman's frame analysis is his belief that whatever the resources are whereby we convince others that we are as we appear to be, they are the same resources confidence tricksters use to deceive people. As he put it: "whatever we use as a means of checking up on claims provides a detailed recipe for those inclined to cook up reality" (1974: 445). Goffman's idea that we "cook up reality" reconciles the apparent differences between his analyses of trust and deception by showing that both make use of the same mechanisms in order to succeed. The same resources whereby we appear trustworthy are the ones used when we betray. Goffman was not therefore primarily interested in trust, ritual accommodation, or deception; rather, he was interested in developing a theory of credibility. Put differently, Goffman analyzed the ways in which people make their performances convincingly real.

A good test case for the possibility of analyzing how we make ourselves and our social settings convincingly real is interaction among the unacquainted. This is because this setting might be simple enough to find a parsimonious account of the rules that must be followed to maintain a convincingly real sense that everything is as we expect it to be: namely, that "nothing" is really taking place. This is why children, comics, and the mentally ill are so useful to sociologists: their lives are what Garfinkel (1967) called "breaching experiments" in that their behavior consistently involves rule violations. In these groups, often "something" (rather than the desired "nothing") is taking place, and the something is often disruptive, tiring, or embarrassing to at least someone present. Because of this, children, comics, and the mentally ill, among others, teach us by default what has to occur for people and social situations to be, or at least to appear, convincingly real. In this sense, Goffman's work attempted to understand the resources by which we maintain a shared sense of what the world is like.

Tensions in Goffman's Account of the Self

The danger in focusing on the ways in which people sustain a credible world is that the people themselves begin to appear hollow. For the most part, Goffman provided us with a model of the structure of social interaction, not a model of the performing agent. For example, reading *The Presentation of Self in Everyday Life* teaches us a lot about the presentation of self and not much about the self. As Dennis Wrong (1998: 22–3) argues, Goffman and most symbolic interactionists fail to offer a convincing account of what motivates people to do what they do. Jeffrey Prager (1998: 70) makes a similar point when he suggests that a sociological focus on ritual deflects attention away from the analysis of the interpreting self.

Several commentators have recognized that Goffman often avoided analyzing the inner world or mental life of people in favor of the structure of social interaction. Lyman and Scott (1975: 107) put it well when they suggested that in *The Presentation of Self*, Goffman "moved the theater of performances out of 'the head' and into public places." More recently, Williams has described Goffman's position eloquently:

> He [Goffman] wanted to provide what he regarded as a distinctly sociological account of the person. In doing this, he treated as irrelevant the large variety of ways that people think about their own or other people's "inner lives". He was not concerned with individuals in the way that psychologists or novelists are when they attempt to display the full depth of human motivation, feeling, intention, unconsciousness and so on. . . . To understand the self sociologically it had to be approached as a social institution, and researched by observing and analyzing externally observable forms of conduct. (1998: 154)

In the Verhoeven interview, Goffman was unusually candid about his analysis of the self, describing his research in a way that confirms the assessments by Lyman and Scott, Williams, Wrong, and Prager:

> [w]hat I'm doing is the structural Social Psychology that is required, or is natural for, Sociology. That is, given Sociology is a central thrust, what can it say about the individual? Not that the individual is the central unit that permits us to study society; but if you take society as the basic and substantive unit . . . what is it we have to assume about individuals, so that they can be used or be usable socially? . . . I am an ethnographer of small entities. (1993: 322–3)

He added later:

> sociologists in some ways have always believed in the social construction of reality. The issue is, at what level is the reality socially constructed? . . . But where I differ from social constructionists is that I don't think the individual himself or herself does much of the constructing. (1993: 324)

This passage suggests that Goffman deliberately downplayed the importance of analyzing the interpreting self in favor of an analysis of the interpreted self. A more skillfully worded version of this idea can be found in the frequently cited introduction to *Interaction Ritual*:

> I assume that the proper study of interaction is not the individual and his psychology, but rather the syntactical relations among the acts of different persons mutually present to one another. . . . What minimal model of the actor is needed if we are to wind him up, stick him in amongst his fellows, and have an orderly traffic of behavior emerge? . . .
>
> Not, then, men and their moments. Rather moments and their men. (1967: 2–3)

However, as suggested earlier, this "minimal model" strategy is partially reversed in his investigations of the behavior of the mentally ill, in which an elaborate analysis of the self emerges.

Goffman's preference for theoretical abstraction, although well hidden in a thicket of revealing examples, made it difficult for him to offer an adequate theory of selfhood. He made tremendous progress in understanding the resources used by people to preserve or manipulate a shared sense of what is taking place, but he did so at the expense of a viable account of the people themselves who use these resources. In Goffman's role-analytic account, the self is in danger of collapsing into its roles; it becomes, in an infamous phrase, a peg on which something can be put for a while. In this sense, Goffman offers us something quite different from Freud.

The secondary literature contains important and in many ways consistent criticisms of Goffman's account of the self. The model of the self in *The Presentation of Self* and the paper "Role Distance" (1961b) suggests that our public performances are all that we are. There is nothing underlying these performances, except perhaps a necessary fiction of a unified self. But Goffman suggests that it is just a fiction. This is a radically depersonalized world in which we are simultaneously performer and audience: we hear our own voices as disembodied cries, we watch ourselves perform in a frightening version of the looking-glass self.

However, in one sense, these criticisms are misplaced, as Goffman's analysis of the interaction order does not require a theory of the self, as his main focus concerned the ground rules or enabling conventions that people use in daily life. He analyzed the resources people use in managing daily living rather than the people who use them. Since the interaction order is an analysis of the structure of group life, it is separable from the members of groups. This argument is recognizably

Durkheimian and one which Goffman himself might readily have accepted as a reasonable account of both sociology in general and of his own work in particular. Nevertheless, it is also true that Goffman succumbed at times to a theory of the self, or more accurately, to different theories of the self.

His most criticized theory of the self arose out of his role analysis, where, in his attempt to integrate "role distance" into a distinctly sociological rather than psychological theory, he argued that the self is played out in its different performances. For example, Alasdair MacIntyre has complained that Goffman has "liquidated the self into its role-playing" (1982: 30), adding that for Goffman the critical mistake is to "suppose that there is a substantial self over and beyond the complex presentations of role-playing" (1982: 31). MacIntyre suggests that, for Goffman, the social world is everything, permitting only a "ghostly 'I' " with almost no selfhood (1982: 31).

Jonathan Glover (1988) has also explored and criticized Goffman's role theory. Glover notes that Goffman's analysis suggests that "the things we do which seem to escape from social roles are themselves refinements to this roles" (1988: 171). In response, Glover claims that:

> Of course we are shaped by people's expectations of us, and of course these vary with our job, our sex, our age, and so on. But it is an illusion to think that we are utterly malleable, submitting entirely to social molding. This picture might fit people who had no inner story. They would have no conception of themselves apart from the conception other people had. They would lack desires and values in the light of which to criticize the demands made of them, and would have no independent views about how their story should continue. We are not such people. (1988: 175)

Glover's suggestion that Goffman's model of the person implies someone who has no "inner story" connects with MacIntyre's sense that Goffman's world is amoral (1982: 108–10). It also resonates with Sennett's (1970: 36) belief that Goffman describes a two-dimensional world in which there are scenes but no plots.

Even *Frame Analysis* contains a description of the self that is quite compatible with these critical readings. Here, Goffman suggested that we all endeavor to understand people using what he calls a "tacit theory of expression" (1974: 462). This theory assumes that there are things such as relationships, feelings, and character that are revealed in various ways. Goffman, however, implies that this theory is quite wrong. Instead, he suggests that all we have are just "expressions and gestural equipment" for providing certain kinds of displays – and this equipment can easily be used either to convey genuine feeling or to deceive.

Goffman's ideas about the interaction order and deception converged into an analysis of the production and reproduction of credibility. Maintaining credibility involves the use of various kinds of resources and a willingness to abide by rules of conduct. When the social world is credible it is "convincingly real" which, in the context of everyday behavior, often means that participants have a sense that "nothing" in particular is going on. That is, the setting and the people in it appear unremarkable, in the sense of not being worthy of a remark. I have also suggested that interaction among the unacquainted is not only a substantive topic in its own right, but also a test case for the ability of sociological analysis to describe the rules and resources underlying a relatively simple and frequently occurring social practice. It is relatively simple in the sense that managing a stranger in a shopping mall should be simpler than, for example, managing a friendship that has not just a present but also a history and a projected future.

For the most part, Goffman's work contains a sustained attempt to analyze what he called the enabling conventions of the interaction order, or what I have described as the conditions of credibility. Goffman wanted to show that the interaction order is an autonomous realm that can be analyzed separately and in its own terms. Described in this way, Goffman did not need a theory of the self.

However, Goffman discovered that he needed a theory of the self when he analyzed aspects of mental illness and institutionalization. This suggests that *Asylums* and related papers are theoretically different from his general analyses of face-to-face interaction, in that they show that he needed a viable theory of the self and they also show what the theory might look like. Goffman needed this theory so that he could investigate what might be called the inmates' "strategies of resistance" embedded in various secondary adjustments. To further his account of the behavior of patients at St Elizabeth's, Goffman had to draw upon what he often rejected: namely, a theory of an inner core to the self that is expressed in various performances and which stretches between them. Goffman is at his most compelling in *Asylums* because there is the potential for both scenes and a plot, as Sennett put it. It also opened a door to psychoanalysis, but this was not a door he wanted to walk through himself.

4

Parsons' Freud:
The Convergence with
Symbolic Interactionism

Overview

Talcott Parsons only realized the importance of Freud and psycho-analysis for sociology after he had published his assessment of the converging strands of European social theory, *The Structure of Social Action* (1949 [1937]). Twelve years later, in the preface to the second edition of this book, he bemoaned his earlier failure to recognize the potential of a pared-down version of Freud's ideas for sociology. The theoretical task was to identify the strands of Freud's work that were relevant for sociology and to find a non-clinical way of exploring them empirically.

The key to Parsons' appropriation of Freud's ideas is his overriding concern with theoretical convergence. It was obvious to Parsons that the litmus test of the importance of theoretical ideas was whether different major theorists had arrived at them independently. Parsons was therefore able to include Freud in his general theory of social action by demonstrating that Freud's later object-relations approach and structural model converged with both the implicit social psychology of Durkheim and with the proto-symbolic interactionism of Cooley and Mead. Parsons pursued this by arguing that Freud's account of introjection is very similar to a sociological account of internalization. More than any other American sociologist, Parsons kept his eye on the big prize: a convincing, general theory of social action. In so doing, he was often blinded to the empirical difficulties – perhaps impossibilities – of realizing the overall project as he had conceived it. He also downplayed the more modest inquiries favored by Robert Merton and others as projects that can only win consolation prizes.

Parsons' analysis of Freud raises specific issues. These concern the transition from his demonstration of the potential relevance of psychoanalysis for sociology to the actual empirical demonstration of how sociologists might engage Freud, and with what results. These more focused failures are features of his own (1973) empirical investigation of American universities, as became apparent when he could not find an angle from which to bring the aspect of psychoanalysis into clear view. As Neil Smelser (1998) recognized, without this, Parsons' allegiance to Freud had little impact on sociological work, and psychoanalysis as a discipline became merely another way of telling the story of the impact of internalization. Parsons' Freud turned out to be not very different from Parsons' Mead. Ironically, as we will see in chapter 6, the cross-fertilization of sociology and psychoanalysis has re-emerged since Parsons' death in 1979, and has required boundary crossing from both sides. Parsons was the key precursor to this development, as he planted the seed that made this cross-fertilization possible. His key contribution occurred when he demonstrated that versions of object relations led Freud and other psychoanalysts to sociology.

The second cluster of questions that I want to address concerns Parsons' underlying assumption of the convergence of different sociological theories into a general theory of social action. I propose that the key error in his approach became evident when he tried to present his ideas as two-dimensional diagrams, most of which consisted of boxes within boxes. Despite the analytic attractiveness of this mode of presentation, it preserved the illusion that a sociological theory could present (i.e. see) all aspects of the social world at the same time. Had Parsons used three-dimensional boxes instead, it would have become immediately clear that each sociological vantage point inevitably produces its own blind spots. Empirical research therefore involves a decision – made consciously or not – to see the social world from a certain vantage point and therefore not to see it from others.

There is a third cluster of questions also. These concern the implications of Parsons' attempt to tame Freud's ideas. Parsons made psychoanalysis appear more reasonable, even intuitive. In this sense, as I show in the next chapter, Parsons' symbolic interactionist Freud is in many ways antithetical to Rieff's moral Freud. Parsons wanted to push Freud into the mainstream so that he converged with other theorists, all of whom contributed to Parsons' general theory of action. By contrast, Rieff wanted to pull Freud away from any collaboration; Rieff's

Freud was a figure in need of greater radicalization. Rieff's mission was not, therefore, to incorporate Freud but to follow through the logic of Freud's ideas to their natural conclusion.

Introduction

Talcott Parsons (1902–79) is often remembered as a key figure in the development of structural functionalism, a perspective that appears to have little in common with psychoanalysis. The realization that Parsons held Freud in such high regard, and in fact saw him as one of the key theorists of the modern age, should at the very least unsettle anyone who had thought of him simply as a "macro-theorist" with little interest in problems of agency, intention, and motivation. More than any other American sociologist, Parsons viewed sociology's confrontation with Freud – and the incorporation of Freud into sociology – as absolutely necessary. Sociology, he believed, needed psychoanalysis in order for it to progress. But what did psychoanalysis supply that was missing from sociology? Parsons saw psychoanalysis as the discipline concerned with the study of motivation. As such, he believed that psychoanalysts could identify what motivated people to act in ways that sustained (or failed to sustain) the groups in which they lived. This provides the key to Parsons' work: he wanted to understand the conditions that any group – in his language, any action system – must meet if it is to survive. For Parsons, therefore, sociology is the investigation of how action systems survive or why they fail. Insofar as people must be motivated to participate in activities that sustain these systems, Parsons came to believe that Freud was central to his vision of sociology.

Freud was a transitional figure for Parsons in two quite separate ways. First – as Parsons made clear in his autobiographical statement (1977) – he was drawn to psychoanalysis because of personal difficulties in his own life. Second, Parsons found a way to use Freud to reinvigorate his earlier (1949 [1937]) analysis of the "unit act." In so doing, he also brought to light convergences between psychoanalysis and homespun American symbolic interactionism.

As perhaps the preeminent theorist of elaborate conceptual schemata, Parsons' mission was not directly scientific, in the sense that it was closely allied to hypothesis testing. Rather, Parsons wanted to provoke certain styles of thinking and to encourage discussion about particular questions. The schemata produced by his theoretical inquiries are general and abstract: they have to be so because they are empty of both content and answers. Parsons tried to persuade social scientists to dig in certain places; he did not tell them how to dig or what they might find, except in the most general of terms.

As will be discussed later, Parsons identified two strands to Freud's work. The first presented Freud as a theorist of instincts and the second as a theorist of object relations. Parsons favored the latter but tried to incorporate elements of the former by emphasizing the importance of pleasure and gratification as opposed to the display of mere instinct. As a result, Parsons' Freud was a moving target and certainly different from the Freud identified and often rejected or downgraded by earlier generations of American sociologists.

Like Goffman, Parsons hoped that he might be able to formulate foundational classifications for the social sciences; unlike Goffman, he believed that he came close to achieving his goal. Parsons' challenge was to build an account of motivation into his general action system – an ambition Goffman, Garfinkel, and other near contemporaries rejected as a hopeless task. However, while Goffman remained quietly sympathetic to Parsons' general theoretical research, Garfinkel was clearly opposed to it. Ethnomethodology, his respecification of the social sciences, shifted the focus and the research questions away from formal analysis and onto the *in situ* practical reasoning of agents, whereby the social world is made "accountable," that is, intelligible. In limiting inquiry to the nevertheless potentially endless difficulties of description, Garfinkel took another step toward the anti-Durkheimian project of separating sociology and ethics. This went against the storyline running through both the classical European sociology of Durkheim and Weber and the American sociology of Cooley, Mead, Parsons, and Goffman, all of whom advocated a reconstructive logic that identified what was worthwhile and tried to bring it either into being or at least into fuller expression. The point of Garfinkel's ethnomethodology is far more modest: to establish what is the case by specifying how it is done (and understood by others to be done). Freud, as Rieff demonstrated compellingly, was above all a moralist, albeit a reluctant one, and not just a describer. His personal ambition was great, although his ambitions for both his treatments and humanity were far more modest. In this regard, Parsons hid Freud's pessimism by making Freud converge with the major strands of the thought of Durkheim, Cooley, and Mead.

Parsons' thought was necessarily both very general and very abstract. He did not want to learn from case studies of the survival or demise of particular action systems. Rather, he wanted to isolate the common, minimum conditions that each and every system, on whatever scale, must meet to ensure survival. He then wanted to state these general conditions in as abstract a language as possible in order to facilitate comparative analysis. These two principles of maximum generality and maximum abstraction made for technical, dry treatises. However, in his view, these consequences were a necessary evil. Parsons was not trying to contribute to sociological theory; rather he was trying to re-establish sociological theory with a new conceptual scheme that would be adopted widely in the social sciences. His work was intended to be a foundation stone of a new sociology, much as Crick and Watson laid a foundation stone for a new field: molecular biology.

Parsons' life long interest in Freud and psychoanalysis began after the publication of *The Structure of Social Action* in 1937. He interpreted Freud as a social theorist who had established an aspect from which to see the social world. What Freud offered therefore was one among many vantage points from which to observe human systems. If we think of the action system not as a two-dimensional object but as a three-dimensional object, then we can grasp this point more easily. If we hold the action system in our hands – or admire it as a sculpture in a museum – we see it from a certain aspect. We know that the object would look different from other vantage points, although the object itself of course has not changed. This is how Parsons thought about Freud. In the context of Parsons' action theory, the aspects revealed by psychoanalysis were the personality system and the behavioral-organism; the blind sides of psychoanalysis were the cultural and social systems. Although the system as a whole survives or dies because of the interdependent actions of its subsystems, our vantage point only guides our eye to part of the object. Parsons' two-dimensional diagrams – like Freud's – mislead us into thinking that we see the action system as an object from all aspects simultaneously. In fact, thinking about the social system as a three-dimensional object makes us recognize that even before we investigate the social world (and independent of the methods we use to do so) we commit ourselves knowingly or otherwise to a position from which to see.

Understood in this way, it is possible to state part of his achievements as follows. Among his many accomplishments, Parsons made two interconnected contributions to sociological theory that required him to connect Freud to mainstream sociological concerns. The first contribution was the invention of a theoretical language with which to analyze the social world as a system; the second was an ambitious attempt to specify the conditions that any system must meet if it is to survive. He endeavored to extend the analysis of system survival up to but not beyond the limits of two-dimensional representation. Parsons feared what Derrida has called the "play" of any discursive account of the social world and so worked within the structure and limits of graphic representation. That is, Parsons wanted sociological theory to advance, and possibly to reach a point where practitioners could consider many foundational issues to have been settled. He therefore understood socio-logical theory in the Mertonian sense of a "systematics" that can (and must) be used repeatedly and successfully in empirical research if it is to have any value. Parsons was an ambitious promoter of sociological theorizing, seeing it as having the potential to blossom in the manner of theories in the natural sciences. As stated earlier, this optimism mani-fested itself in his work through increasingly complex, schematic, graphic representations that initially appeared in his work as two-by-two boxes and then (and increasingly) as boxes within boxes in an infinite regress. This approach produced two countervailing kinds of tension: the first concerns whether his graphic representations of social systems can actually be used in empirical, sociological projects, and the second concerns whether any two-dimensional characterization of the social world can do justice to its inherent complexity. However, before turning to these meta-theoretical questions, it is useful to trace Parsons' increasing interest in Freud and psychoanalysis.

In his autobiographical statement, Parsons dated his interest in Freud to a conversation with Elton Mayo.

> For me the decisive event was a talk with Elton Mayo [around 1936] about my interest in medical practice, in which he asked point blank how well I knew the work of Freud. My reply had to be, only very fragmentarily. He then earnestly advised me to read Freud seriously and comprehensively. This was fortunately a time when I had a good deal of free time, thanks to an assistant professor's term leave, and I followed his advice. It was too late to build the implications of Freud's ideas into *The Structure of Social Action*, but this proved to be one of the few crucial intellectual experiences of my life. This, of course, prepared the way for formal psychoanalytic training – at the level permitted – about a decade later. (Parsons, 1977: 34)

So, Parsons' first serious engagement with Freud's texts occurred about three years before Freud's death. It was in many ways a natural extension of the qualitative investigation of the social world of phys-icians that was then occupying Parsons. In 1946, almost certainly prompted by the deaths of family members – his brother (in 1940) and his parents (in 1943 and 1944) – Parsons began formal academic training at the Boston Psychoanalytic Institute (Parsons, 1977: 38–9). He went through psychoanalysis himself with a prominent analyst, Dr Grete Bibring. As a "Class C" candidate he was not allowed to practice and could not take control cases. However, in all other regards, Parsons completed the training given to candidates with a medical background (1977: 39). Despite the contemporary doubts about the clinical efficacy of psychoanalysis, Parsons was one of its success stories. Even while writing his monumental *Structure of Social*

Action, he proceeded slowly, despite the constant institutional pressure to succeed. The project itself, parts of which germinated during his studies in England and Germany, took many years to complete. His empirical investigation of the social world of the hospital moved even slower, until it reached a dead stop. However – and almost miraculously – Parsons became a highly productive scholar following his analysis with Dr Beibring. Indeed, he was prolific from the mid-1940s until his death in 1979. Curiously, in terms of the sheer quantity of material, there is an eerie resemblance between Parsons and his most sympathetic follower, Niklas Luhmann, who was also able to write fluently – if not always accessibly – throughout his life, and who also left a formidable corpus of theoretical writings.

Parsons' Action Theory

For Parsons, sociological theory is an umbrella term referring to a set of conceptual schemes that aid empirical research. By themselves, these conceptual schemes do not answer any questions about the social world, they do not specify a moral, political, or ideological agenda, and they do not propose hypotheses to be tested. Rather, in a methodologically neutral way, Parsons understood theory as simply an orienting device that facilitated the formulation of questions, hypotheses, and research projects. Stated in this way, his project sounds unduly modest – but this is misleading. If he had accomplished his aim, not just sociology but all the social sciences would now be oriented to their diverse interests in the same way. Comparative and perhaps even cumulative research might be possible. Certainly, every social scientist after 1950 would have internalized a Parsonsian way of thinking that then regulated empirical research.

In many different publications, produced for different audiences and with varying degrees of complexity, Parsons attempted to outline this way of looking at – or thinking about – the social world. His aspiration was to make this way of looking at and thinking about social matters so compelling that a diverse group of social scientists would be united in an interdisciplinary investigation of the social world. Although Parsons anticipated that these social scientists would keep their disciplinary affiliations as sociologists, anthropologists, economists, and so on, their disciplinary ties would be considerably weakened. Instead of departments, Parsons envisaged research groups that share a paradigmatic vision while employing a wide range of methods to investigate the full array of social issues. Whereas methods will likely evolve and substantive social issues will certainly change, Parsons anticipated that the conceptual scheme linking the different social sciences would be relatively stable. That is not to say that he ever believed that he had finished his own theoretical work (after all, he was still revising his formulations in the weeks before he died), but it is to suggest that Parsons could at least imagine a time when most theoretical issues in the social sciences were more or less settled. Counterintuitively, these two massive ambitions – to unite the warring disciplines of the social sciences and to produce a stable, shared conceptual scheme – explain why much of Parsons' work is inaccessible. This is because whenever he believed that he was making a foundational contribution to the conceptual scheme of the social sciences, he attempted to write in the formal, technical language he associated with economics. At other times, when he was writing for general discussion or when lecturing, Parsons' prose is lucid and even entertaining. Nevertheless, when his game face was on, he wrote with off-putting austerity, believing that his work was then a contribution to an intellectual revolution that would usher in a new phase of "normal science," as Thomas Kuhn had conceived it.

In this sense, Parsons bears comparison to Erving Goffman (Manning, 2000), the differences between them being primarily matters of scale and readability. Goffman aspired to provide a conceptual scheme for all occasions of face-to-face interaction, a domain he called the "interaction order." Parsons aspired to something even grander: a conceptual scheme for the study of society.

As stated earlier, the central term of Parsons' theory is the "action system" and both words require explication. "Action" refers to the symbolically oriented character of human behavior, especially as it is codified and transmitted through language (Parsons and Platt, 1973: 8). The word "system" dates from the early seventeenth century to denote the whole of creation, the universe. In more recent times, a system is generally thought of as the component parts of an interdependent network. This latter definition is close to Parsons' use of the term, as his focus was on the minimum conditions for any system's survival. Although the decision to define sociology as the investigation of systems seems to plunge sociologists into murky waters, it is worth remembering that economists routinely investigate the "behavior" of markets – a project that, if anything, is even more conceptually troubling, since it is hard to give a clear definition of a market and harder still to believe that it "behaves" in anything other than a metaphorical way. For Parsons, Freud was central to the analysis of systems because he contributed to our understanding of what motivates people to participate in various social systems in ways that ensure the survival not only – or even – necessarily of themselves, but of these systems.

Perhaps Parsons' clearest definition of a system is the collaborative statement he co-authored with his Harvard colleagues in *Toward a General Theory of Action* (1951b), a book often remembered by students as the "yellow terror" because of both the color of the book's dust jacket and their experience of reading the book's contents. There, a system is defined as the "determinate relations of interdependence [that] exist within the complex of empirical phenomena" (1951b: 5, footnote 5). In *The Social System* Parsons gave a longer definition: "A CONCRETE action system is an integrated structure of action elements in relation to a situation. This means essentially integration of motivational and cultural or symbolic elements, brought together in a certain kind of ordered system" (1951a: 36; emphasis in original).

For Parsons, a theoretical system denoted an abstract understanding of what any system had to have in order to reproduce itself and therefore survive. A concrete system, as discussed above, referred to an empirical example of a system. Thus, a family, a university, and a baseball team are all examples of systems which theoretically share common elements and face common problems, but which concretely must be analyzed in their different contexts. Parsons described these contexts as environments, and all systems must be bounded and hence clearly separable from their environments.

In the early 1950s, Parsons identified three interdependent components, that is, three subsystems, to every system. These were the social system, the cultural system, and the personality system. In 1970, in the last decade of his life, he added a fourth, the behavioral-organism. To analyze a concrete system therefore involves the analysis of the interplay and interdependency of these four subsystems. Put very simply, the key elements of each subsystem are as follows.

I The social system

This refers to the network of statuses and roles present in the system. These often go together, and a macro analysis of the social world uses the status-role as the basic unit of analysis. This is the approach Parsons took in *The Social System* (1951a). Status locates a person hierarchically within a system, whereas role defines what people do as a contribution to the reproduction of the system (1951a: 25). The hierarchical blueprint of a system's network of statuses is its social structure. In some systems, such as businesses or universities, the social structure may be formalized and generally known. In other systems the "map" of the social structure may be secret and even internally contested. For example, a gang of drug-traffickers may go to considerable trouble to ensure that the Drug Enforcement Agency (DEA) does not discover its chain of command; at the same time, group members may jockey for position, trying to promote not just themselves but also the status-role they occupy within the gang (i.e. system). In addition to these distinctions, a status network can operate manifestly and latently. Its operation is manifest whenever the chain of command functions as the social structure dictates that it should. It is latent whenever the chain of command is circumvented. For example, the basketball coach of a university does not occupy a very high position in the social structure of the school, but may still have the ear of the president and the provost.

Parsons contributed to the theoretical exploration of the concept of role, a term that has attracted a range of theorists with different interests. In particular, functionalists and symbolic interactionists have found it profitable to explore this realm, with the result that a proliferation of useful concepts has emerged. Three terms are worth highlighting: Merton's concept of role set (1957: 368–84), and Goffman's account of role conflict and role distance (1961b: 73–134).

Parsons' analysis is further complicated by the fact that each of us is a "composite bundle of statuses and roles" because we participate in and contribute to different systems at the same time (1951a: 26). Thus, although systems must maintain the boundaries between themselves and their environment, the members of systems are always simultaneously living in and contributing to different systems that regulate and constitute their lives. It is easy to realize that each person has simultaneous membership in multiple systems, but extremely hard to find a way of analyzing this complexity in an empirically convincing way. Indeed, it may be too hard to analyze a person's membership in just one system in an empirically convincing way.

2 The cultural system

This refers to the network of norms and values that are internalized by each person and which then regulate behavior. Parsons understood values as abstract standards that do not directly influence behavior in particular situations. Rather, values are "conceptions of the desirable" (Parsons, quoted in Kim, 2003: 34). By contrast, to use Jon Elster's useful formula, norms are concrete guides to action that instruct people, outlining what to do in given circumstances. Thus, if there is a way of specifying the "x" in the instruction, "in these circumstances, do x," then, Elster argues, norms are present. For example, if a man says that his cat has just died, the expected response is "I'm sorry." The "I'm sorry" is therefore the content to the "x" in this case.

Parsons thought of norms in this way, while recognizing the significant difficulties that researchers must overcome if they are to study norms empirically. Norms "involve a reference to a situation" (Parsons, 1967: 9), but they are rarely as clear or explicit as the example above suggests. Instead, Parsons understood norms to "offer only general guidelines" that "are always open to question or reinterpretation" (Kim, 2003: 38). Parsons also recognized that the classification of different types of norms still required further clarification. In his own work, Parsons (1967: 9) raised three issues: jurisdiction, enforcement, and interpretation. This allowed him to classify (and thereby distinguish) norms in terms of (1) their range of application, (2) the type and severity of the sanctions associated with norm violation and (3) the difficulty of interpreting whether particular examples are in fact in keeping with specific norms. The investigation of these issues brought him closer than is often realized to the ethnomethodological studies of his former student, Harold Garfinkel.

3 The personality system

Parsons defined the personality system as the "learned behavioral system" (1966: 7). The components of each person's psychological make-up emerge developmentally. Psychoanalytic thinking about child socialization heavily influenced Parsons; in fact, he often accepted as established fact psychoanalytic ideas that strike a contemporary reader as being simply speculations. In this regard at least, Parsons' sociology is very much a creature of the 1950s. The novelty in Parsons' reading of Freud concerned his belief that Freud took a sociological turn in his later structural model – when he conceptualized the self as a tripartite model of id, ego, and super-ego. According to Parsons, the super-ego was a key pathway by which conscience and guilt regulated each person's behavior. Freud's analysis of the super-ego was certainly present in his 1923 paper on the "Ego and the Id," but was cast in a strikingly sociological way seven years later in *Civilization and its Discontents* (1930, *SE*, XXI: 64–145). In this, Freud's most transparent sociological work, the person's super-ego is generalized into a "cultural super-ego" that regulates group behavior.

Parsons initially recognized that Freud's ideas at this point converged with Durkheim's respecification of the *conscience collective* as the collection of different "collective representations" in the preface to the second edition of *The Division of Labor in Modern Society* (1984). Parsons later recognized (much to his chagrin) that much closer to home George Herbert Mead had traveled down the same road when he specified the self as a dialog between "the I and the Me." For Mead, the "Me" was the internalized "attitude of the generalized other;" that is, the absorption of community standards. By the late 1950s – if not before – Parsons believed that he had identified a key convergence between the theoretical ideas of Freud, Durkheim, Mead, and, to a lesser extent, Cooley (see Parsons, 1964). The combination of these ideas specified the content of the personality system.

4 The behavioral-organism

This subsystem refers to the person as a real, living, and dying element of the system. Parsons recognized in the 1960s that because individuals simultaneously belong to multiple systems, for analytic, theoretical purposes they must be recognized as a separate component of the overall system. Although this seems obvious enough, for a long time Parsons retained Durkheim's belief that sociology studies a discrete, *sui generis* social reality that is properly its domain. In a sense, Durkheim traded the familiar analysis of individuals for the esoteric analysis of social facts. In return, he got a subject matter that was in his view clearly separate from philosophy and psychology (and also, although he did not comment on this, from orthodox, narrative history). Parsons did not exactly trade back, but he did reclaim this familiar, individualistic domain for sociology.

He had to do so – as soon as he recognized that each person's simultaneous membership in multiple systems produces the "inherent potential for conflict and disorganization" (1966: 7). It is tempting to put the matter in even stronger terms, and suggest that this potential will be frequently realized: active participation in any system is likely to require inactive participation in other systems, and this inactivity is likely to threaten the overall stability – and survival – of those systems.

The analysis of the behavioral-organism introduced a useful distinction between static and dynamic analysis – and committed Parsons to the latter. Understood statistically, Parsons' conceptual schema of systems and subsystems served as a checklist of things for researchers to consider, and, depending on their talents, researchers could produce empirical studies of greater or lesser sophistication. Status hierarchies, role analyses, normative inquiries, and investigations of internalization processes are all subjects that, in turn, network analysts, symbolic interactionists, ethnomethodologists, psychoanalysts, and molecular biologists have shown can be handled with tremendous subtlety. Each system in the social world contains the four interdependent components. The task for empirical research is to understand in each concrete case how these four subsystems work or fail to work over time. Empirically, researchers must figure out (1) how each of these subsystems contributes to the system, and (2) how the subsystems interact (or fail to interact) with each other.

Understood dynamically, however, Parsons' conceptual schema plunged sociology into both a reflexive and analytic quagmire, as Luhmann has demonstrated (1982: 47–68, 1998). The quagmire is the result of Parsons' realization of two things. First, each person is a complicated analytic composite, consisting of multiple status-roles spread out across multiple systems. Further, each person is both a subject of his or her actions and simultaneously the object of the actions of others. This constitutes what Parsons saw as the reflexive challenge of double contingency. Second, just as each system consists of the four subsystems (the social, the cultural, the personality, and the behavioral-organism), so each subsystem itself consists of the same four sub-subsystems, in an infinite regress. Therefore, a compelling empirical demonstration of Parsons' general theory must do more that just incorporate the disparate interests of network analysts, symbolic interactionists, ethnomethodologists, and psychoanalysts (and perhaps molecular biologists). In addition, it must show (1) that these interests are both interdependent, and (2) that each subsystem can itself be analyzed as a system consisting of the four subsystems and so on, until empirical resources are exhausted.

The Survival Test: AGIL

For any action system to survive, its four subsystems must work interdependently to pass the AGIL survival test. Once passed, every action system must gear up to pass it again ad infinitum, until that day when the test is failed and the system dies. It is important to remember that Parsons' conceptual scheme was amoral: evil men and women working in horrific action systems therefore face identical problems of system management to those of, for example, the Progressive politicians who Parsons personally admired. Thus, for Parsons, the social world was not stable but both problematic and precarious (see Kim, 2003: 40–52).

The AGIL schema was first presented in 1953 in the collection *Working Papers in the Theory of Action*, co-written by Parsons, Bales, and Shils. These papers were sympathetic to a version of sociological theory in which Freud figured heavily. Three years later, working now with Smelser on the project that became *Economy and Society*, Parsons presented the AGIL schema in a rather different way, emphasizing instead an integration of sociological and economic ideas that left little space for psychoanalysis.

The four survival conditions are: adaptation (A), goal-attainment (also called goal gratification (G)), integration (I), and latent pattern maintenance (L). Adaptation refers to the processes whereby any action system manages its environment. This involves the accommodation of the "reality demands" and proactive strategies (Parsons et al., 1953: 183). Adaptation is thus achieved instrumentally; i.e. by a rational, efficient, means-driven plan. As circumstances change (in both expected and unexpected ways), each action system must recognize that its environment has changed and adapt itself. Thus, there is not a formula or template for success that can simply be applied over and over. Rather, as Weber (1949: 111) argued in his methodological work, the stream of culture moves forward creating new situations. Neither sociologists nor the social systems they study can remain static.

Goal-attainment refers to the specification of relationships between any action system and its environment through which gratifications are earned through performance (Parsons et al., 1953: 184). That is, the (typically) broad mission of an action system must be specified, understood, and accepted by its members. The goals are not those of individual members but of the system itself. There may be compatibility between personal and systemic goals, but this is not guaranteed. For example, the goal of a corporation is likely to be profitability, whereas the goal of an executive who works for the corporation may be a high salary. The executive is likely to believe that, although these two goals are quite different, the personal goal will follow from the system goal. However, there will be many situations in which this elective affinity is missing, as is the case if the executive's goal is to develop into a fine golfer. According to Parsons, the system itself must take responsibility for socializing and internalizing a survival mentality into the minds of its members, not necessarily by making personal and systemic goals one and the same, but by making them, at a minimum, readily compatible.

Parsons' name for the test for any system in this regard is latent pattern maintenance. This refers to the processes of motivation and socialization that attempt to secure the appropriate participation in the system by its members (Parsons et al., 1953: 185). Empirically, there will obviously be tremendous variation in these processes. In some cases, these processes will be almost life long; in others they will be extremely short. Similarly, there will be variation in the willingness of members to undergo the different kinds of training necessary for the inculcation of those personal traits that will maximize the chances of system survival. For example, the willingness of members to undergo medical training may be linked to the desirability of the status-role that results from it, whereas the willingness of marathon runners to undergo athletic training may be linked to the perceived desirability of the training itself.

Finally, integration refers to the management of internal tensions between the often competing and sometimes contradictory functions of A, G, and L. In one sense, integration concerns the maintenance of solidarity; however, it also refers to structural inconsistencies (Parsons et al., 1953: 184). Although the empirical investigation of actual action systems will reveal a very large number of internal tensions, it is not difficult to anticipate the kinds of systemic strain that research will uncover. For example, one way to motivate members to participate in an action system and to retain membership of that system is to reward them. This solution to one of the AGIL problems creates another, if one of the goals of the system is to maintain a high level of overall profitability. Similarly, changes in the environment of an action system may be so drastic that it is hard for it to meet any of its goals. The question is then whether the system itself can introduce new goals without wreaking havoc on itself.

Integrating Freud into Sociological Theory

For Parsons, one of Freud's key insights was made early in his career when he realized that a person's instincts are regulated by "society's moral standards," even though they are often in conflict with each other. The resulting regulation is absorbed by the person to the point of saturation, at which time introjection occurs. For Parsons, this meant that the person had internalized group norms to the extent that they had become part of his or her identity or outlook (Parsons 1968a: 432). Parsons believed that Freud's realization of the importance of introjection led him to the study of object relations. We are all objects to each other in three ways: first, through conceptualization, by recognizing what the object is; second, through cathexis, by recognizing what the object means to us emotionally; and third, through the evaluation of the combined force of conceptualization and cathexis (1964: 20–1). Insofar as people share a common culture, the introjection of object relations is one of the conditions of possibility for the stability of any action system. The seed of this stability is initially introduced during early childhood, when children are confronted by a powerful "meaningful anxiety" that the much desired love they receive from their mothers may be lost if their behavior is unacceptable. The super-ego, Parsons thought, is built out of this anxiety (1964: 28).

Parsons also believed that Freud understood this, but was led astray by his insistence on isolating each person from the embrace of this common culture. In its place, Freud analyzed the "lonely struggle" of each person against his or her id (1964: 25). Freud's error is, in Parsons' view, corrected by recognizing that internalization is the combination of integration and affect. The result is identification through a positive cathexis of relevant objects (1964: 29). This produces the motivation to sustain action systems and provides each of these with a sense of gratification brought about by generalized emotional feelings, shared cognitive categorizations, and a shared system of moral values (1964: 29).

Through his own extensive reading and clinical training, Parsons undoubtedly had a deep knowledge of both Freud's work and the psychoanalytic literature. However, this has to be largely inferred because Parsons did not publish detailed analyses of Freud's work. Unlike the other two great intellectual influences in his life, Durkheim and Weber, about whom he wrote at length, Freud is confronted at a distance through general discussions in essays. In this regard, Freud receives the same treatment as those thinkers who Parsons understood as his American counterparts: Cooley and Mead. I do not believe that this strategy was accidental; rather it reflected Parsons' decision to work with an element of Freud's theory that only emerged in his mature work. The result was a recognizable but partial description of Freud. Parsons' Freud was rather tame and uncontroversial, a representative of an approach identified and endorsed by others at or around the same time. After all, as Parsons pointed out, Durkheim had just beaten Freud to the punch, although they both converged by independent means on the centrality of internalization for any theory of human behavior.

Freud's work was not therefore for Parsons an inexhaustible repository of ideas. Writing initially in 1974, Parsons commented that it was a pleasure to read *The Interpretation of Dreams* again after having put it to one side for "a good many years" (1978: 82). What was true for Parsons' reading of Freud's magnum opus was almost certainly true for his reading of Freud's other works too. Parsons had absorbed them into his general theoretical orientation and thereby, in a sense, dispensed with them. They had disappeared by and through convergence, resurfacing now only as components of his general theory of action systems. It had to be so, unless Parsons was willing to overhaul the general theory to which Freud's ideas contributed.

On the positive side, Parsons is the author of a "big," counterintuitive, theoretical idea: namely, that four apparently very different thinkers, Freud, Durkheim, Cooley, and Mead, all highlighted the importance of internalization, and then contributed to our understanding of its discursive and emotional role in identity formation. On the negative side, Parsons was not interested at all in nurturing many "smaller" ideas into the light of day, and as a result he wrote at the most general level about only the overall tenor of their diverse contributions to sociological social psychology. Thus, Parsons did not have any of the ambitions of, for example, Rieff, as we shall see in the next chapter, and he had no use for the close, deconstructive readings of Derrida and others. Freud therefore disappears temporarily from Parsons' work, only to reappear in amalgamated form.

However, there is a second, quite different sense in which Parsons' Freud disappears, as became evident in his empirical study of the university. This disappearance is the result of the difficulty of bringing the aspects of the personality system and the behavioral-organism into full relief. Instead they remained hidden and unexplored. "On paper" – literally on paper – these aspects were constantly visible and hence "in play." However, as Parsons and Platt proceeded with their institutional research, these largely Freudian aspects disappeared, hidden by a focus on the social and cultural subsystems of the action system of the university. This too was not accidental; it turned out that Parsons and Platt had no use for these subsystems in their investigations. The three-dimensional research model was "turned" so as to hide the personality and behavioral-organism subsystems. What Parsons was not able to show was how sociologists could turn the object in such a way as to bring these two subsystems into full view.

The Empirical Demonstration: *The American University*

Parsons and Platt published *The American University* in 1973, after beginning the project in the fall of 1969, at the behest of Martin Meyerson and Stephen Granbard of the American Academy of Arts and Sciences. They were all blessed to live through interesting times in the history of American universities, although the book itself makes only cursory references to the student upheavals, civil disobediences, and civil rights activism of the era. The formal properties of action theory are laid out in the first two chapters and in a technical appendix. From the beginning, Parsons and Platt recognized that although their book was a demonstration of action theory, they would not be able to offer a general analysis of the university. As they put it, theirs was not a study of the American academic system but rather a "specialized analysis of certain aspects of it" (1973: 1). Although not stated explicitly, the "certain aspects" are what is seen in three dimensions at the expense of other aspects. This quiet realization of the necessity of a modest analysis of the university is actually a very significant moment: the difficulties facing Parsons and Platt are not unique; rather they face all empirical researchers. Action theory therefore anticipated a scope of inquiry that researchers have no chance of realizing. Action theorists are set up to fail, albeit – hopefully – in interesting ways. In fact, Parsons and Platt vacillated between the modest realism of studying aspects of the university and the fantasy of capturing the complexity of the university. Thus, not long after advocating modesty, they committed themselves to the impossible task of analyzing the interdependence of the academic system with other elements of society, including the political and the economic systems (1973: 7).

Parsons and Platt chose to focus on the characteristics of elite American universities, recognizing that it would be hard to generalize across the range of academic institutions. They were initially motivated by the idea that enhanced educational opportunities distributed primarily on merit signified a "revolution" in American society, comparable in significance to the earlier industrial and democratic revolutions. The "quasi-aristocratic elitism" of the nineenth-century university has been replaced by professionalism in which "universalistically defined qualification" has replaced ascribed status (1973: 6).

The result is a focus on the "cognitive complex." Parsons' and Platt's explanation of this key term is deferred until the end of chapter 2. It refers to the institutionalization of four key skill areas. The function of the university is to foster the development of these four competences in its students. They are: (1) knowledge, understood as what we might call today "cultural literacy;" (2) rational action, understood as the ability to act on the basis of calculated decisions; (3) competence, understood as personality development; and (4) intelligence, understood as the development of the innate skills built into the body of each person (1973: 55). The conceptual elegance of the cognitive complex is that each of its functions corresponds to one of the basic subsystems of the general theory of action. Thus, knowledge belongs to the cultural system, rationality belongs to the social system, competence belongs to the personality system, and intelligence belongs to the behavioral-organism (1973: 57).

These four skill areas are related to the four general themes of the implicit mission statement of the new American university that emerged out of the pre-Civil War colleges and seminaries. These four emerging themes (or functions) are the general education of students, the training of researchers to be employed in the economy, the reproduction of the university itself through the training of students who will become professors themselves, and the training of professionals (such as physicians and lawyers) who will solve practical problems through the use of expert knowledge (1973: 5–6).

The potential conceptual complexity of Parsons' and Platt's model is daunting, and the reader is given a glimpse of this in the early chapters of *The American University*. Thus, many aspects of contemporary society can be understood as "general action systems," each consisting of social, cultural, personality subsystems, and behavioral-organisms, each of which interacts with other general action systems at various boundary points. Further, each subsystem of each general action system can itself be understood as (or broken down to) four further subsystems, each of which consists of social, cultural, personality subsystems, and behavioral-organisms. Further, every general action system, subsystem, and sub-subsystem (and so on) is separately confronted by the AGIL survival test, each of which must be passed. It is clear, then, that Parsons was hardly a theorist who assumed stability; rather he was constantly amazed by the existence of any stability at all.

At least in the early chapters of *The American University*, where they were still free of any empirical detail, Parsons and Platt tried to specify the level of detail required to analyze aspects of the university. For example, the general action system of the university consists of the cultural, social, personality subsystems, and the behavioral-organism. The cultural subsystem consists of four sub-subsystems: constitutive symbolization, moral-evaluative symbolization, cognitive symbolization, and expressive symbolization. The social subsystem consists of four sub-subsystems: the fiduciary sub-subsystem, the societal community, the economy, and the polity. The fiduciary sub-subsystem itself consists of four further sub-sub-subsystems: civic religion, the moral community, the rationality sub-sub-subsystem, and the telic sub-sub-subsystem (1973: 15–21).

Clearly, by the time Parsons and Platt have identified sub-sub-subsystems, it is no longer possible to use either two- or three-dimensional representations of their conceptual architecture, and each two-by-two set of boxes has to stand alone, leaving the reader to reconstruct the conceptual hierarchy of the overall model of the general action system. And all of this takes place before any analysis of the dynamic processes that occur through double contingency, as action systems confront each other. To call the ensuing analysis unwieldy is a bit like saying that chess is a complicated game. Ironically, in his epilogue to the book, Smelser points out – quite correctly – that Parsons' and Platt's model is a massive simplification of the actual problems facing contemporary American universities, since they only considered the situation of the dozen or so elite universities, thereby ignoring the in many ways independent problems encountered by public universities, such as the California system analyzed by Smelser himself (1973).

In the later chapters of *The American University*, Parsons and Platt focused on particular concerns that are part of the picture of particular subsystems or sub-subsystems. As they provided more specific details, the overall conceptual architecture receded until it was finally out of view. For example, Parsons and Platt consider how the university can survive by adapting in an environment of other general action systems. They propose an interesting idea: that universities control two generalized media of exchange; namely, intelligence and influence. In this regard, universities offer banking services in which they hold deposits of intelligence and influence. Not only do universities provide "custodial services" whereby they safeguard these deposits; they also loan them out, thereby strengthening other communities. This is the "capitalization of intelligence" that produces widespread "cognitive upgrading" (1973: 306). According to Parsons and Platt, academic freedom is comparable to the entrepreneurial character of contemporary capitalism. Many "loans" will be made but not all will be successful. However, as long as the university "loan officers" choose each faculty carefully, the institution should receive a profitable return on its investment.

Parsons and Platt argued that there will be both inflationary and deflationary pressures on the generalized media of exchange of intelligence and influence. During inflationary periods, intelligence and influence become less valuable. In these circumstances, the network of universities may undergo a significant drop in value while at the same time particular universities may have to pay more to obtain inflation-proof intelligence and influence assets. For example, during a time when both the value of a university education is being widely questioned and the legitimacy of particular disciplines is under attack, there is clearly inflationary pressure. However, particular gold standard institutions and particular untouchable academics (such as Nobel Laureates) may experience an increase in value. They remain sacred. At many points, Parsons and Platt draw upon Merton's analysis of the

"Matthew effect," by which proximity to greatness conveys greatness (such as working in the laboratory of a Nobel-winning chemist).

Clearly, Parsons' and Platt's interesting but increasingly economic focus (even if rather metaphorical) signaled the difficulty of incorporating a psychoanalytic account into their action theoretic account of the university. The elegance of their approach, the analytic sophistication of their increasingly complicated two-by-two boxes, and their ambitious attempt to investigate an ideal-type of the university from many simultaneous aspects derailed the empirical hopes they had for the project. It remained, therefore, an interesting contribution to action theory, not a persuasive demonstration of action theory. It could not play the same role that *Asylums* played in Goffman's work.

5

Philip Rieff and the Moral Ambiguity of Freud

Introduction

Although there have been efforts to portray symbolic interactionism as an approach with a general theory of society, the consensus among sociologists has been that it is a micro rather than a macro approach. Notwithstanding the ingenious attempts by some of the leading contemporary symbolic interactionists, such as David Maines (2001), Mead, Blumer, and others have to be squeezed hard if they are to be recast as grand theorists in the tradition of Marx or Parsons.

Until his later work, most notably *Civilization and its Discontents* (*SE*, XXI), Freud also seemed to shy away from general proclamations in favor of something closer to a case method. However, in this and other later texts, Freud outlined a theory that was pessimistic enough to be reminiscent of Max Weber. However, unlike Weber, who, at the end of *The Protestant Ethic and the Spirit of Capitalism*, famously anticipated the unstoppable growth of a crass consumerism at the expense of all spiritual and cultural values (2002: 121–5), Freud was deeply pessimistic about our ability to control our own aggressive and self-destructive impulses (*SE*, XXI: 145). Freud considered the "ideal" demand "Thou shalt love thy neighbor as thyself" as an admirable attempt to limit our destructive potential. Unfortunately, it is a precept that cannot be followed (*SE*, XXI: 109–16). Freud deliberated at some length over this, recognizing that our failure to love our neighbors as ourselves may condemn us to mass destruction. Nor did Freud have an alternative. With false bravado, Freud added a final sentence in 1931 suggesting that the future could not be known (*SE*, XXI: 145), but the deadly arrival of national socialism and his own suspicions of communism suggested otherwise.

The greatest sociological reading and engagement with Freud is by Philip Rieff, not only in his widely admired *Freud: The Mind of the Moralist* (1959), but throughout his corpus. As I hope to show in this chapter, Rieff became increasingly suspicious of the timidity of Freud's moral judgments. His evolving understanding of the moral ambiguity of Freud's social theory prompted Rieff to develop his own powerful cultural theory.

Thus, I think that it is appropriate to consider Rieff as a theorist and moralist of cultural change. The trajectory of his work is from the elusively descriptive to the elusively prescriptive. Descriptively, Rieff identifies the elements of what he calls our current "negative communities" and contrasts them with moribund "positive communities" and their "therapies of commitment." Rieff believes that, among others, Weber and Freud both recognized that negative communities emerge once positive communities are recognized as illusory. Prescriptively, while still accepting the intellectual justification for negative communities, Rieff became transparently critical of their by-products: a "remissive" culture incapable of distinguishing "god-terms" from "transgressive depths." This culture produces a relativist, permissive culture, a version of the cult of the individual, alienation, consumerism, and indifference to tradition. In most of his work, Rieff acknowledged the inevitability of negative community but not the inevitability of its by-products. In his most recent work he has tried to preserve the monotheistic "second culture" and oppose the approaching "third culture" of modernity. Through his teaching and scholarship, Rieff has tried to envisage what a contemporary model of the sacred might be like in a negative community. In doing so, he has been drawn back to the positive communities that he had believed were no longer viable. Rieff's dilemma is that the sacred order that he wishes to preserve can only be defined by what it forbids. Therefore any effort to specify it is self-defeating. It is not preserved through celebrations but by the negative, and, in his view, vital emotion of guilt.

I want to suggest that the key to Rieff's work is his concern to understand the moral vacuum produced by contemporary cultural change. His procedure for doing so involves the interrogation of key texts of great and usually dead scholars (or, as Rieff often says, of "teachers"). This interrogation proceeds until the teacher's text gives up its "truth." It is part of our collective perception of Rieff that among these dead scholar-teachers, Freud occupies a special place in his thinking. In fact, I consider Rieff to be deeply ambivalent about Freud and indifferent to psychoanalysis as a profession. As I will elaborate in the second half of this paper, Freud slipped in Rieff's view from being "the moralist" to being barely moral at all.

The scholar-teachers who interest Rieff are his "laboratory" – just as, for example, Chicago was a laboratory for Robert Park and his students in the 1920s. However, Chicago sociology and Rieff's sociology appear to have very different fates: the former is bundled with symbolic interactionism and ingrained into the history and discipline of sociology, whereas Rieff is now in danger of being forgotten. Although the wonderful elasticity of Rieff's phrase "the triumph of the therapeutic" is still stretched in many different directions and often quoted – even by proponents of mutually exclusive views – the underlying arguments of his moral and cultural sociology are left untouched. We are therefore in danger of overlooking his analysis of our contemporary plight, as we undergo what he sees as a profound cultural transformation. Rieff writes for "troubled readers in whose minds and hearts one culture is dying while no other gains enough power to be born" (1966: 2). In this sense, Rieff is very much a man of the moment, perhaps even the man of the moment, because his work is an unrepentant critique of what he takes to be the excesses of mass culture. Rieff's challenge is to find a way to conceptualize the sacred order that stands above profane culture, without defining it. That is, the "space" of the sacred has to be delineated by, to echo his later language, negative edicts. These take the form "Thou Shall Not," rather than positive edicts declaiming "Thou Shall." This is because the latter is inherently limiting and stifling, whereas the former allows for endless re-creation.

In what follows therefore the focus is on the challenges facing Rieff's moral theory of cultural change. I present this in three parts: the first concerns the culture we lost, the second the culture we gained, and the third the culture Rieff imagines that we might find or, perhaps, the one to which we might return. The first two parts are descriptive, and Rieff modestly suggests that his descriptions are only his interpretations of descriptions first offered by the scholar-teachers he admires. The third part, which tries to glimpse a desirable future based on what he had earlier described as an unsustainable past, indicates his hopes for a new moral culture, and as such contains prescriptive judgments. In his most recent writings, Rieff has been much more explicit in outlining his own moral vision, which appears to be deeply conservative. However, before unpacking the different layers of Rieff's theory of culture, it is worth considering the way he works.

Rieff's Textual Laboratory

Readings – by both Rieff and his students – were deliberately separated from and valued above established commentaries. Thus, students were encouraged and required to confront the written page without recourse to familiar and "safe" interpretations. At the beginning of *Fellow Teachers* Rieff instructs us that:

> As teachers of the humane studies, our sacred world must remain the book. No, not the book: the page. We teachers are the people of the page – and not only the page of words but of numbers and of notes. To get inside a page of Haydn, of Freud, of Weber, of James: only so can our students be possessed by an idea of what it means to study. (1985: 2).

In addition to teaching hermeneutic skills, this approach assumes and commands a respectful attitude on the part of the student-reader, as there is no thought of a quick judgment or summary dismissal of any author's arguments. Through his teaching, Rieff fulfills three goals: the substantive acquisition of historical, empirical, theoretical, and even emotional knowledge, interpretive skill, and a moral stance in which through careful deliberations students show respect for the authors and texts they read.

Rieff's style of teaching theory reiterates an established and revered pedagogy. This is not to say, of course, that Rieff's approach is typical; on the contrary, the teaching of sociological theory is now largely a textbook-based survey of ideas in which students encounter, or at least fly over, entire traditions of thought in one course. By contrast, Rieff's students may encounter, for example, only the first few pages of Nietzsche's *Beyond Good and Evil* (1973), and then subject it to lengthy discussions as they unpack its layers of meaning.

Curiously, Rieff's own writings may not be a clear guide to his teaching. This is because in his writing he often flamboyantly jumps from text to text, challenging the reader to make the connections that he himself has made. As a result, a few tantalizing – but not self-explanatory – remarks on, for example, Kafka, can be followed by equally tantalizing remarks on Nietzsche, or perhaps Beethoven. The result is dizzying and humbling as it demonstrates to many of us the thinness and fragility of our own knowledge. However, Rieff the teacher – as opposed to Rieff the writer – appears to be far more concerned with the letter of the text.

Rieff's emphasis on the textual truths of dead authors inevitably obscures the intellectual context of his work. Although he was without doubt influenced by the leading sociological theorists of his day, his work rarely acknowledged them. Although there are exceptions – for example, he edited and contributed to a book on leadership that considered Parsons' work in depth – for the most part Rieff avoided the interrogation of contemporary sociological work. Situating Rieff's work in the context of either the sociology or the sociological theory of the 1950s and 1960s is therefore a formidable challenge – and one that would be hard to attempt on the basis of Rieff's published work alone. Unlike Parsons' references and footnotes, which reveal the context and content of the debates of his day, Rieff's scholarship draws on a wide and historical tradition. Although very different, his footnotes are as entertaining as Goffman's. The difference is that Goffman's footnotes contain material that is eclectic and obscure, whereas Rieff's footnotes constitute a scholarly education. Thus, Goffman's footnotes contain references that no one can imagine finding, never mind reading, whereas Rieff's are a reading list for the well-educated scholar.

Let me make a comparison between Rieff and Derrida – hesitantly – because I know that Rieff has described Derrida as a "less lyrically persuasive . . . illustrator" (1991: 324) of our emerging culture. Nevertheless, despite the risks involved, I want to suggest that at least in regard to the microscopic examination of texts, Rieff's *teaching* is in some ways comparable to Derrida's *writing* and that their interests show considerable overlap. Thus, for example, both Rieff and Derrida have been captivated by the opening lines of Nietzsche's *Beyond Good and Evil*, where Nietzsche asks: "Supposing truth to be a woman – what?" (1973: 13). Their writings on Freud reveal an interesting difference: whereas Rieff the writer (if not the teacher) approaches Freud for the most part holistically, floating above individual texts to consider the meanings of Freud's work as a whole, Derrida tenaciously attacks a small fragment, as when he interrogates Freud's apparently throwaway comment about the "navel" of a dream (1998: 10–25).

So, it may be worth distinguishing Rieff's writing from his pedagogical approach. The former is flamboyant and a maze of ideas and possibilities, the latter is in keeping with the teaching of great literature in which each text is understood as an inexhaustible and unique resource. Rieff comes across therefore as a quirky amalgam of Jacques Derrida and, say, George Steiner, although he no doubt feels much closer to the latter.

Among sociologists, the implications of Rieff's approach can be usefully contrasted with another great American theorist, Talcott Parsons. In his early work, notably *The Structure of Social Action* (1949 [1937]), Parsons closely examined the works of Pareto, Marshall, Weber, and Durkheim, arguing that these great scholar-teachers all contribute to a single way of thinking about the social world, as their ideas converge into a general theory. Parsons could therefore imagine, as Rieff cannot, that contemporary theorists might "overcome" earlier theoretical ideas by integrating them into a general theory.

In this regard, Parsons' assumptions are compatible with those of researchers in the natural sciences. This is signaled by his later effort during his "middle period" to develop a neutral, technical language for sociological theory, comparable to that found in physics or economics, and quite different from Parsons' "voice" in *The Structure of Social Action*. The neutral, technical language found in, for example, *Toward a General Theory of Action* (1951b) is meant to be, in a sense, independent of any one individual. Indeed, it is striking that many of Parsons' key texts from the 1950s were co-authored or even multi-authored. This symbolizes collaboration and unity, but also indifference to authorship, as if the reported ideas were a direct representation of the social world itself. Rieff's view is clearly a long way from this: a collection of his papers is titled *The Feeling Intellect* (1990), suggesting the interplay between rational, emotional, and moral thought. Indeed, this phrase is a slogan for Rieff, appearing several times in his work. There is no space in Rieff's intellectual world for Parsons' technical language; nor is there ambition to develop such a language. For Parsons, theory was an activity designed to find a general meta-theoretical scheme for the social sciences, whereas for Rieff, theory is a collective noun for the authority figures who can, if we let them, teach us something important about our cultural predicament.

Ironically, the language of both Parsons and Rieff changed over time and in both cases the changes made their work less accessible. Although Parsons has a reputation for what Bershady (1973) once described as "elephantine" prose, his earlier and later writings are quite lucid. The clarity of *The Structure of Social Action* is often thought to be the result of the intervention of Parsons' father, who was said to be appalled at his son's dense prose. However, Parsons' later papers – for example, his autobiographical statement – are also wonderfully clear. It is primarily the middle phase of his work that is hard to penetrate, as he strove to write collaboratively in an exact way that would permit cumulative research. By comparison, Rieff is also often thought to have written lucidly at the beginning of his career, only to become increasingly poetic, quasi-mystical, quasi-religious, self-consciously aphoristic and circuitous. It is as if Rieff increasingly wanted his readers to struggle to understand him. As one commentator put it: "My initial exposure to Rieff came with *The Triumph of the Therapeutic*, and my first reaction was that it was a fascinating work, which merited translation into English" (Muller, 1995: 193).

Rieff's Sociology of Culture: A Culture Lost

In *The Triumph of the Therapeutic* Rieff defined culture as "the system of significances attached to behavior by which a society explains itself to itself" (1966: 68–9). This definition raises the question of what it is that a culture must explain to itself. Rieff had answered this earlier: "A culture must communicate ideals, distinguish right from wrong and facilitate agreement. Culture directs the self toward communal purposes. It manages the interplay between Yes and No" (1966: 4). Toward the end of the book, Rieff suggested that this communication must be symbolic so as to preserve conditions of mutual trust. He then added a separate and important role for culture: the organization of the "expressive remissions" by which we release ourselves, temporarily, from the controlling, internalized aspects of culture itself (1966: 232–3).

Some cultures are part of what Rieff calls "positive communities." These offer "therapies of commitment;" that is, they promise individual salvation through participant membership (1966: 71). Salvation occurs because individuals subordinate themselves to communal purposes. Rieff frequently gave religious and revolutionary political groups as examples of positive communities with commitment therapies. Perhaps the military has the same potential also.

Rieff believes that the impetus for positive communities has been lost, and that they have been largely replaced by negative communities. Whereas positive communities try to *transform* individuals, negative communities only *inform* them. As a result, there is no prospect of salvation. What is left is merely therapy (1966: 73). Rieff's title, *The Triumph of the Therapeutic*, is now understandable: therapy's triumph is a result of the failure of positive communities to provide salvation. Contemporary therapy (in all its various psychological forms) is comparable to experience: it is what we get now that we no longer get what we want.

This is the thought that connects the final chapter of *Freud: The Mind of the Moralist* to *The Triumph of the Therapeutic*: Freud alerted us to a kind of epistemic cultural break that we are presently living through. This break marks a transition from these positive communities to negative communities. Positive communities retain the fiction of knowing what makes living worthwhile: they present a template of the well-lived life to their members. This well-lived life involves interdictions, community service, and personal sacrifice. By contrast, negative communities consist of people who recognize that every positive community is built on a fiction, albeit one which is often appealing. Members of negative communities accept the following truth: their activities and aspirations are meaningless, and alienation is a constant, understandable, and expected risk. For Rieff, Freud's genius was in being able to describe this cultural shift and then in proposing a way of trying to manage the ensuing malaise. The later Freud's modest solution to the problem of living in negative communities was to use therapy to strengthen the ego:

> Freud maintained a sober vision of the man in the middle, a go-between, aware of the fact that he had little strength of his own, forever mediating between culture and instinct in an effort to gain some room for maneuver between hostile powers. Maturity, according to Freud, lay in the trained capacity to keep the negotiations going. (1966: 31)

Rieff's Sociology of Culture: A Culture Gained

As mentioned earlier, the culture we gained is described in Freud's work and is referred to by Rieff as a negative community. This community is a result of intellectual progress because it signals our realization that all systems of thought that promise salvation through commitment therapies are bankrupt. Negative communities are therefore the default option. In *The Triumph of the Therapeutic* Rieff considered the disquieting poem "The Second Coming," in which Yeats indicates that the people we admire the most no longer have a faith in anything whereas those that we cannot admire display passionate but misplaced convictions. Rieff took this thought very seriously: what will a culture be like when its most talented citizens lack all conviction? Negative communities are marked by both a "dissolution of a unitary system of common belief" and a "disorganization of personality." This has led to several systems of belief competing with each other (1966: 2). There is no longer an internalized, generalized other connecting the person to his or her communities, as Mead or Cooley envisaged. What, then, can prevent the fragmentation of groups, since it is irrational for anyone to commit him- or herself to any particular belief system? In answering this question, Rieff moved from Cooley to Freud.

Current discussions about Freud are a poor guide to Rieff's Freud. They typically emphasize one of three issues: (1) clinical effectiveness, especially when measured against the effectiveness of psychopharmacology; (2) the scientific basis of psychoanalysis; and (3) the compatibility of psychoanalytic ideas with one or other version of deconstructive, postmodern, and feminist theories of identity. By contrast, Rieff famously emphasized that Freud was the moral thinker. It bears restating that the title of his study was not *Freud: The Mind of a Moralist* but rather *Freud: The Mind of the Moralist* (1959). The second definite article reveals the highest esteem in which Rieff – at least at that time – held Freud as the guide to our present moral predicament. Thus, Rieff was unfazed by the suggestions that psychoanalysis may not be clinically effective, especially when stacked up against Zoloft, Paxil, or Prozac; or that it may prove to be unscientific; or that it may fail to contribute to contemporary social theoretical debates. None of these issues is of immediate concern for Rieff, who reads Freud quite differently – as a cultural theorist who has identified a new, albeit modest, moral framework for our transitional times. In fact, part of Rieff's genius was shown in his ability to explore Freud's ideas in a manner that was consistent with Freud's texts but alien to existing interpretations of psychoanalysis.

According to Rieff, Freud's key insight was not only that we are living through an epistemic break, but that the drifting experience of this break will continue because there is nothing to replace it. There is no new culture on the horizon. As he put it in *Fellow Teachers* (1985: 215), "Freud is best interpreted as the chief figure at the endless transitionality of our era." It follows, then, that Freud's moral framework must concern the appropriate pattern of behavior in endlessly transitional times, as there is no point suspending moral judgments until a new moral culture emerges, because none is forthcoming.

The moral standards imposed by psychoanalysis are not very high – and that is what makes them distinctive and compatible with our present era. Freud emphasized that, without the hope of salvation, our aim must be lowered to honest compromise. Since we suspect that all ideals and communities are objects to guard against rather than to embrace, "ironic insight" about ourselves is all we can achieve (1959: 330). Since we cannot be enlightened, our goal instead should be merely not to be deceived. As Rieff put it, in our present negative communities, moral virtue amounts to being able to say that "one has not been taken in" (1966: 51). Probably Goffman's significance in Rieff's view was that he was our foremost sociologist of deception, and as such Goffman accurately described our contemporary quasi-moral sensibility. In this regard, Rieff's reading of Goffman is close to Alasdair MacIntyre's (1981) reading of Goffman, which in turn suggests that there is an affinity between MacIntyre and Rieff.

According to Freud, the threat of meaninglessness in negative communities remains ever present in the background because life's contradictions cannot be resolved. Freud therefore promises only to return his patients to normal unhappiness and ambivalence in which they learn to tolerate ambiguity (1966: 55–7).

Freud had a "cautious wisdom" (1966: 59) that offered the following advice to Americans: "survive, resign yourself to living within your moral means, suffer no gratuitous failures in a futile search for ethical heights that no longer exist – if they ever did" (1966: 58). At best, then, Freud promised "detachment without alienation" (1966: 60).

Rieff's Sociology of Culture: A Culture Imagined

In the final chapter of *Freud: The Mind of the Moralist*, Rieff introduced a developmental schema in which our dominant ideal-type has "evolved" from Religious Man to Political Man to Economic Man to Psychological Man. This last reincarnation, in Rieff's view so well described by Freud, appeared in this book as a terminal state. There is no post-Psychological Man, and so there is no new moral culture to anticipate and perhaps even to wait or strive for. The attempt to build a new moral culture was the impossible project pursued by D. H. Lawrence, Reich, and Jung. All three tried by different means to make more of psychoanalysis than Freud himself thought was possible, and in trying to extend psychoanalysis they made it resemble the moral systems that Freud came to believe could no longer be sustained. According to Rieff's view, when Freud gave up on catharsis, he replaced it with analysis that was, theoretically if not practically, as interminable as the transitional, thin culture in which we live.

Over time, the changing tone of Rieff's writing suggests changes in his reaction to Freud's message. In *Freud: The Mind of the Moralist* Rieff's tone is as detached as Freud's. It is as if he has accepted the limitations of an ethic of honesty and learned to tolerate the ambiguities of our time. At the same time, Rieff seems to be a man who cannot be taken in, someone who is as "bleakly knowing" as his colleague-to-be, Erving Goffman.

In *The Triumph of the Therapeutic* Rieff was still following Freud's advice and not that of Freud's disciples. However, the new tone is one of reluctance and this reveals both a clear break with the earlier work and his increasing concern about Freud's message. "What comes next?" asks Rieff. His answer is not hopeful: either a post-scarcity, affluent society that is thoroughly remissive, or a culture dominated by analytic therapy in which we all seek to manage the unconscious deceit of salvation (1966: 48–9). If psychoanalysis can, as he suggests in this book, only offer the "ultimate freedom" of "having nothing to lose," then it has failed (1968: 60). Contemporary American society is not promising either: in it wealth has become a "substitute for symbolic impoverishment," quantity matters more than quality, and cultural blandness blankets us while standing for nothing at all (1966: 65).

As with his study of Freud, the tone of Rieff's *Fellow Teachers* also suggests that he is "bleakly knowing." However, now he is clearly no longer happy to be so. At the beginning of the new preface to this book he tells us that he is writing a "postmortem letter to the dead, myself self-addressed among them" (1985: vii). The tone of *Fellow Teachers* is, for the most part, angry despair. Neither his diagnosis nor his prognosis of our time has substantially changed, but his judgments of them have. He is no longer willing to be merely a detached observer, commenting, usually ironically, on the massive limitations of Psychological Man. Rieff understands and in a sense appreciates the detached observations of some of his peers, such as Goffman, who masked their moral outrage in what Ignatieff (1983) has aptly described as a misleading "neutral tone." Rieff also understands that the moral critique just below the surface of Goffman's books is already at the limit of what the sociologist as sociologist can do. Rieff's reaction is simply that this is not enough. One of his students, Kenneth Piver (1994), put it well when he suggested that Rieff has increasingly sought to instill personal, interdenominational, religious faith into his work.

Metaphorically, this development appears to have raised Rieff from the dead, and from his own theoretical death as chronicled in *Fellow Teachers*. At the beginning of his paper on the "second culture camp," Rieff uses James Joyce's pun "Let there be fight? And there was" (1991: 316). Rieff is now willing to fight a cultural war to prevent the emergence of a "third culture" which is thoroughly remissive and therefore also deeply transgressive.

Rieff's fight is simultaneously intriguing, confusing, challenging, and deliberately offensive to liberal sensibilities. It is intriguing and confusing because Rieff's decision to fight appears to require him to assert the existence of positive communities with viable therapies of commitment that are capable of transforming the individual whilst providing salvation. That is, Rieff must now defend the existence of the thing that his scholar-teachers, notably Freud, Weber, and Nietzsche, believed to be mere illusion. Thus, Freud can no longer be "the moralist;" in fact he now barely qualifies as "a" moralist. Worst of all, Freud's work might provide the impetus for the third culture that Rieff has armed himself to fight against.

Rieff's work is also increasingly challenging. This is not simply a reference to the intellectual sophistication of his work that requires us to make connections between the diverse scholar-teachers who educated Rieff himself. It also refers to Rieff's challenge to us to live with guilt, and not the watered down sense of guilt that Freud bequeathed us. Rieff believes that unless guilt polices our actions, there is no possibility of preserving a sacred, social order.

Finally, Rieff presents a traditional, conservative, moral agenda that is defiantly at odds with liberal sentiment. The liberal who seems to personify what Rieff stands against is Derrida. The two moral failures that have been the focus of his most recent attention are homosexuality and abortion. Even knowing the conservative nature of his agenda, Rieff's choices are surprising.

As mentioned earlier, Rieff shares considerable common ground with Derrida: the targets of Derrida's deconstructive efforts are almost exactly the same scholar-teachers whom Rieff reveres. Further, Derrida's attitude to these scholar-teachers is very similar to Rieff's; Derrida once remarked that you can only deconstruct what you love. It also seems fruitless to complain about Derrida's opaque, pun-ridden, playful, aphoristic style, since that is essentially Rieff's style now also, and both men enjoy inventing new words. Perhaps, for Rieff, Derrida's claim to love what he deconstructs falls short of honoring – or even recognizing – the sacredness of the text. Nietzsche speculated that truth might be a woman, and perhaps as such the object of intense, temporarily satisfying, but fickle attention. Is Derrida guilty – in Rieff's view – of loving Nietzsche's young women rather than honoring the sacred truths known by old men?

In a different way Rieff's reflections on the evils of homosexuality and abortion are also surprisingly abrasive. He often uses these examples as an opportunity to quote the Bible, as if biblical reference alone were adequate resolution to any moral dilemma.

I like to think of the intellectual space created by Rieff's interdictory culture as something that, at its best, is negative, in the sense that it demarcates a realm of what is both possible and permissible without giving any content to this negative space. It is as if Rieff were standing at the edge of a relativistic abyss and telling us to watch our step. However, when Rieff follows his own declaration, "Let there be fight," he begins to tell us far more than just a cautionary "be careful!" It is not only the content of the "far more" that is then troubling, but also his willingness to impose it by both biblical and military force.

To conclude, I find it useful to contrast Rieff's later work both with his earlier work and with that of someone with whom he is often compared, Alasdair MacIntyre. Part of what is so compelling about Rieff's study of Freud is that he demonstrated an invigorating way of reading Freud that was completely new; that is, he stretched the limits of our understanding of a school of thought that was becoming overly familiar. Part of what is compelling about MacIntyre's study, *After Virtue* (1981), is that he demonstrates the continuing relevance of Aristotle's account of the virtues without specifying a precise content to these virtues. We are entrusted to act, limited only by the restrictions of following what MacIntyre calls "practices." Put simply, practices are things in which we try to excel, subject to certain limitations. This is an important part of MacIntyre's response to the permissive, consumerist, bureaucratic culture of the moment. Increasingly, Rieff appears to be unwilling to entrust culture with the responsibility of maintaining sacred practices in a negative culture. To paraphrase an astute commentator on Rieff, the threat to contemporary culture is not Derrida's deconstructive writings but the lyrics of songs by Too Live Crew and other performers who, through the use of profanities, seek to demonstrate that the "abyss of possibility . . . [has] now been absorbed in community standards" (Muller 1995: 204). Rieff's reaction to what he now sees is to fight to re-establish sacred laws. However, his own earlier work on the rise of negative communities is, ironically, an insightful guide as to why he will lose this battle.

6

Sociologists as Analysts and Auto-Ethnographers: Hochschild, Chodorow, Prager, and After

Introduction

In earlier chapters I have argued that both theoretical and empirical issues influenced the reactions American sociologists had to Freud. The theoretical issues were vast: once Freud and psychoanalysis were no longer understood as one discrete object, but as a maze of possibilities, sociologists had the dizzying task of establishing whether any version of the psychoanalytic project was compatible with different versions of their own. The empirical issues were troubling for different reasons: because American psychoanalysis had developed as a branch of medicine, there was an understandable concern that its methods would be difficult to employ outside of clinical encounters. For sociologists who did not undertake empirical research, this second problem was obviously irrelevant. This was the situation facing Cooley, Mead, and Rieff. It was not the case, however, for Parsons, who, despite an intimidating level of abstraction, always anticipated empirical applications for his ideas. Thus, although he did not solve the problem of how to use psychoanalytic ideas in empirical research, he did recognize this as part of the challenge facing him. In this sense, Parsons and Rieff were antithetical contemporaries. Parsons anticipated the establishment of a unified general theory in which psychoanalysis played a significant role that was routinely used in social scientific research. For this reason, I consider the assessment of Parsons' and Platt's *The American University* as the litmus test of his approach. By contrast, Rieff understood Freud as a moral teacher. Interestingly, *The Triumph of the*

Therapeutic may be a better guide to his understanding of psycho-analysis than *Freud: The Mind of the Moralist* because it is easier to detect his sustained ambivalence to the moral lessons taught by psychoanalysis. Certainly, *The American University* and *The Triumph of the Therapeutic* represent two extremes in sociology's appropriation of Freud.

Blumer and Goffman both opposed all versions of psychoanalysis on theoretical grounds, and therefore the question of whether its ideas could be applied empirically was moot. However, especially in Goffman's case, his opposition to Freud contributed to the development of both a theory and a method that competed with rather than complemented psychoanalysis. This required him to consider the content of a person's internal world to be irrelevant for sociology. The litmus test for an assessment of Goffman is therefore the assessment of *Asylums*, a book I read as both an extension of Sumner's ethological research and a reaction against Cooley's advocacy of sympathetic introspection, which could lead sociology toward a rapprochement with psychoanalysis.

In this chapter I consider a new way sociologists can react to psychoanalysis. This is by benefiting from the demedicalization of psychoanalysis to receive clinical training. Unlike Parsons' generation, sociologists who now train as psychoanalysts do so with the prospect of obtaining a license to practice. Does this change their understanding of the relationship between sociology and psychoanalysis? I consider three cases: Arlie Hochschild, Nancy Chodorow, and Jeffrey Prager. Later I want to consider whether there is a version of Goffman's project that could be receptive to the study of internal worlds. Understood non-psychoanalytically, I take this to be a project that synthesizes the ambitions of Sumner and Cooley. This requires a rethinking of both theoretical and empirical concerns. I understand this to involve a merger of the Sumner/Goffman ethological approach that leads to "ethnographies of concepts" with the Cooley/Rieff tradition of sympathetic introspection. Chodorow has suggested that a "reflexive anthropology" holds the best prospect for the synthesis of social science and psychoanalysis. Here I want to look at work by sociologists who have employed auto-ethnography to explore a similar set of issues.

The Current Context

In the last 40 years the psychoanalytic profession has experienced extraordinary downward mobility. The psychoanalysis of Parsons' day was the prestigious centerpiece of psychiatry; today it is often assumed to be quackery. Luhrmann recently reported that a candidate in psycho-analysis described the annual meeting of the American Psychoanalytic Association as a place to watch "dinosaurs deliberate over their own extinction" (2000: 183). Although it is probably impossible to identify exactly the causes of the widespread loss of confidence in psychoanaly-sis, several factors contributed in varying degrees to its demise. The most obvious of these was the emergence of psychopharmacology in the 1950s, which was certainly a threat to psychoanalysis, because the perceived benefits of chlorpromazine (sold as Thorazine in the US and Largactil in Britain) convinced many physicians and lay people that serious mental illness could at last be treated conventionally with medi-cation (Baldessarini 1999: 446–7). Conrad and Schneider suggest that by 1957 a "new feeling of optimism permeated the psychiatric world" (1992: 61). However, the impact of psychopharmacology on psycho-analysis is more complicated and subtle than this observation suggests. Chlorpromazine was a serendipitous discovery (the French scientists credited with its discovery were actually trying to make a sedative). There was therefore no scientific understanding at that time about the illness that the new drug was found to treat. In fact, there was even doubt about which mental illness the drug was meant to treat and an underlying concern that perhaps chlorpromazine simply alleviated or exchanged symptoms. These initial concerns were not settled by clinical experience and for critics this new drug was no more than a masking agent. In a sense, then, the first steps of the psychopharmacological era could have been its last, and its perceived failures could have been a boon to the already struggling field of psychoanalysis.

However, the key phrase here is "already struggling" as it indicates that there was no longer a willingness to engage in psychoanalysis. Psychopharmacology was therefore successful, not simply because of its own merits, but by default and because it promised future break-throughs. By the time it became clear that these breakthroughs were not around the immediate corner, psychopharmacology already had hold of psychiatry, public opinion, and many of the mentally ill them-selves, who were relieved that they could now be treated and accepted as people who are conventionally ill.

There is no doubt that other factors contributed to the demise of psychoanalysis. These include concerns about its lack of scientific cred-ibility, the general "anti-psychiatry" movement of the 1960s, interdis-ciplinary critiques of totalizing theories, and the many forms of feminist and cultural attacks. These disparate elements all contributed to a widespread sense that psychoanalysis was bankrupt. Psychiatry itself was not exactly thriving and so it had no resources of its own to lend. In retrospect, the ensuing demedicalization of psychoanalysis was inevitable and the surprise was that it took so long: it only came about in 1988. However, demedicalization was not a complete disaster for psychoanalysis as a profession, as it opened the door to new possibilities and collaborations. This development is not particularly shocking, as psychoanalysis had operated in Europe from inception using both medical and lay analysts. In the United States, social workers were quick to recognize that psychoanalysts' loss could be their gain, as their downward mobility brought them within reach. Therefore, after psychoanalytic training became available to people without a medical degree, social workers became one of the main beneficiaries. Although not the focus of this project, the study of the merger between psychoanalysis and social work is an interesting contribution to the sociology of the professions (see, generally, Luhrmann, 2000).

Sociologists have been the source of a different kind of collaboration with post-1988 psychoanalysis, the contours of which are clearer when they are contrasted with the kind of collaboration attempted by Parsons and his colleagues 30 years earlier. Parsons and other sociologists who completed psychoanalytic training did so without any intention or interest in pursuing careers as psychoanalysts. They signed waivers promising not to engage in clinical work, and maintained the professional identity of academic sociologists. Their interests were therefore primarily theoretical and intellectual. Post-1988 sociologists who trained as psychoanalysts did so under quite different conditions. Obviously, they were aware that they would be able to practice psychoanalysis and they were often interested in pursuing clinical practices that could run parallel with or perhaps even against their academic careers. In addition, unlike social workers, sociologists and other academics could, potentially at least, lend the institutional prestige of the university to the psychoanalytic world. While this is certainly not as attractive as an affiliation to medicine, it promised to stop the threat of disciplinary free fall that occurred after 1988.

Put simply, the key issue for pre-1988 sociologists was the prospect for a synthesis between sociology and psychoanalysis, whereas the dilemma for post-1988 sociologists was whether it made sense for them to leave sociology altogether and embark on what is essentially a new career.

The sociologist who embodies both sides of this issue is Parsons' protégé, Neil Smelser. Smelser trained with Parsons, completing his doctoral training at the Department of Social Relations in 1957. He collaborated with Parsons in the analysis of the ramifications of the AGIL schema. This is the project that emerged from Parsons' lectures at the University of Cambridge in 1952–3 and was published as

Economy and Society. Smelser was also Parsons' and Bales' research assistant on the project that was published as *Family, Socialization and Interaction Process* (1955). When he left Harvard to take a faculty position at the University of California at Berkeley he did so with the firm intention of undertaking psychoanalytic training himself. Like Parsons, he did so out of both intellectual interest and because of personal difficulties, in his case resulting from a failing marriage. Like Parsons, he completed the training without any expectation of undertaking clinical work. However, Smelser's circumstances were different, and new legislation in California meant that he was later able to obtain a license to practice psychoanalysis. This he did with the blessing and encouragement of the San Francisco Psychoanalytic Institute (Smelser, 1998: viii–x).

However, Smelser preserved his primary identification as sociologist and did not establish a private practice, although he did engage in clinical work at the University Medical Center. His decision was based on two very different arguments. The first was practical: as a successful sociologist, Smelser traveled extensively and therefore could not guarantee patients regular appointments. The second reason was intellectual: unlike Parsons, he believes that sociology and psychoanalysis are quite different activities, based on different assumptions and requiring different empirical approaches (Smelser, 1998). Thus, the idea of a psychoanalytic sociology makes little sense to him; he is, in a very loose sense, a recent version of William Ogburn.

There are two different lines of inquiry at this point. The first concerns the impact sociology can have on contemporary psychoanalytic practice. The second concerns the empirical content of a putative psychoanalytic sociology. The first line of inquiry is clearly very new, since it is only in the last 20 years or so that there has been any thought in the United States that lay analysis might contribute to clinical understanding. By contrast, the second line of inquiry is almost as old as American sociology itself. As I have argued earlier, theories often imply methods. Thus, for example, the symbolic interactionist tradition has an affinity with a qualitative methodology, just as mainstream psychoanalysis is tied to the methodology of the "talking cure" through free association. The underlying issue for sociologists interested in psychoanalysis, therefore, concerns the appropriate methodology for a psychoanalytic sociology.

In the next section I want to examine aspects of the work of three contemporary sociologists, Arlie Hochschild, Nancy Chodorow, and Jeff Prager, the last two of whom followed in the footsteps of Parsons and Smelser by completing analytic training. Chodorow and Prager began by seeking an answer to the question of the composition of a psychoanalytic sociology, but ended up by giving an answer to the question of the contribution sociology can make to clinical, psycho-analytic practice.

Hochschild, Chodorow, and Prager

The arguments that I explore in this chapter have been anticipated, albeit in a slightly different way, by Arlie Hochschild, who has ele-gantly pointed out that Goffman's "black-box psychology" is in need of elaboration (2003: 92). As I have done, Hochschild also points to Freud and psychoanalysis as a resource for developing Goffman's game-theoretic, impression-management approach to sociology, and like me she favors a psychoanalytic approach that downplays the role of internal drives.

In *The Managed Heart* (1983) Hochschild contrasts an "organ-ismic" model of emotion that she connects with, among others, Freud's earlier work with an "interactional" model that she identifies predom-inantly with Goffman. The organismic model is primarily biological and as such is concerned with the discharge of energy or with instinct. By contrast, the interactional model is concerned with the continuing effort we all make to preserve social interaction by applying unclear rules to social situations. Hochschild presents the strengths and weak-nesses of Goffman's account of this project very clearly:

> In Goffman's theory, the capacity to act on feeling derives only from the occa-sion, not from the individual. The self may actively choose to *display* feelings in order to give outward impressions to others. But it is passive to the point of invisibility when it comes to the private act of managing emotion. The "I" is there, of course, in the many stories from the *San Francisco Chronicle*, in the passages from novels, in hangmen's accounts, in Ionesco plays, in Lillian Gish's autobiography. But the private "I" is simply not there in theory. Feelings are contributions to interactions via the passive medium of a bodily self. We act behaviorally, not affectively. The system affects our behavior, not our feelings. (1983: 218, emphasis in original)

Reconciling these two positions is the task of her path-breaking attempt to establish the sociology of emotions. By emotion, Hoschchild refers to "bodily cooperation with an idea, thought, or attitude and the label attached to that awareness" (2003: 75). "Feelings" are simply milder emotions. Sociologists are well placed to study emotions because, as at least potential members of the groups they study, they have "direct access" to them (2003: 75).

To achieve her theoretical ambitions, Hochschild had to fuse these two images of the self: the conscious, cognitive self and the unconscious, emotional self. Her proposed synthesis yields the "sentient self" that is capable of both recognizing and reflecting upon internal, emotional states. The sentient self is revealed in everyday expressions such as "I'm not usually this anxious" (see Hochschild, 2003: 77).

In Hochschild's view, once sociologists recognize the sentient self as a legitimate target for sociological investigation, then emotions are no longer an "impediment" to research but an appropriate subject matter for research (2003: 75). Again, Hochschild does not use the concept of auto-ethnography, but she does emphasize that sociologists are interested in both the "normal emotions" that group members typically feel and in the "feeling rules" for these emotions. Feeling rules are the social guidelines that we internalize and which allow us to experience normal emotions (2003: 97). In *The Managed Heart* Hochschild argued that many – arguably most – jobs involve emotional work for which people must be able to reflect upon their own reactions to clients and events and produce appropriate emotions. Hochschild's decision to investigate the training of flight attendants was an inspired one, as it is clear that they sell the company to the public by being its visible face (1983: 92).

In her most recent work (2003), Hochschild has become interested in the commercialization of feeling rules through the proliferation of self-help books. Through a kind of identity shopping, consumers select self-help books that promise to teach them to have the emotional responses to people and events that they want to have but presently don't. This may mean being a submissive, dutiful wife, as taught by Marabel Morgan in *The Total Woman*, or it may mean being an independent woman, as taught by Colette Dowling in *The Cinderella Complex*. For Hochschild, these authors are both "emotion investment counselor[s]" (2003: 19).

Hochschild identified weaknesses in Freud's earlier conception of emotion and limitations in Goffman's restricted view of emotion. She also recognized that sociologists had either failed to appreciate the significance of emotions or had simply discounted them as irrational forces. In my view, while developing a new area of sociological research – the sociology of emotions – Hochschild forged a new theoretical alliance between the later Freudian model of object relations and the broad tradition of symbolic interactionism. The missing link was the realization of the centrality of transference and countertransference in this new theoretical alliance. For this, it is necessary to turn to Chodorow, Prager, and the new group of often reluctant "auto-ethnographers."

Nancy Chodorow first came to prominence in 1978 following the extraordinary impact of her feminist study *The Reproduction of Mothering*. This book began its life as a doctoral dissertation and was later identified by *Contemporary Sociology* as one of the 10 most influential books in sociology over the last 25 years. After finishing this book, Chodorow undertook psychoanalytic training and has emerged as a leading psychoanalyst. She has therefore contributed significantly to three fields: sociology, feminist theory, and psychoanalysis. In 1999, she published *The Power of Feelings*. In many ways, this is a fully psychoanalytic response to her first work. It is not a repudiation of it at all, but it does recast her earlier insights, using her clinical experience and greater theoretical understanding.

Jeffrey Prager had already established a successful career as a sociologist at UCLA when he undertook psychoanalytic training. In *Presenting the Past* (1998) Prager states explicitly that he did so in order to "bring the knowledge and insights of psychoanalysis to bear on my sociological research interests" (1998: 1). Therefore he shared, initially at least, Parsons' ambition for a rapprochement between the two disciplines. However, he became less optimistic about the prospects for this. Unlike Smelser, Prager saw continuities in the epistemological assumptions of sociology and psychoanalysis; however, like Smelser he found the differences between the two disciplines more striking than the similarities. For example, Prager revealed that "at my most psychoanalytic I came to believe that genuine communication and understanding could be achieved only in a psychoanalytic setting (and there only rarely). Finding a way to connect psychoanalytic findings with sociological ones seemed more difficult than ever" (1998: 3).

Chodorow's work began with the kind of question that parents regret their children asking them. It is reminiscent of Ludwig Wittgenstein's approach: he once taught an advanced class at the University of Cambridge on the philosophy of mathematics in which he only explored very elementary problems of addition. Chodorow displayed the same intellectual audacity in her first book, *The Reproduction of Mothering* (1999a [1978]) when she asked the apparently trivial question(s), why do women mother and why do they want to? Chodorow showed that our understanding of the question is heavily influenced by assumptions about gendered expectations because, as she pointed out, we can make sense of the idea that a man "mothered" a child but suffer to make sense of the apparently parallel idea that a woman "fathered" a child, as this verb has an overriding biological connotation (1999a: 11).

The simplicity of Chodorow's query belied the complexity of the answer. In fact, her answer had three parts: in the first she showed the inadequacy of either biological or social explanations; in the second she showed the complexity of the "psychoanalytic story" and high-lighted a reformulation of Freud's analysis of the Oedipal complex; in the third she identified sociological contributions to the answer to the problem. So, on the face of it, Chodorow appeared to be seeking the middle ground that was responsive to feminism between sociology and psychoanalysis. However, this is misleading, as the clear focus of the book is the psychoanalytic component.

This allows us to identify the key to her work: Chodorow wanted to explore the typical content of gendered, unconscious, internal worlds and the accompanying conscious and unconscious senses of personal identity that typically emerge from them. In her first book, Chodorow was not generalizing from actual clinical case studies, which at that time she didn't have; rather she was constructing an ideal-type of the dynamics of mother–daughter relationships and the differences between them and the dynamics of mother–son relationships. Although these experiences are in significant ways different, they are all processed in the same way. Thus, as Chodorow summarized in her new preface to the second edition of *The Reproduction of Mothering*:

> On a general level I would reiterate that everyone has a psyche that operates in the ways that psychoanalysis describes (through unconscious fantasy; projection and introjection; defenses against anxiety and guilt such as repression and splitting; creating an inner world, managing desire and aggression; and so forth): this psyche is part of our human psychobiological makeup. (1999a: xii)

Chodorow went on to claim that this terrain is not primarily theoretical but rather "empirical-clinical" (1999a: xii). In arguing in this way, she takes a position that is quite close to Prager's claim that genuine communication when it occurs at all occurs in the clinical psychoanalytic setting. Clearly, the issues facing both of them are, first, whether it still makes any sense to theorize generally about the typical content of gendered interactions and, second, whether the viable methodological options have been so narrowed down that the "empirical-clinical" is really the only one left standing. Chodorow is of course aware of the critics of her work who claim that her analysis is too general, with the result that it universalizes and essentializes heterogeneous experiences. She must maintain a delicate balance between criticizing Parsonsian action theory (as she understands it) and the Frankfurt School for being too general, while at the same time salvaging the idea that some kind of general theoretical and empirical observations are still possible.

For sociologists interested in psychoanalysis, the key question concerns the availability to them *as sociologists* of Chodorow's empirical-clinical field. If this domain is properly and exclusively psychoanalytic, then it makes no sense to seek out any version of the synthesis that motivated Parsons' theoretical research. The logic of Chodorow's position supports the idea of two discrete fields, making her a successor to Smelser rather than to Parsons. Insofar as Chodorow is primarily concerned with the analysis of identity and psyche together, and insofar as she specifies the analysis of the psyche as the investigation of unconscious fantasy, projection, introjection, defenses against guilt and anxiety, and the management of desire and aggression (see above), then her exodus from sociology to psychoanalysis seems inevitable. Smelser found himself in a similar predicament and chose differently, but understood his situation exactly as Chodorow appears to understand hers.

The onus is in fact on sociologists to demonstrate exactly how investigations of internal worlds could be achieved without psychoanalytic methodology: that is, outside of a clinical-empirical field. In her most recent work, Chodorow has suggested (1999b: 172–218) that a reflexive anthropology can fuse psychoanalytic insights with ethnographic methods, and I want to suggest that this is a promising direction for sociology also. However, although I will indicate that this can be accomplished, it is important to recognize that even sociologists who appear to be only one remove from psychoanalysis have often discounted even the possibility. Thus, leading qualitative sociologists, such as Blumer, Goffman, and Garfinkel, whatever their differences, were united in understanding sociology in opposition to psychoanalysis. And if their investigations were unsympathetic to psychoanalysis, imagine the reaction of the rest of sociology.

An instructive example of the problem is Chodorow's handling of one of the key elements of Parsons' action theory: the concept of internalization. As Chodorow herself has pointed out, there are significant overlaps between the sociological account of internalization and the psychoanalytic account of introjection. In *The Reproduction of Mothering*, Chodorow warns us that internalization does not simply involve the "direct transmission" of elements of the social world into the "unconscious experience of self-in-relationship" (1999a: 50). Rather, internalization is an idiosyncratic process that varies with each person's emotional state and is "mediated by fantasy and by conflict" (1999a: 50). Matters are further complicated by the fact that we all inhabit multiple, largely unconscious inner worlds that contain conflicts that "give meaning to external situations" (1999a: 51), and also build upon childhood experiences. This is a far richer understanding of internalization than the one offered by Parsons, but one that seems impossible to incorporate into social science methodology. Perhaps recognizing this, Chodorow switched from her theoretical discussion to a practical evaluation of the adequacy of psychoanalytic evidence, tacitly stating that the evidence concerning internalization will in fact be psychoanalytic in character (1999a: 52–4).

Nevertheless, although Chodorow's account of internalization (or introjection) is richer than Parsons', it is compatible with it. What is different is her belief that sociology has yet to develop the empirical means to investigate it. There is a predictable drift in Chodorow's work away from the social sciences and into psychoanalysis, and what was anticipated in *The Reproduction of Mothering* is realized in *The Power of Feelings*, where her perspective is authoritatively that of an analyst. Thus, the difficulties of investigating the social world psychoanalytically but without mainstream psychoanalytic methods are central to Chodorow's assessment of reflexive anthropology. By contrast, these same difficulties are easily overlooked in reviewing Parsons' own work, in which there are already many other unresolved theoretical and other problems, and, in any case, many other parts of Parsons' action theory appear to be resistant to empirical analysis. A different approach was taken by, for example, Blumer and Goffman, who, despite their other differences, regarded a person's internal world as simply not part of the subject matter of sociological analysis. By limiting sociological research to the meanings given to situations by group members, they found a way of sidestepping the questions that energize Chodorow's own investigations.

Prager makes an interesting contribution to this debate about the appropriate methods to pursue psychoanalytic sociology. In the preface to *Presenting the Past* he had made it clear that he was ambivalent about the prospects for any meaningful interdisciplinary investigations. Although later chapters suggest that a form of psychoanalytic sociology may in fact be possible, the central chapter indicates otherwise, as it contains the protracted and fascinating clinical case study of "Ms A."

For clinical readers of this case study, it must be disappointing to discover that Ms A. turns out to be not one person but a composite of several of Prager's patients, whom he saw as an integral part of his own psychoanalytic training (1998: 224). From a clinical perspective, this may significantly undermine the value of the study, which is no longer a case study in the typical sense. However, it remains a powerful investigation of the role of transference and counter-transference in social relationships.

Prager used the experiences of Ms A. to explore the characteristics of internal worlds. His specific interest was central to the object-relations perspective: the dynamics of transference and counter-transference as they occur in different relationships, some simultaneously, some over time.

The Analysis of Transference and Ms A.

Here is a short summary of the case. Ms A. was a graduate student in California. She was intelligent, articulate, and attractive. Her own account of her reasons for seeking an analysis concerned her perceived disconnection between her internal state and her external appearance: although she appeared confident and successful to others, to herself she felt overwhelmed, sad, unattractive, a little overweight, and "unsure about her femininity" (1998: 17).

Ms A.'s parents were fundamentalist Christians. Her mother was the mainstay of the family, while her father became increasingly incapacitated by alcohol. Ms A. had a number of older brothers and sisters, who initiated her into a world of alcohol, cigarettes and marijuana at the age of seven or eight. She also witnessed her teenage brothers and sisters having sex with their friends. When Ms A. was in her early twenties she thought of herself as an alcoholic – and with good reason. Like her father, she experienced blackouts and was involved in a car accident in which alcohol played a role. As a result, she joined Alcoholics Anonymous, found a sponsor, and began analysis (making Prager's her second). The combination of these activities seemed to work, as Ms A. successfully abstained from drugs and alcohol from that point on (1998: 18–20).

Ms A.'s relationships with men had been less successful. Her first boyfriend left her after realizing that he was gay. He later learned that he was HIV positive. Another boyfriend was clinically depressed and in fact killed himself while they were still dating. She considered her relationship with her boyfriend at the time of her analysis with Prager to be unsatisfactory. Her closest friend in Los Angeles was a man who developed AIDS and died a few months after Ms A. began analysis (1998: 22). She reported to Prager that she conscientiously remembered and memorialized all these events.

During her analysis with Prager, Ms A.'s mother became seriously ill and died. This had the unexpected result of reuniting her with her father and siblings. In her retelling of events, this conjured up lost (repressed) childhood memories that revealed that her father had sexually abused her many years before.

This could have been interpreted as a breakthrough for the analysis: Ms A.'s present problems were rooted in a traumatic childhood. Ms A. connected her own experiences with those of thousands of other women whose stories of abuse were becoming headline news at the time. She eagerly encouraged Prager to attend meetings at which he could educate himself about the lives of incest survivors. In the same vein, she also provided him with a reading list featuring Ellen Bass' and Laura Davis' *The Courage to Heal: A Guide for Women Survivors of Child Sexual Abuse* (Prager, 1998: 44). It must have been tempting for Prager to pat himself on the back and explore the ramifications of Ms A.'s dysfunctional family with her. To bolster her story, Ms A. reported that, when she confronted her father with the allegation, he could neither confirm nor deny it because his alcoholism had severely impeded his memory. However, while unwilling to reject the abuse narrative completely, Prager was suspicious of it. How else to make sense of it?

Part of what is intriguing about Prager's retelling of Ms A.'s story is that it is both diachronic and synchronic. The diachronic components concern her childhood development and familial difficulties; the synchronic components concern the repetition of apparently bad choices. Investigating the first requires the use of Ms A.'s own accounts, which are difficult to verify. Investigating the second is different, because if her behavior is indeed repetitive, then Prager both saw it first hand and could also anticipate experiencing it for himself, as he had become, in effect, her new "relationship."

The pattern to Ms A.'s relationship was apparently as follows: she selected men who were for different reasons unavailable to her (perhaps because of sexual orientation or illness); she then formed some kind of relationship with them from which she obtained satisfaction until it subsequently failed for reasons that any reasonable observer would conclude were the fault of the men themselves. Ms A. therefore emerged from each encounter as a blameless victim. If this was her modus operandi, then Prager could expect that, as another man who is unavailable to her, she will form a strong attachment to him, only to be let down (again) by something that Prager himself was responsible for. Whatever the something turned out to be, the facts of the matter would prove to be such that any reasonable observer would conclude that the blame rested squarely with Prager, and that Ms A. was once again an unlucky victim.

There are three related versions of transference at work in this case study. The first is the conventional understanding of transference in which the patient develops strong feelings for her analyst, of either a sexual or a hostile character, that originate in childhood experiences. Although sometimes understood as an obstacle to analysis, the investigation of the transference can also be understood as the principal work of the analysis itself.

The second sense of transference is more sociological: it is the idea that people have a template with which to manage their relationships and they use it again and again in similar ways. Rather than thinking of each relationship as a unique, emerging creation, this sense of trans-ference encourages us to think of the person as having a more or less limited repertoire of skills with which to manage their disparate social interactions. As a result, analysts are therefore privy to first-hand data about how patients manage their worlds by seeing how patients manage them. Further, an analyst's counter-transference is itself poten-tially first-hand data about the experiences people have in managing their patients in everyday settings. For example, if an analyst finds a patient boring, irritating, or flirtatious, this is likely to be the typical reaction many people have to the template or repertoire used by that patient. These templates are formed from our familial and other per-sonal experiences and from cultural categories that we internalize. In Ms A.'s case, the cultural category that was probably most important was that of the survivor. This allowed her to identify with the suffer-ing and rehabilitation of a movement.

The third sense of transference refers to the psychoanalytic concept of a "transference neurosis." Prager explains this rather intimidating idea in a revealing way, as the

> point in a psychoanalysis when the analytic relationship becomes the most important feature of a patient's life and the feelings concerning the treatment make all other life experiences pale in comparison. The analysis fills the fore-ground for the patient; "life itself" is, for a time, in the background. (1998: 27)

Understood generally, therefore, transference neuroses are not ill-nesses, but intense feelings of attachment that are so important to the person that they become overwhelming and all other spheres of the person's life suffer. Whether or not this is appropriate is a social, not an objective judgment. In a trivial sense, the term is a near synonym for the everyday notion of concentration, since to do just about any-thing requires a concentrated focus that involves "switching off" other thoughts. At the other end of the continuum are the destructive, obses-sive behaviors for which everyday life appears to have been put per-manently on hold. However, there may well be social-moral judgments operating here as well: an accomplished molecular biologist who declares that she has been thinking non-stop about the inner workings of cells for three decades might be considered to be both hardworking and a genius, but a football fan who idolizes his team to the same extent may well be thought of as someone who needs to get a life. At work here is a social-moral judgment that science is worth doing well, whereas supporting a football team is not.

The clinical challenge facing Prager in his treatment of Ms A. was therefore not to eliminate her transferences or transference neuroses all together, but rather to rechannel them into more productive domains. In order to accomplish this he had first to understand Ms A.'s transferential template and then find a way of explaining it to her such that she could change it. His second task was to allow her to pass through a transference neurosis with regard to the analytic process itself.

Prager wondered whether her claim of sexual abuse could be interpreted instead as a form of sabotage, since it left him in a double bind: if he accepted her account then she had healed herself without his help, but if he rejected it he became an uncaring, incompetent analyst. Ms A. was apparently reusing an old transferential template. Initially she was attracted to Prager, only to be let down by his refusal to accept her discovery of her own sexual abuse. He is therefore a version of the gay boyfriend; she has been unlucky again and her transferential love for Prager can turn to understandable hate.

Curiously, the resulting analytic tension between them was never really resolved; rather, it dissipated as Ms A.'s interest in discussing her father dwindled. In a sense, she passively abandoned her claim of abuse and, perhaps, the template that produced it. Similarly, her transference neurosis with her analysis also began to run out of steam, as she regained energy for her academic studies and became involved in a fulfilling sexual relationship, and began to wonder about marriage.

Rethinking Transference

Prager's account of Ms A. is therefore a powerful demonstration of the many facets of transference that initiates a dialog with sociological theory (Elliott, 2004: 60–6). Transference is not a singular concept, but a strand woven into all relationships and interactions that adds color to them. Its impact therefore extends far beyond the clinical setting. The appreciation of this broad significance and the nuanced exploration of transference is striking in both Prager's and Chodorow's work. In *The Power of Feelings*, Chodorow declared that "In my view, the discovery of transference constitutes, perhaps, *the root psychoanalytic discovery*" (1999b: 26; emphasis in original). She had earlier defined transference as "the hypothesis and demonstration that our inner world of psychic reality helps to create, shape, and give meaning to the intersubjective, social, and cultural worlds we inhabit. It is the original psychoanalytic vehicle documenting for us the power of feelings" (1999b: 14). Transference occurs through both projection and introjection, as we all inject our own emotions into others, assuming that what is true about us is actually true about others, while also receiving the emotions of others and then embodying them. Thus, we often choose to avoid sad people not only because we see the sadness in them, but also because they are able to transfer their sadness to us in such a way that we really feel it ourselves: we embody it.

There are clearly tremendous clinical implications that follow from this, and it is probably true to say that the clinical elaboration of the implications of transference has been one of the main tasks of contemporary psychoanalysis. It is also the locus of many central doctrinal disputes between different psychoanalytic schools and traditions. Understandably, both Prager and Chodorow chose to sidestep the confrontation between often warring schools, and both chose instead to use transference as an invitation to rethink our understanding of our memories and our present relationship to the past. Prager signaled this in the title of his book, *Presenting the Past*, which alludes to the ideas that our past is always with us and that we reconstitute the past by using the resources and interpretations of the present.

For Chodorow, memories of the past produce "anxieties of uncertainty." This is because existing deterministic models of development and the causal role of the past on the present are no longer compelling (1999b: 35). In their place, both analysts and analysands, like people in general, have to manage a reflexive, indeterminate world. Chodorow explained this as follows:

> Because psychological meaning is constitutive of internal and external perceptions and experiences from childhood on, the past is always drawn in to the present. But this drawing in is always complex and indeterminate, perhaps not invented anew at each moment but continually constructed, reconstructed, and changed. The past does not cause the present, but the present includes and incorporates the past. (1999b: 60)

It is interesting to rethink Ms A.'s experiences in the light of Chodorow's comments. Prager's key argument is that Ms A.'s allegation that she had been sexually abused by her father is her way of realizing a transferential and interactional template that, in different circumstances and in different ways, she had drawn on before, albeit in ways that she ultimately found unsatisfying. The allegation is therefore part of the shifting contours of transference between Ms A. and Prager that constituted her way of retaliating against him by trying to sabotage the analysis itself. And yet it is also true that Ms A. was reacting to – and introjecting – part of the culture of American life at the time, which was then saturated with discussions of repressed memories of familial sexual abuse and with the upbeat symbolization of the survivor. That in varying degrees Ms A. both projected and introjected these disparate elements at different times speaks to the complexity of the analytic encounter that Prager described.

From the perspective of a non-clinician, the case is especially remarkable because Prager handled it during his training, suggesting that his supervisors judged Ms A. to be a relatively straightforward client. This gives force to Prager's confession that although he had hoped that psychoanalysis could enrich his sociological research, he increasingly thought of the analytic process as a unique approach that could not be translated into the practices of social science. Chodorow's own decision to establish a dual career as both academic and analyst suggests a similar attitude. However, in *The Power of Feelings* she makes a powerful argument for the integration of psychoanalytic ideas into the practices of reflexive anthropology (1999b: 172–218). Drawing upon a variety of anthropological sources that integrate psychoanalysis, social theory, and ethnography, Chodorow made the following claim:

> there is never a single way in which a cultural meaning is personally construed. Anthropologists, like other cultural thinkers, have in recent years stressed how complex, contradictory, multiple, and situated cultural meanings are. From psychoanalysis and psychoanalytic anthropology, we also can see how cultural meanings, like any dream image or other psychological symbol or fantasy, are also personally multiple, individualized, and situated, with no fixed and unchanging meaning. In addition, contemporary accounts stress that the relations between cultural meanings and personal meanings, and between culture and personality, are not so seamlessly intertwined as psychological anthropology once affirmed. There is no simple internalization of culture, no single way in which psyches hook onto culture. Rather, the same disjunctions, contradictions, and tensions that inhere in meaning in general also inhere in the various relations between culture and psyche. (1999b: 197)

I take Chodorow's summary to be a cautionary account of the difficulty of ethnography, as this passage emphasized the multiplicity and fluidity of meanings. If culture is understood to inhabit the internal worlds of the members of groups, then it will be both appropriated and manipulated in idiosyncratic ways. As a result, it will be hard for the ethnographer to generalize about the norms, values, and symbols that constitute the internalization of culture. Chodorow uses the anthropological work of Jean Briggs as an instructive example of both this theoretical difficulty and the practical difficulty of managing counter-transference. Briggs's classic study, *Never in Anger* (1970) began as an investigation of shamanism among the Inuit, but became an exploration of her own emotions and frustrations as the Inuit trained her to be one of them. As part of this training, Briggs was regarded for long periods by the Inuit not as an anthropologist but as a "recalcitrant child" (Chodorow, 1999b: 211). In her later work, Briggs emphasized that her "ethnographic understanding of Inuit emotional values and practices has developed through her own inter-personal and intra-psychic experience of these values" (Chodorow, 1999b: 212). This example shows the blending of counter-transference, ethnography, and auto-ethnography.

Although Chodorow believes that Briggs and other anthropologists have been sensitive to these issues and hence receptive to a psycho-analytic perspective, she does not believe that other social sciences have been able to rise to the challenge. In particular, she singled out quali-tative sociology as an approach that could have but to date has not developed a framework capable of absorbing psychoanalytic insights. Most elements of fieldwork "cry out for introspective, psychodynamic investigation of both the other and the self" (1999b: 132), but sociolo-gists, Chodorow argues, have largely resisted – and rejected – this kind of work. Their mistake has been caused by a pre-commitment to "macro-explanatory concepts" that effectively eliminate the need for the investigation of subjectivity (1999b: 132–3).

As a generalization about qualitative sociology, Chodorow may be right to criticize the one-dimensionality of much of the work. However, within qualitative sociology, a reflexive ethnography has gained ground. Unlike its anthropological counterpart, it does not identify itself with psychoanalysis. Ironically, then, and despite itself, this body of work may provide a framework for the integration of the two dis-ciplines, thereby mirroring the developments Chodorow identified for anthropology and psychoanalysis.

From Ethnographies of Concepts to Reflexive Ethnography

In chapter 3 I suggested that, albeit in a subtle way, Erving Goffman directed sociology away from psychoanalytic concerns and on to a dis-tinctively sociological way of studying the social world through ethnography. Goffman completed his sociological training at a time when psychiatry was a powerful branch of medicine, when psycho-analysis was the dominant approach within psychiatry, and when American sociology was dominated by Parsons' theoretical work that was itself transparently sympathetic to Freud and psychoanalysis in general. Despite this, and despite his broad admiration for Parsons' work, Goffman was antagonistic toward psychoanalysis as either a theory or a practice and toward psychiatry as a branch of medicine.

In fact, he considered psychiatry to be a questionable science populated by physicians who routinely did more harm than good. The tone and barely hidden agenda of *Asylums* (1961a) serves to indict psychiatry, a discipline that he described more than once as "grotesque." Thus, if Parsons represents the high point of sociology's interest in Freud and psychoanalysis, Goffman saw himself as its nemesis.

Goffman's opposition to psychiatry and psychoanalysis occurred in part because he questioned their scientific standing, in part because he objected to the treatment patients received after hospitalization, in part because he felt a disciplinary duty to side with the underdog, and in part because he believed that the insights obtained from qualitative sociology were better than clinical observations. His alternative approach entailed comparative observations of theoretically comparable sites. I have referred to this approach as the ethnography of concepts, to suggest that, for example, *Asylums* is not simply an ethnography of St Elizabeth's Hospital but also an ethnography of the concept of the total institution. Goffman's comparative focus discouraged him from pursuing the kind of reflexive work that would have been required had he considered his own reactions to the social world of the hospital. For Goffman, this was too close to the clinical-empirical material encountered by Chodorow and Prager. Thus, rather than enter into the investigation of transference and counter-transference and the study of internal worlds, Goffman chose instead to make himself invisible as part of his own research. The focus of his work is limited to public observations that anyone present could make. There is nothing confessional or personal: Goffman's primary contributions are conceptual and classificatory.

In my retelling of the story of sociology's encounters with psychoanalysis, Goffman took the road marked out by Sumner and stayed away from the implications of Sumner's contemporary, Cooley. In his masterpiece, *Folkways*, Sumner displayed the insight, comparative analysis, and classificatory zeal that became Goffman's trademark. By contrast, Cooley had emphasized that, in the manner of Adam Smith's (2000 [1854]) moral philosophy, a key element of sociology had to be sympathetic introspection.

Cooley's reworking of Adam Smith can itself be reworked. The result is that Adam Smith's concept of sympathy – when understood sociologically through Cooley – emerges as sociology's version of counter-transference. The remaining issue is how to make use of counter-transference non-clinically. What is missing, then, is the sociological equivalent of reflexive anthropology.

Although Chodorow was right to argue that although ethnographic sociology had undergone a reflexive turn this had not included a noticeable psychoanalytic component, I believe that she underesti-mated examples of sociologists who have appropriated and renamed psychoanalytic concepts and approaches. The example I want to highlight is Loic Wacquant's ethnography of his experiences of learn-ing to box, *Body and Soul* (2004), which employs a kind of auto-ethnography (Hayano, 1982) where Wacquant's own internal world is used as data that serve as a guide to the internal worlds of others participating in the same activities. Wacquant did not understand his own counter-transferential reactions to events and people as some-thing merely subjective or idiosyncratic. Rather, Wacquant used sym-pathetic introspection to examine empirically the aspect of the social world that Goffman considered to be beyond sociological reach. I therefore consider Wacquant to have extended Cooley's investigation of "thought-worlds" (in Rieff's suggestive phrase) by transforming his own counter-transference into a researchable topic. This work involves the tacit appropriation of psychoanalytic insights stripped of psychoanalytic methods.

Before turning to this, I think that it is important to note that Sumner and Cooley did not necessarily propose mutually exclusive options, any more than Goffman and Blumer did 50 years later. Thus, it is certainly possible – and desirable - for sociologists to explore ethnographies of concepts and classificatory models, while at the same time reflexively examining the emotional, counter-transferential internal world that emerges during the research itself. However, as tendencies, these two approaches have to date taken sociologists in two different directions. Max Weber has characterized this problem very well:

> Many mystical experiences which cannot be adequately communicated in words are, for a person who is not susceptible to such experiences, not fully under-standable. At the same time the ability to perform a similar action is not a neces-sary prerequisite for understanding; 'one need not have been Caesar in order to understand Caesar.' 'Recapturing the experience' is important for accurate understanding, but not an absolute precondition for its interpretation. (1978: 5)

Auto-ethnography is, in Weber's phrase, a way of "recapturing the experience." It is not always possible to do so, but when it is, it is desir-able. This is because it is not just "mystical experiences" but many experiences that, if possible, are better understood first hand.

There is also an intermediate position that examines the internal worlds of participants without considering the ethnographer's response to or involvement in these worlds. This is compatible with Blumer's (1969: 68) characterization of social objects. An excellent example of this is Ruth Horowitz's *Teen Mothers* (1995), in which she shows that the social world of the young women she studied was dramatically impacted by the fantasies or "dramatic dreams" they had about mother-hood, sex, and having a boyfriend (1995: 114–45). As with Ms A., their dramatic dreams were influenced by external events, the difference being that Ms A., was influenced by books and media reports of repressed memories, whereas Horowitz's subjects were more concerned with role models derived from television soap operas (1995: 116). The teen mothers participated in the joint construction of a shared internal world – described by Horowitz as dreamlike – to capture both the fantasy and the impossibility of the description. The joint construction of these dreams was achieved during informal group gatherings in which they shared stories. Horowitz presents their stories to show that they were fabricated and idealized presentations of self:

> As they told their stories, they were always in control of the situation and it was always the other person who was being manipulated. The events were dra-matized as rituals of what they viewed themselves as capable of achieving or becoming, which, most often, was not indicative of their actual performance: in the storytelling, the young woman telling the story was never manipulated but was always the manipulator. (1995: 120)

However, Horowitz herself is obviously not wrapped up in the fan-tasies and rationalizations that she observed. As she tersely put it: "I was not part of the world of teenage mothers" (1995: 16). And, although she is certainly "present" in her study (rather than absent, as Goffman was in *Asylums*), her own reactions to the teenagers mothers she studied are not the focus of her project and are therefore not understood as viable data. Rather, as in earlier psychoanalytic inter-pretations of transference and counter-transference, Horowitz under-stood her reactions as a problem to solve so that she could preserve a marginal but tolerated position with both the teenage mothers them-selves and with the teachers and social workers who monitored them.

By contrast, the auto-ethnographic work attempted by Wacquant required complete immersion. This was undertaken voluntarily (and serendipitously) by Wacquant (unlike the involuntary auto-ethno-graphic research conducted by Karp (1996) with regard to his painful, personal experience of depression). The term "auto-ethnography" derives from the research of Hayano (1982) concerning the world of the professional gambler. It describes situations in which researchers become so embroiled in the social worlds they study that it is no longer possible to distinguish them from their informants. In a literal sense, they become one of their own informants. Hayano characterized his auto-ethnographic research among poker players as something that "is completely interwoven with my personal involvement and analysis as an inside member. At this stage it is not possible to separate subjects' strategies and realities from my own because of the many points of contact and similarity" (1982: 150-1).

Hayano became, then, a version of the anthropologist who began by studying witchcraft only to become a witch doctor himself. His internal world became that of a professional poker player. For example, away from the poker table Hayano retained a keen interest in numbers and patterns. This was revealed when once, while driving, he noticed that the license plate of the car in front of him contained three sevens. He immediately recalled the odds of making "trips" in poker and then relived all the hands in the past weeks and months when he had been dealt three sevens. He replayed them in his mind, reviewing his decisions (1982: 148-9). His thought processes had thus become those of the poker player rather than those of the social scientist.

Hayano also used his complete immersion in the poker world to reveal the physical stresses of the game. Even though it is extraordinary to people unfamiliar with poker, it was not uncommon for him to play for 20 or even 30 hours at one sitting. This produces a widespread sense of numbness in the body; concentration also becomes difficult and players have to rely on "learned reflexes." As the hours go by, the mood of the players at the table becomes more discouraging, as the winners leave and the remaining players continue merely in an effort to get even before they become too exhausted to think (1982: 5-6).

Hayano is able to describe these different elements first hand. However, and unfortunately, this is not his focus. Rather, he has more conventional ethnographic goals: to describe the social structure of the poker world, to discuss career contingencies, to reveal illegal activities, and to analyze the dramaturgy that accompanies the game itself. Auto-ethnography is therefore his explanation of why he undertook the project rather than its focus. For the most part it is a means of confirmation rather than of discovery. There are exceptions: near the end of the book, Hayano recalls a night of poker in which, despite his best efforts, he could not get even. In the morning, discouraged, hungry, and tired, he decided to go home. As he was leaving, a friend in the same predicament stopped him in the parking lot and suggested that they go for breakfast instead and then rejoin a 9 a.m. game. Hayano thought for a moment – and agreed: he could not get poker out of his system.

Despite these occasional vignettes, *Poker Faces* is primarily a conventional ethnography that did not exploit its own potential. Hayano is more apologetic than radical, perhaps because he had internalized the poker player's mentality that the game really is a waste of time and that there must be better things to do with one's life. He was therefore unable or unwilling to exploit his own immersion in the game by fully exploring the emotional, moral, and physical aspects that he experienced profoundly himself. The book makes frequent reference to Goffman, implying perhaps that Goffman's work is serious research whereas his own is contaminated by his complete immersion in the social world of poker. In fact, I think that Hayano underestimated the value of his own exposure to every aspect of this world, and by seeking to produce a "respectable" ethnography he failed to realize the promise of the auto-ethnographic method that he described so well.

Unlike Hayano, and despite his avoidance of the term, Wacquant has embraced a version of auto-ethnography and the "blurred genres" (Geertz, 1983) it produces. His ethnography of the social world of boxing (and particularly the boxing gym) signposts this in its subtitle, *Body & Soul: Notebooks of an Apprentice Boxer* (2004), which affirms that the focus of the study is Wacquant's own experiences. The book is also unconventional in organization, since it does not contain chapters but set pieces that reveal the complex dimensions of the experiences and emotions of the neophyte boxer in the context of both the gym and the wider community.

In these set pieces Wacquant characterized the Woodlawn boxing gym in Chicago as a haven from the drudgery and poverty of the surrounding community. Wacquant portrays boxing as an escape but not as an easy option. The boxers in training must acquiesce to the authority of DeeDee Armour, the trainer at the gym. Under his guidance, the boxers learn not only technique but also the ascetic lifestyle that boxing training requires. This involves physical training – road work, muscular development, and feet and hand skills, together with personal commitment – to be punctual, to follow a strict diet, to live a quiet life, and to persevere with repetitive drills. This is part of the hidden curriculum of boxing. As Wacquant reveals, training to box often involves relatively little sparring. Those boxers who are motivated by the thrill of competition will fail unless they are able to endure long periods of non-contact training.

Wacquant's distinctive contribution is to document the physical and emotional world of the boxer using his own experiences as a guide. In this way he is able to get inside both the physical hardships of the sport and the conflicting emotions that accompany it. The physical hardships are in part the necessary by-product of training, such as tiredness and soreness, but they are also the realities of a sport in which the athlete's body is the target of attack. Thus, Wacquant reported that his nose was broken while sparring. Further, at several points he also wondered whether one of his partners had broken several of his ribs, and he had the frequent pain of bruises and facial swelling. These physical discomforts are matched with an array of emotions: exhilaration, cunning, remorse, and fear. Thus, boxing is a sport in which the training is primarily repetitive, individualized, and cumulative, but there are nevertheless moments of extraordinary intensity. One such moment for Wacquant was his first exposure to sparring, after just eight weeks of training. Wacquant describes his apprehension and excitement while waiting to enter the ring. At that moment he caught sight of himself in the mirror and was shocked to see that he looked alien to himself, sporting a large, protective leather belt, huge red gloves and a leather helmet (2004: 73). The result was a "hyperacute awareness" of his body's fragility that was quickly confirmed by a stream of painful jabs (2004: 74). Wacquant's world is reduced to a circle with a 1-meter diameter as he tries to hang on, pleading for the three-minute round to end.

About nine months later Wacquant had sufficiently internalized the skills of boxing as to be able to execute a plan when sparring. He developed a "patented" move whereby he feigned a left jab in order to encourage his opponent to move to his left – and into the big right hook he really intended all along. When successful this attack brought a flush of pride to his face and a fast apology, motivated in part by the certain knowledge that vengeance was only moments away, and there was little he could do apart from wait to be hit very hard. For the neophyte boxer learning to spar, there is therefore the awareness that every display of competence will be met with a greater reaction.

Theoretically, then, Wacquant is trying to incorporate an understanding of the visceral and emotional aspects of boxing within the conventional ethnographic investigation of social structure and normative regulations. Although Wacquant does not present this additional material in a psychoanalytic way, it is suggestive of the clinical-empirical analyses found in both Chodorow's and Prager's work.

This may be most striking in the relationship between the ethnographer and the "gatekeeper" who provides entrée and acts as a guide, mentor, friend, ally, fixer, and facilitator. The trainer at Woodlawn gym, DeeDee Armour, fulfilled this role for Wacquant, and, in Wacquant's telling of their relationship, became like a second father to him. This involves an interesting reversal of the analyst and analysand relationship, since the sociologist adopts the role of analysand in order to learn from the gatekeeper. In Wacquant's case, as in many other ethnographic studies, it appears that a kind of transference neurosis developed, in the manner described by Prager, where life is put on hold and the new activity becomes everything that is on the horizon. Although it is hard to imagine Goffman reacting in this way, he suggested (1989) something very similar when he commented that sociologists have only penetrated the social worlds they study when they can imagine falling in love and abandoning their academic careers. This was exactly the situation for Wacquant, who revealed that he was bored by the prospect of attending Harvard and was considering leaving the university for a full-time career in boxing. The detachment of the scientist is therefore replaced by the emotional intensity and confusion of the analytic setting. This is clear at the end of the book, in a scene occurring the day after Wacquant's first amateur fight in Chicago's Golden Gloves tournament. Wacquant lost the fight, during the course of which he was battered and bruised by a bigger and stronger opponent. Nevertheless, Wacquant was inspired and energized by the fight. He therefore returned to the gym in an excited mood, already thinking about resuming training and preparing for his second tournament. His trainer, DeeDee, however, had other ideas, and announced to everyone that Wacquant had fought his last fight. Since he now had enough material for his book, DeeDee said, he could and should retire from boxing. There was no discussion, and the book ends without Wacquant commenting on this unexpected turn of events. It seems to show that DeeDee retained a clearer understanding of the limits of Wacquant's involvement than did Wacquant himself. As Wacquant himself put it early in his account, his relationship with boxing had gone far beyond "seduction."

Unlike Hayano's sustained ambivalence about poker, Wacquant does not appear to have doubted the meaningfulness of his immersion into the world of boxing. This allowed him to see his auto-ethnography as useful data rather than as pretence. Hayano's account of poker is better than he believed and his own reactions are more revealing than he realized. Even his reluctance to accept the legitimacy of poker itself is very significant: it was identical to the attitude of the poker players themselves to their own activities. In Mead's vocabulary, he had fully absorbed the attitude of the generalized other.

Concluding Thoughts

In my view, Goffman's *Asylums* (1961a) occupies a special position in the history of American sociology in general and symbolic interactionism in particular. This is because it extended the framework proposed by Sumner and developed by Mead, Blumer, and others, while at the same time demonstrating that the ideas could be applied successfully in empirical research. The transformation of ethnographies of places into ethnographies of concepts was something that Everett

Hughes had anticipated, but it was fully realized by Goffman himself. The impact of comparative data on ethnographic research did not make ethnography akin to a natural science, but it did add a rigor that prevented the worst excesses of subjectivism. It also facilitated the theorizing and generalizations later associated with grounded theory. In addition, sociology retained a critical, moral role, as is evident from the tone and content of *Asylums*. What Goffman advocated for sociology, Rieff advocated for both sociology and psychoanalysis. It is a tribute to the power of Goffman's varied, Sumnerian classificatory schemata that today it is easy to miss the moral conviction in his work. Goffman remained steadfastly a champion of the underdog.

Goffman, Blumer, and many qualitative non-Parsonsians saw their work in opposition to psychoanalysis, which they rejected for a variety of reasons. This complete opposition prevented them from contemplating a partial rapprochement in which only parts of the psychoanalytic apparatus were adopted for sociological use. Had Goffman and Blumer before him been open to this, then the analysis of transference and counter-transference could have been integrated into their research projects. Particularly for Goffman, this could have been the opportunity for him to analyze the emotions and experiences of those living in the situations he studied. He was occasionally close to such an account in *Asylums*, but backed away from this in most of his other work, perhaps most strikingly in "The Insanity of Place." His decision to do so produced the curiously "flat" feeling of many of his books, in which his intent appears to be simply to exemplify his conceptual schemata.

Although I appeal to psychoanalysis as a remedy for this, particularly the relational approaches that are outlined by Chodorow and Prager, I believe that the seeds of this remedy could also be found in Mead and especially in Cooley. Rieff's admiration for Cooley is his way of signaling the moral-introspective-emotional-experiential aspect of Cooley's proto-symbolic interactionism. Cooley himself recognized Freud as a fellow traveler down this road, although Freud was clearly not the person he admired the most.

I consider Cooley's empirical successors to be those contemporary sociologists who have incorporated an analysis of their own experiences, emotions, and reactions into their work, and in this chapter I have touched upon the contributions of Hayano, Karp, and Wacquant. Although none of these sociologists considered himself to be engaged in a psychoanalytic project, I believe that all auto-ethnography is an analysis of what psychoanalysts call counter-transference. Their theoretical and clinical experience is a treasure trove for sociologists, particularly for symbolic interactionists and ethnographers.

It is not, however, an alternative to the ethnography of concepts, which remains a vital insurance policy against a groundless, indulgent subjectivism that blurs the line between sociology and short-story writing. Auto-ethnography is not autobiography, in that the latter deals with extraordinary lives and the former with typical lives. Auto-ethnographers inhabit the world of what Hochschild called normal emotions and feeling rules, where the focus remains on the typical.

A final precautionary word – the clinical lesson from psychoanalysis taught to us by both Chodorow and Prager is this: the rewards from the analysis of transference and counter-transference are high, but so are the difficulties. Chodorow and Prager recognize that this material places unusual demands upon sociologists who are used to maintaining a healthy degree of separation. It remains to be seen whether they will be up to this new challenge.

References

Abbot, Andrew. 1999. *Department and Discipline: Chicago Sociology at One Hundred*. Chicago: University of Chicago Press.

Abbott, Andrew. 2001. *Time Matters: On Theory and Method*. Chicago: University of Chicago Press.

Anderson, Elijah. 1978. *A Place On the Corner*. Chicago: University of Chicago Press.

Anderson, Elijah. 1990. *Streetwise: Race, Class and Change in an Urban Community*. Chicago: University of Chicago Press.

Aronovici, Carol. 1919. "Organized Leisure as a Factor in Conservation." *American Journal of Sociology* XXIV(4): 373–88.

Austin, John. 1962. *How To Do Things With Words*. Oxford: Clarendon Press.

Bain, Read. 1936. "Sociology and Psychoanalysis." *American Sociological Review* 1(2): 203–16.

Baldessarini, Ross. 1999. "Psychopharmacology." In *The Harvard Guide to Psychiatry*. Cambridge, Mass.: The Belknap Press of Harvard University Press.

Bannister, Robert. 1979. *Social Darwinism: Science and Myth in Anglo-American Thought*. Philadelphia: Temple University Press.

Barham, Peter. 1992. *Closing the Asylum: The Mental Patient in Modern Society*. Harmondsworth, Middlesex: Penguin.

Bernard, L. 1936. "Henry Hughes, First American Sociologist." *Social Forces* 15(2): 154–74.

Bershady, Harold. 1973. *Ideology and Social Knowledge*. Oxford: Blackwell.

Blumer, Herbert. 1937. "Social Disorganization and Individual Disorganization." *American Journal of Sociology* 42(6): 871–7.

Blumer, Herbert. 1969. *Symbolic Interactionism*. Berkeley: University of California Press.

Blumer, Herbert. 1975. "Exchange on Turner, 'Parsons as a Symbolic Interactionist'." *Sociological Inquiry* 45(1): 59–68.

Bollas, Christopher. 1992. *Being a Character*. New York: Hill and Wang.

Bott-Spillius, Elizabeth. 1993. Letter to Gregory Smith, unpublished.

Bowie, Malcolm. 1991. *Lacan*. Cambridge, Mass.: Harvard University Press.

Brick, Howard. 2000. "Talcott Parsons's 'Shift Away from Economics'." <www.historycooperative.org>.

Briggs, Jean. 1970. *Never in Anger: Portrait of an Eskimo Family*. Cambridge, Mass.: Harvard University Press.

Bulmer, Martin. 1984. *The Chicago School of Sociology*. Chicago: University of Chicago Press.

Burgess, Ernest. 1939. "The Influence of Sigmund Freud Upon Sociology in the United States." *American Journal of Sociology* XLV: 356–74 (Nov.).

Burns, Tom. 1992. *Erving Goffman*. London: Routledge.

Burrow, Trigant. 1926. "Insanity as a Social Problem." *American Journal of Sociology* 32(1): 80–7.

Cahill, Spencer. 1987. "Children and Civility: Ceremonial Deviance and the Acquisition of Ritual Competence." *Social Psychology Quarterly* 50: 312–58.

Cahill, Spencer and Eggleston, Robin. 1994. "Managing Emotions in Public: The Case of Wheelchair Users." *Social Psychology Quarterly* 57: 300–12.

Chodorow, Nancy. 1999a [1978]. *The Reproduction of Mothering*. Berkeley: University of California Press.

Chodorow, Nancy. 1999b. *The Power of Feelings*. New Haven: Yale University Press.

Cioffi, Frank. 1998. *Freud and the Question of Pseudoscience*. Chicago: Open Court.

Conrad, Peter and Schneider, Joseph 1992. *Deviance and Medicalization: From Badness to Sickness*. Philadelphia: Temple University Press.

Cook, Gary. 1993. *George Herbert Mead: The Making of a Social Pragmatist*. Urbana: University of Illinois Press.

Cooley, Charles. 1916. *Social Organization: A Study of the Larger Mind*. New York: Charles Scribner's Sons.

Cooley, Charles. 1927. *Life and the Student: Roadside Notes on Human Nature, Society and Letters*. New York: Alfred Knopf.

Cooley, Charles. 1964 [1902]. *Human Nature and Social Order*. New York: Schocken Books. (1922 edn. New York: Charles Scribner.)

Crawford, Margaret. 1992. "The World in a Shopping Mall." In Sorkin, M. (ed.), *Variations on a Theme Park: The New American City and the End of Public Space*. New York: Farrar, Strauss and Giroux.

Curtis, Bruce. 1981. *William Graham Sumner*. Boston: Twayne.

Davie, Maurice. R. 1963. *William Graham Sumner*. New York: Cromwell.

Davies, Christie. 1989. "Goffman's Concept of the Total Institution: Criticisms and Revisions." *Human Studies* 12(1–2) (June): 77–95.

Delaney, William. 1977. "The Uses of the Total Institution: A Buddhist Monastic Example." In Gordon, R. and Williams, B. (eds), *Exploring Total Institutions*. Champaign, Ill. Stipes.

Derrida, Jacques. 1998. *Resistances of Psychoanalysis*. Stanford, California: Stanford University Press.

Ditton, Jason (ed.). 1980. *The View From Goffman*. London and Basingstoke: Macmillan.

Dollard, John. 1934. "The Psychotic Person Seen Culturally." *American Journal of Sociology* 39(5): 637–48.

Drew, Paul and Wootten, Anthony (eds). 1988. *Erving Goffman: Exploring the Interaction Order*. Cambridge: Polity.

Duneier, Mitchell. 1992. *Slim's Table*. Chicago: University of Chicago Press.

Durkheim, Emile. 1984. *The Division of Labor in Society*. London: Macmillan.

Eliot, Thomas. 1920. "A Psychoanalytic Interpretation of Group Formation and Behavior." *American Journal of Sociology* 26(3): 333–52.

Elliott, Anthony. 2001. *Concepts of the Self*. Cambridge: Polity.

Elliott, Anthony. 2004. *Social Theory Since Freud: Traversing Social Imaginaries*. London and New York: Routledge.

Elster, Jon. 1989. *Nuts and Bolts*. Cambridge: Cambridge University Press.

Fine, Gary. 1983. *Shared Fantasy: Role-Playing Games as Social Worlds*. Chicago: University of Chicago Press.

Fine, Gary. 1987. *With the Boys: Little League Baseball and Preadolescent Culture*. Chicago: University of Chicago Press.

Fine, Gary (ed.). 1995. *A Second Chicago School?* Chicago: University of Chicago Press.

Fine, Gary. 1996. *Kitchens: The Culture of Restaurant Work*. Berkeley: University of California Press.

Fine, Gary and Manning, Philip. 2000. "Erving Goffman." In George Ritzer (ed.), *Blackwell Companion to Major Social Theorists*. Oxford: Blackwell.

Fine, Gary and Manning, Philip. 2003. "Preserving Philip Rieff: The Reputation of a Fellow Teacher." *Journal of Classical Sociology* 3(3): 227–34.

Fine, Gary and Martin, D. 1990. "A Partisan View: Sarcasm, Satire and Irony as Voices in Erving Goffman's *Asylums*." *Journal of Contemporary Ethnography* 19(1): 89–115.

Folsom, Joseph. 1918. "The Social Psychology of Morality and Its Bearing on Moral Education." *American Journal of Sociology* 23(4): 433–90.

Foner, Eric. 1989. *Reconstruction: America's Unfinished Revolution*. New York: Perennial.

Freud, Sigmund. 1966. *The Standard Edition of the Complete Psychological Works*. Ed. and tr. J. Strachey et al., 24 vols. London: Hogarth Press. (Abbreviated to *SE* throughout this book.)

Gardner, Carol. 1995. *Passing By: Gender and Public Harassment*. Berkeley: University of California Press.

Garfinkel, Harold. 1967. *Studies in Ethnomethodology*. Englewood Cliffs: Prentice Hall.

Gay, Peter. 1988. *Freud: A Life for Our Time*. New York: Anchor Books, Doubleday.

Geertz, Clifford. 1983. *Local Knowledge: Further Essays in Interpretive Anthropology*. New York: Basic Books.

Giddens, Anthony. 1984. *The Constitution of Society*. Cambridge: Polity.

Giddens, Anthony. 1987. *Sociology and Modern Social Theory*. Cambridge: Polity.

Glover, Jonathan. 1988. *I: The Philosophy and Psychology of Personal Identity*. London: Allen Lane, The Penguin Press.

Goffman, Erving. 1951. "Symbols of Class Status." *British Journal of Sociology* 11: 294–304.

Goffman, Erving. 1952. "On Cooling the Mark Out: Some Aspects of Adaptation to Failure." *Psychiatry* 15(4) (Nov.): 451–63.

Goffman, Erving. 1953. "Communication Conduct in an Island Community." Ph.D. dissertation, University of Chicago.

Goffman, Erving. 1959. *The Presentation of Self in Everyday Life*. New York: Doubleday, Anchor Books.

Goffman, Erving. 1961a. *Asylums*. Harmondsworth: Penguin.

Goffman, Erving. 1961b. *Encounters: Two Studies in the Sociology of Interaction*. Indianapolis: Bobbs-Merrill.

Goffman, Erving. 1963. *Behavior in Public Places: Notes on the Social Organization of Gatherings*. New York: The Free Press.

Goffman, Erving. 1967. *Interaction Ritual: Essays on Face-to-Face Behavior*. New York: Anchor.

Goffman, Erving. 1970. *Strategic Interaction*. Oxford: Blackwell.

Goffman, Erving. 1971. *Relations in Public: Microstudies of the Public Order*. New York: Basic Books.

Goffman, Erving. 1974. *Frame Analysis: An Essay on the Organization of Experience*. New York: Harper and Row.

Goffman, Erving. 1983a. "Felicity's Condition." *American Journal of Sociology* 89(1): 1–53.

Goffman, Erving. 1983b. "The Interaction Order." *American Sociological Review* 48: 1–17.

Goffman, Erving. 1989. "On Fieldwork." *Journal of Contemporary Ethnography* 18(2): 123–32.

Gronfein, William. 1992. "Goffman's Asylums and the Social Control of the Mentally Ill." *Perspectives on Social Problems* 4: 129–53.

Gronfein, William. 1999. "Sundered Selves: Mental Illness and the Interaction Order in the Work of Erving Goffman." In G. Smith (ed.), *Goffman and Social Organization: Studies in a Sociological Legacy*. London and New York: Routledge.

Groves, Ernest. 1917. "Sociology and Psycho-Analytic Psychology: An Interpretation of the Freudian Hypothesis." *American Journal of Sociology* 23(1): 107–16.

Habermas, Jürgen. 1987. *The Theory of Communicative Action*. vol. 2. Cambridge: Polity.

Hale, Nathan. 1971. *The Beginnings of Psychoanalysis in the United States, 1876–1917*. New York: Oxford University Press.

Hale, Nathan. 1995. *The Rise and Crisis of Psychoanalysis in the United States. Freud and the Americans 1917–1985*. New York: Oxford University Press.

Joas, Hans. 1985 [1997]. *G. H. Mead: A Contemporary Re-examination of his Thought*. Cambridge, Mass.: MIT Press.

Hayano, David. 1982. *Poker Faces: The Life and Work of Professional Card Players*. Berkeley: University of California Press.

Healy, David, Bronner, Augusta, and Bowers, Anna Mae. 1930. *The Structure and Meaning of Psychoanalysis*. New York: Alfred Knopf.

Hinkle, Gisela. 1957. "Sociology and Psychoanalysis." In Howard Becker and Alvin Boskoff (eds), *Modern Sociological Theory in Continuity and Change*. New York: Holt, Rinehart and Winston.

Hochschild, Arlie. 1983. *The Managed Heart: Commercialization of Human Feeling*. Berkeley: University of California Press.

Hochschild, Arlie. 2003. *The Commercialization of Intimate Life: Notes from Home and Work*. Berkeley: University of California Press.

Holt, Edwin. 1915. *The Freudian Wish*. New York: Henry Holt and Company.

Horowitz, Ruth. 1995. *Teen Mothers: Citizens or Dependents?* Chicago: University of Chicago Press.

Ignatieff, Michael. 1983. "Life at Degree Zero." *New Society* (January 20).

Jandy, Edward. 1969 [1942]. *Charles Horton Cooley: His Life and his Social Theory*. New York: Octagon Books.

Jaworski, Gary. 2000. "Erving Goffman: The Reluctant Apprentice." *Symbolic Interaction*, 23(3): 299–308.

Jones, Alan Robert. 1974. "Freud and American Sociology, 1909–1949." *Journal of the History of the Behavioural Sciences*, 10 January 1974: 21–39.

Jones, Ernest. 1953. *The Life and Work of Sigmund Freud*. Vol. 1: *The Formative Years and the Great Discoveries* 1856–1900. New York: Basic Books.

Jones, Ernest. 1955. *The Life and Work of Sigmund Freud*. Vol. 2: *Years of Maturity* 1901–1919. New York: Basic Books.

Jones, Ernest. 1957. *The Life and Work of Sigmund Freud*. Vol. 3: *The Last Phase* 1919–1939. New York: Basic Books.

Kantor, J. 1922. "An Essay Toward an Institutional Conception of Social Psychology." *American Journal of Sociology* 27(5): 611–27.

Karp, David. 1996. *Speaking of Sadness*. Oxford: Oxford University Press.

Keller, Albert Galloway. 1927. "Introduction." In Sumner, William Graham and Keller, Albert Galloway, *The Science of Society* (4 vols). New Haven: Yale University Press.

Kim, Kwang-ki. 2003. *Order and Agency in Modernity: Talcott Parsons,*

Erving Goffman and Harold Garfinkel. Albany: State University of New York Press.

Laslett, Barbara. 1990. "Unfeeling Knowledge: Emotion and Objectivity in the History of Sociology." *Sociological Forum* 5(3): 413–33.

Laslett, Barbara. 1991. "Biography as Historical Sociology: The Case of William Fielding Ogburn." *Theory and Society* 20: 511–38.

Lemert, Edwin. 1942. "The Folkways and Social Control." *American Sociological Review* 7(3): 394–9.

Lewis, David J. 1979. "A Social Behaviorist Interpretation of the Meadian 'I'." *American Journal of Sociology* 85(2): 61–87.

Lofland, Lyn. 1998. *The Public Realm: Exploring the City's Quintessential Social Territory.* New York: Aldine de Gruyter.

Luhrmann, Niklas. 1982. *The Differentiation of Society.* New York: Columbia University Press.

Luhrmann, Niklas. 1998. *Observations on Modernity.* Stanford, California: Stanford University Press.

Luhrmann, Tanya. 2000. *Of Two Minds: The Growing Disorder in American Psychiatry.* New York: Alfred Knopf.

Lyman, Stanford and Scott, Marvin. 1970. *A Sociology of the Absurd.* New York: Meredith Corporation.

Lyman, Stanford and Scott, Marvin. 1975. *The Drama of Social Reality.* New York: Oxford University Press.

McDougall, William. 1924. "Can Sociology and Social Psychology Dispense with Instincts?" *American Journal of Sociology* 29(6): 657–73.

MacIntyre, Alasdair. 1981. *After Virtue: A Study in Moral Theory.* London: Duckworth.

Maines, David. 2001. *The Faultline of Consciousness: A View of Interactionism in Sociology.* New York: Aldine de Gruyter.

Manning, Philip. 1991. "Drama as Life: The Significance of Goffman's Changing Use of the Dramaturgical Metaphor." *Sociological Theory* 9(1): 71–86.

Manning, Philip. 1992. *Erving Goffman and Modern Sociology.* Stanford: Stanford University Press.

Manning, Philip. 1998. "Procedure, Reflexivity and Social Constructionism." In Irving Velody and Robin Williams (eds), *The Politics of Constructivism.* London: Sage.

Manning, Philip. 1999a. "The Deinstitionalization and Deinstitutionalization of the Mentally Ill: Lessons from Goffman." In James Chriss (ed.), *Counseling and Therapeutic State.* New York: Aldine de Gruyter.

Manning, Philip. 1999b. "Ethnographic Coats and Tents." In Gregory Smith (ed.), *Goffman and Social Organization: Studies in a Sociological Legacy.* London: Routledge.

Manning, Philip. 2000. "Credibility, Agency and the Interaction Order." *Symbolic Interaction* 23(3): 283–97.

Manning, Philip. 2003. "Philip Rieff's Moral Vision of Sociology: From

Positive to Negative Communities – and Back?" *Journal of Classical Sociology* 3(3): 235–46.

Marx, Gary. 1984. "Role Models and Role Distance: A Remembrance of Erving Goffman." *Theory and Society* 13(5): 649–62.

Masson, Jeffrey Moussaieff. 1985. *The Complete Letters of Sigmund Freud to Wilhelm Fliess 1887–1904*. Cambridge, Massachusetts: The Belknap Press of Harvard University Press.

Mead, George Herbert. 1962 [1934]. *Mind, Self and Society from the Standpoint of a Social Behaviorist*. Edited and with an Introduction by Charles W. Morris. Chicago: University of Chicago Press.

Mechanic, David. 1989. *Mental Health and Social Policy*. Englewood Cliffs, New Jersey: Prentice Hall.

Mechanic, David and Rochefort, D. A. 1990. "Deinstitutionalization: An Appraisal of Reform." *Annual Review of Sociology* 16: 301–27.

Menand, Louis. 2001. *The Metaphysical Club: A Story of Ideas*. New York: Farrar, Straus and Giroux.

Merton, Robert K. 1957. *Social Theory and Social Structure* (revised and enlarged edn). New York: The Free Press.

Muller, Jerry. 1995. "Philip Rieff." In David Murray (ed.), *American Cultural Critics*. Exeter: University of Exeter Press, pp. 193–205.

Muller, Jerry. 2003. *The Mind and the Market: Capitalism in Modern European Thought*. New York: Alfred Knopf.

Nietzsche, Friedrich. 1973. *Beyond Good and Evil: Prelude to a Philosophy of the Future*. Harmondsworth, Middlesex: Penguin.

Ortiz, Steven. 1994. "Shopping for Sociability in the Mall." In D. Chekki, S. Cahill, and L. Lofland (eds), *Research in Community Sociology*. New York: JAI Press.

Park, Robert. 1915. *The Principles of Human Behavior*. Studies in Social Science series, vol. 6, ed. by W. I. Thomas. Chicago: Zalaz Corporation.

Park, Robert and Burgess, Ernest. 1921. *Introduction to the Science of Sociology*. Chicago: University of Chicago Press.

Parsons, Talcott. 1949 [1937]. *The Structure of Social Action*. New York: The Free Press.

Parsons, Talcott. 1951a. *The Social System*. New York: The Free Press.

Parsons, Talcott. 1951b. *Toward a General Theory of Action*. Editor and contributor with Edward Shils and others. Cambridge, Mass.: Harvard University Press.

Parsons, Talcott. 1964. *Social Structure and Personality*. New York: The Free Press.

Parsons, Talcott. 1965. "Unity and Diversity in the Modern Intellectual Disciplines: The Role of the Social Sciences." *Daedalus* 94: 39–65.

Parsons, Talcott. 1966. *Societies: Evolutionary and Comparative Perspectives*. Englewood Cliffs, New Jersey: Prentice Hall.

Parsons, Talcott. 1967. *Sociological Theory and Modern Society*. New York: The Free Press.

Parsons, Talcott. 1968a. "Interaction." *International Encyclopedia of the Social Sciences*, vol. 7. New York: Cromwell Collier and Macmillan.

Parsons, Talcott. 1968b. "The Position of Identity in the General Theory of Action." In Colin Gordon and Kenneth Gergen (eds), *The Self in Social Interaction*. New York: Wiley.

Parsons, Talcott. 1968c. "Cooley and the Problem of Internalization." In Albert Reiss Jr. (ed.), *Cooley and Sociological Analysis*. Ann Arbor: University of Michigan Press.

Parsons, Talcott. 1975. "Exchange on Turner, 'Parsons as a Symbolic Interactionist'." *Sociological Inquiry* 45(1): 59–68.

Parsons, Talcott. 1977. *Social Systems and the Evolution of Action Theory*. New York: The Free Press.

Parsons, Talcott, Bales, R. F., and Shils, Edward. 1953. *Working Papers in the Theory of Action*. New York: The Free Press.

Parsons, Talcott and Bales, R. F. 1955. *Family, Socialization and Interaction Process*. Glencoe, New York: The Free Press.

Parsons, Talcott and Platt, Gerald. 1973. *The American University*. Cambridge, Mass.: Harvard University Press.

Parsons, Talcott. 1978. *Action Theory and the Human Condition*. New York: The Free Press.

Paskauskas, R. Andrew (ed.). 1993. *The Complete Correspondence of Sigmund Freud and Ernest Jones 1908–1939*. Cambridge, Massachusetts: The Belknap Press of Harvard University Press.

Phillips, Adam. 1988. *Winnicott*. Cambridge, Mass.: Harvard University Press.

Piver, Kenneth. 1994. "Philip Rieff: The Critic of Psychoanalysis as Cultural Theorist." In Mark Micale and Roy Porter (eds), *Discovering the History of Psychiatry*. New York and Oxford: Oxford University Press.

Prager, Jeffrey. 1998. *Presenting the Past: Psychoanalysis and the Sociology of Remembering*. Boston: Harvard University Press.

Ricoeur, Paul. 1970. *Freud and Philosophy: An Essay on Interpretation*. New Haven and London: Yale University Press.

Rieff, Philip. 1959. *Freud: The Mind of the Moralist*. New York: The Viking Press.

Rieff, Philip. 1968. *The Triumph of the Therapeutic: Uses of Faith After Freud*. New York: Harper and Row.

Rieff, Philip. 1985. *Fellow Teachers: Of Culture and Its Second Death*. Chicago: University of Chicago Press.

Rieff, Philip. 1990. *The Feeling Intellect*. Edited and with an introduction by Jonathan Imber. Chicago: University of Chicago Press.

Rieff, Philip. 1991. "The Newer Noises of War in the Second Culture Camp: Notes on Professor Burt's Legal Fictions." *Yale Journal of Law and the Humanities* 3: 315–88.

Ross, Dorothy. 1991. *The Origins of American Social Science*. Cambridge: Cambridge University Press.

Ross, Edward Alsoworth. 1901. *Social Control*. New York: Macmillan.

Rothman, David. 1990. *The Discovery of the Asylum: Social Order and Disorder in the New Republic*. Boston: Little Brown.

Schegloff, Emanuel. 1988. "Goffman and the Analysis of Conversation." In P. Drew and A. Wootten (eds), *Erving Goffman: Exploring the Interaction Order*. Cambridge: Polity.

Schegloff, Emanuel. 1990. "Betwen Macro and Micro: Contexts and Other Connections." In J. Alexander et al. (eds), *The Micro-Macro Link*. Berkeley: University of California Press.

Schegloff, Emanuel. 1992. "Introduction" to H. Sacks, *Lectures on Conversation*. Ed. Gail Jefferson. Oxford: Blackwell.

Scull, Andrew. 1984. *Decarceration. Community Treatment and the Deviant: A Radical View*. Cambridge: Polity.

Scull, Andrew. 1989. *Social Order/Mental Disorder: Anglo-American Psychiatry in Historical Perspective*. Berkeley: University of California Press.

Searle, John. 1995. *The Construction of Social Reality*. New York: The Free Press.

Searle, John. 1998. *Mind, Language and Society*. New York: Basic Books.

Sedgwick, Peter. 1982. *Psycho Politics*. London: Pluto Press.

Sennett, Richard. 1970. *The Fall of Public Man*. New York: The Free Press.

Smelser, Neil. 1998. *The Social Edges of Psychoanalysis*. Berkeley: University of California Press.

Smith, Adam. 1976. *An Inquiry into the Nature and Causes of the Wealth of Nations*. Chicago: University of Chicago Press.

Smith, Adam. 2000 [1854]. *The Theory of Moral Sentiments*. New York: Prometheus Books.

Smith, Dennis. 1988. *The Chicago School: A Liberal Critique of Capitalism*. New York: St Martin's Press.

Smith, Gregory. 1997. "Incivil Attention and Everyday Intolerance: Vicissitudes of Exercising in Public Places." *Perspectives on Social Problems* 9: 57–79.

Smith, Gregory. 1999a. "'The Proprieties of Persondom': The Individual in the Writings of Erving Goffman." Unpublished paper.

Smith, Gregory (ed.). 1999b. *Goffman and Social Organization: Studies in a Sociological Legacy*. London and New York: Routledge.

Sorkin, Michael (ed.). 1992. *Variations on a Theme Park: The New American City and the End of Public Space*. New York: Farrar, Strauss and Giroux.

Sumner, William Graham, 1959 [1909]. *Folkways: A Study of the Sociological Importance of Usages, Manners, Customs, Mores, and Morals*. New York: Dover Publications.

Sumner, William Graham and Keller, Albert Galloway. 1927. *The Science of Society* (4 vols). New Haven: Yale University Press.

Sumner, William Graham. 1978 [1883]. *What Social Classes Owe to Each Other*. Caldwell, Idaho: Caxton Printers.

Thomas, William. 1907. *Sex and Society*. Boston: The Gorham Press.

Thomas, William and Znaniecki, Florian. 1958. *The Polish Peasant in Europe and America* (2 vols). New York: Dover Publications.

de Tocqueville, Alexis. 2002 [1835]. *Democracy in America.* The Folio Society: London.

Turner, Jonathan. 1974. "Parsons as a Symbolic Interactionist: A Comparison of Action and Interaction Theory." *Sociological Inquiry* 44(4): 283–94.

Turner, Jonathan. 1988. *A Theory of Social Interaction.* Stanford: Stanford University Press.

Turner, Stephen and Turner, Jonathan. 1990. *The Impossible Science.* Newbury Park, California: Sage.

Verhoeven, Jeff. 1993. "An Interview with Erving Goffman, 1980." *Research on Language and Social Interaction* 26(3): 317–48.

Wacquant, Loic. 2004. *Body & Soul: Notebooks of an Apprentice Boxer.* Oxford: Oxford University Press.

Weber, Max. 1949. *The Methodology of the Social Sciences.* New York: The Free Press.

Weber, Max. 1978. *Economy and Society: An Outline of Interpretive Sociology*, 2 vols. Eds Guenter Roth and Claus Wittich. Berkeley: University of California Press.

Weber, Max. 2002. *The Protestant Ethic and the Spirit of Capitalism* Tr. Stephen Kalberg. Los Angeles, California: Roxbury Publishing Company.

Weinstein, Raymond 1994. "Goffman's Asylums and the Total Institution Model of Mental Hospitals." *Psychiatry* 57(4): 348–67.

Wiley, Norbert. 1986. "Early American Sociology and the Polish Peasant." *Sociological Theory* 4(1): 20–40.

Wiley, Norbert. 2003. "The Self as Self-Fulfilling Prophecy." *Symbolic Interaction* 26(4): 501–14.

Williams, Robin. 1998. "Erving Goffman." In Rob Stones (ed.), *Key Sociological Thinkers.* New York: New York University Press.

Winkin, Yves. 1988. *Erving Goffman: Les Moments et Leurs Hommes.* Paris: Minuit.

Winkin, Yves. 1999. "What's in a Life Anyway?" In Gregory Smith (ed.), *Goffman and Social Organization.* London: Routledge.

Winkin, Yves. (forthcoming) *Erving Goffman: A Biography.* London: Macmillan.

Wirth, Louis. 1931. "Clinical Sociology." *American Journal of Sociology* 37(1): 49–66.

Wittgenstein, Ludwig. 1958. *Philosophical Investigations.* Oxford: Blackwell.

Woolgar, Steve and Pawluch, Dorothy. 1985. "Ontological Gerrymandering." *Social Problems* 32(3): 214–27.

Wrong, Dennis. 1990. "Imagining the Real." In Bennett Berger (ed.), *Authors of Their Own Lives.* Berkeley, Los Angeles, Oxford: University of California Press.

Wrong, Dennis. 1998. *The Modern Condition: Essays at Century's End.* Stanford: Stanford University Press.

Young, Kimball. 1927. "Topical Summaries of Current Personality Studies." *American Journal of Sociology* 32(6): 953–71.

Index